Isaac S. Moses

Order of Prayers and Responsive Readings for Jewish Worship

Isaac S. Moses

Order of Prayers and Responsive Readings for Jewish Worship

ISBN/EAN: 9783337130282

Printed in Europe, USA, Canada, Australia, Japan

Cover: Foto ©Lupo / pixelio.de

More available books at **www.hansebooks.com**

Order of Prayers

AND

RESPONSIVE READINGS

FOR

JEWISH WORSHIP.

Second revised and corrected Edition.

ARRANGED BY

ISAAC S. MOSES,

Rabbi of Congregation "Emanu-El", Milwaukee, W

MILWAUKEE, WIS.

1887.

Entered according to Act of Congress, in the year 1884, by

ISAAC S. MOSES,

In the Office of the Librarian of Congress at Washington, D. C.

PREFACE.

After a trial of over two years, the English Ritual published by the undersigned in 1884 has been found inadequate to the wants of our congregation. The majority of those who regularly attend divine service are accustomed to to the Hebrew as the language of prayer, while those for whom the English Ritual was intended, do not take that interest in our public worship as to justify the substitution of the English for the Hebrew. To return to the old Hebrew Prayer-book with its un-English translation would land us where we started from a few years ago; it will not remedy the evil. To satisfy the demands of both, the old and the young generation, the undersigned has recast his former publication, adding all the principal prayers in the Hebrew language contained in the older Prayer-book, yet making the English rendition on the opposite page an independent Ritual, thus enabling the worshipper to follow the service intelligently whether using the Hebrew or the English part. Some changes have been made in regard to the Psalms to be read at Sabbath eve and Sabbath morning service; they have been placed before each service. The Minister, however, may now and then select some other Psalm from the appended Collection which has been left unaltered from the previous edition.

No modern prayer can compare in depth of feeling and simplicity of expression with the Psalms of the Hebrew bards. In them breathes the living spirit of prayer. There is hardly a state of feeling that finds not expression in one or the other of these ancient songs. The opening Psalm before each service may be repeated by the Choir for which abundant compositions are extant. In addition to this Collection of Psalms every pew ought to be provided with one or two Hymn-books, the minister announcing every hymn to be sung. This would avoid the frequently ridiculous if not

PREFACE.

scandalous use of hymns and anthems not calculated for Jewish worship. Excellent Hymn-books have been published by Dr. M. JASTROW, Dr. M. LANDSBERG, and lately by Dr. G. GOTTHEIL which is a rich collection of gems of poetry. The responses should invariably be sung in Hebrew, as the ear of the Jewish worshipper loves to hear those quaint Hebrew melodies.

In this present edition as well as in the first publication I have availed myself of the labors of my predecessors. I do not claim to have composed a new prayer-book; the merit of this book is its lack of originality. I have simply compiled, arranged and rendered into English the ancient forms of our prayers, making free use of the English portion of existing prayer-books, especially that of the late Dr. EINHORN, of Dr. JASTROW's and Dr. LANDSBERG's Ritual, which I hereby acknowledge with thanks. The Hymns on pages 63 and 72 are from Temple Emanu-El Prayer-book; the one on page 81 is by Rev. J. V. BLAKE and the Shofar-Hymn on page 106 from Dr. M. JASTROW's Prayer-book.

For the Service of Day of Atonement a second volume is in preparation.

May this Ritual help to kindle in the hearts of worshippers the spirit of true devotion.

Milwaukee, Wis., July 1886.

ISAAC S. MOSES.

CONTENTS.

ORDER OF PRAYER.

	page
Evening Service for Sabbath and Holidays	3
Morning Service for Sabbath and Holidays	22
Service for New Year's Eve	61
Morning Service for New Year's Day	79
Service in the House of Mourners	113

RESPONSIVE READINGS.

		page
I.	Joy in Worship	1
II.	Acceptable Worship	6
III.	The Glory of God	8
IV.	The Goodness of God	12
V.	Time and Eternity	16
VI.	The Universal Presence of God	19
VII.	Seeking God	22
VIII.	Thanksgiving	27
IX.	Prayer	34
X.	In the Day of Trouble	36
XI.	Repentance and Forgiveness	43
XII.	Trust	45
XIII.	Consolation	53
XIV.	The Justice of God	55
XV.	Beatitudes	59
XVI.	National	61
XVII.	Praise	67

Children's Prayers ... 72

EVENING SERVICE
FOR
SABBATH AND HOLIDAYS.

Organ Prelude.

MINISTER:

מַה־טֹּבוּ אֹהָלֶיךָ יַעֲקֹב מִשְׁכְּנֹתֶיךָ יִשְׂרָאֵל: וַאֲנִי בְּרֹב חַסְדְּךָ אָבֹא בֵיתֶךָ אֶשְׁתַּחֲוֶה אֶל־הֵיכַל קָדְשְׁךָ בְּיִרְאָתֶךָ: יְיָ אָהַבְתִּי מְעוֹן בֵּיתֶךָ וּמְקוֹם מִשְׁכַּן כְּבוֹדֶךָ: וַאֲנִי אֶשְׁתַּחֲוֶה וְאֶכְרָעָה אֶבְרְכָה לִפְנֵי־יְיָ עֹשִׂי: וַאֲנִי תְפִלָּתִי לְךָ יְיָ עֵת רָצוֹן אֱלֹהִים בְּרָב־חַסְדֶּךָ עֲנֵנִי בֶּאֱמֶת יִשְׁעֶךָ:

How beautiful are thy tents, O Jacob, thy tabernacles, O Israel! With faith in thy loving kindness, O God, we enter thy house; with profound reverence we will worship thee in thy holy temple. We love thy dwelling-place, O Lord, the abode sanctified by thy holiness. We will bow down before thee, and offer up our supplication unto thee, O God our Creator. Accept our prayers at this hour in the fulness of thy grace. Hear us, O God, our stronghold and support.

CHOIR: (Either of the following sentences.)

Worship the Lord in the beauty of holiness;
Stand in awe before him all the earth.

Give unto the Lord glory and praise;
Worship the Lord in holy attire.

Serve the Lord with gladness;
Come before his presence with songs.

RESPONSIVE READING.

Select one or more Psalms from the following pages; for the Three Festivals, appropriate Psalms from the appended Collection, then begin Borechu on page 11.

EVENING SERVICE FOR SABBATH AND HOLIDAYS.

Psalm 95. לכו נרננה ליי

O come, let us sing unto the Lord; let us raise a voice of joy to the rock of our salvation!

Let us come into his presence with thanksgiving, and sing joyfully to him with psalms!

For the Lord is a great God; yea a great King over all the world.

In his hands are the depths of the earth; his also are the heights of the mountains.

The sea is his, and he made it; the dry land also his hands have formed.

O come, let us worship and bow down, let us bow down before the Lord, our Maker!

For he is our God, and we are the people of his pasture and the flock of his hand.

O that ye would now hear his voice!

Psalm 96. שירו ליי שיר חדש

O sing to the Lord a new song; sing to the Lord, all the earth!

Sing to the Lord; praise his name, show forth his salvation from day to day!

Proclaim his glory among the nations, his wonders among all people!

For the Lord is great, and highly exalted, and beside him there is no God.

For all the gods of the nations are idols; but the Lord made the heavens.

Honor and majesty are before him, glory and beauty are in his holy abode.

Give to the Lord, ye families of the people, give to the Lord glory and praise!

Give to the Lord the glory due to his name; bring an offering, and come into his courts!

O worship the Lord in the beauty of holiness! stand in awe before him, all the earth!

Say among the nations, the Lord is king; he will judge the nations in righteousness.

Let the heavens be glad, and the earth rejoice; let the sea roar, and the fullness thereof;

Let the fields be joyful, with all that is therein; let all the trees of the forest rejoice;

Before the Lord! for he cometh, he cometh to judge the earth! he will judge the world with justice, and the nations with faithfulness.

Psalm 97. יי מלך תגל הארץ

The Lord reigneth, let the earth rejoice! let the multitude of isles be glad!

Clouds and darkness are round about him; justice and equity are the foundation of his throne.

Before him goeth a fire, which burneth up his enemies around.

His lightnings illumine the world; the earth beholdeth and trembleth.

The mountains melt like wax at the presence of the Lord, at the presence of the Lord of the whole earth.

The heavens declare his righteousness, and all nations behold his glory.

Zion hath heard, and is glad, and the daughters of Judah exult on account of thy judgments, O Lord!

For thou, O Lord! art most high above all the earth; thou art far exalted above all powers!

Ye that love the Lord, hate evil! He preserveth the lives of his servents, and delivereth them from the hand of the wicked.

Light is sown for the righteous, and joy for the upright in heart.

Rejoice, O ye righteous, in the Lord, and praise his holy name!

Psalm 98. מזמור שירו ליי

Sing to the Lord a new song; for he hath done marvellous things.

His own right hand and his holy arm have gotten him the victory!

The Lord hath made known his salvation; his righteousness hath he manifested in the sight of the nations.

He hath remembered his mercy and truth toward the house of Israel, and all the ends of the earth have seen the salvation of our God.

Sing unto the Lord, all the earth! break forth into joy, and exult, and sing!

Sing to the Lord with the harp, with the harp, and the voice of song!

With clarions and the sound of trumpets, make a joyful noise before the Lord the King!

Let the sea roar, and the fulness thereof; the world, and they that dwell therein.

Let the rivers clap their hands, and the mountains rejoice together;

Before the Lord! for he cometh to judge the earth! he will judge the world, with righteousness and the nations with equity.

Psalm 99.　　מלך ירגזו עמים יי׳

The Lord reigneth, let the nations tremble! he dwelleth between the cherubim, let the earth quake!

Great is the Lord upon Zion; he is exalted over all the nations.

Let men praise thy great and awe-inspiring name! it is holy.

Let them declare the glory of the King who loveth justice!

Thou hast established equity; thou dost execute justice in Jacob!

Exalt ye the Lord, our God, and bow yourselves down at his footstool! he is holy.

Moses and Aaron, with his priests, and Samuel, who called upon his name,—they called upon the Lord, and he answered them.

He spake to them in the cloudy pillar; they kept his commandments, and the ordinances which he gave them.

Thou, O Lord, our God, didst answer them; thou wast to them a forgiving God, though thou didst punish their transgressions!

Exalt the Lord, our God, and worship at his holy mountain! for the Lord, our God, is holy.

Psalm 100.   מזמור לתודה

Raise a voice of joy unto the Lord, all ye lands!

Serve the Lord with gladness; come before his presence with songs!

Know ye that the Lord is God! it is he that made us, and we are his, his people, and the flock of his pasture.

Enter into his gates with thanksgiving, and his courts with praise; be thankful to him, and bless his name!

For the Lord is good; his mercy is everlasting; and his truth endureth to all generations.

Psalm 29.   הבו ליי בני אלים

Give unto the Lord, O ye sons of the mighty! give unto the Lord glory and praise!

Give unto the Lord the glory due to his name; worship the Lord in holy attire!

The voice of the Lord is heard above the waters; the God of glory thundereth,—the Lord above the great waters.

The voice of the Lord is powerful; the voice of the Lord is full of majesty;

The voice of the Lord breaketh the cedars; yea, the Lord breaketh the cedars of Lebanon;

Yea, he maketh them to leap like a calf,—Lebanon and Sirion like a young buffalo.

The voice of the Lord divideth the flames of fire.

The voice of the Lord maketh the wilderness tremble;

Yea, the Lord maketh the wilderness of Kadesh tremble.

The voice of the Lord causes the wild deer to start, and layeth bare the forests; while, in his temple, every one declareth his glory.

The Lord dwelleth above the floods; yea, the Lord is king for ever.

The Lord will give strength to his people; the Lord will bless his people with peace.

Psalm 92.   מזמור שיר ליום השבת
A Psalm for the Sabbath-day.

It is a good thing to give thanks to the Lord, and to sing praises to thy name, O Most High!
To show forth thy loving kindness in the morning, and thy faithfulness every night.
For thou, O Lord, hast made me glad by thy doings; in the works of thy hands I greatly rejoice!
How great are thy works, O Lord! how deep thy purposes!
But the unwise man knoweth not this, the thoughtless can not perceive it:
When the wicked spring up like grass, and evil-doers flourish; —to be destroyed for ever!
But thou, O Lord, art for ever exalted!
For, lo! thy enemies, O Lord! thy enemies perish, and dispersed are all who do iniquity!
The righteous shall flourish like the palm-tree; they shall grow up like the cedars of Lebanon;
Planted in the house of the Lord, they shall flourish in the courts of our God.
Even in old age they bring forth fruit; they are green, and full of sap;
To show that the Lord, my Rock, is upright, and there is no unrighteousness in him.

Psalm 93.   " מלך גאות לבש

The Lord reigneth; he is clothed with majesty; the Lord is clothed with majesty, and girded with strength:
Therefore the earth standeth firm, and cannot be moved.
Thy throne was established of old; thou art from everlasting!
The floods, O Lord! lift up their voice; the floods lift up their roaring!
Mightier than the voice of many waters, are the mighty waves of the sea;
But mightiest of all is the Lord in his lofty habitation.
Thy promises are most sure; holiness becometh thy house, O Lord! for ever!

תפלת ערבית לשבת ויו״ט

מִזְמוֹר שִׁיר לְיוֹם הַשַּׁבָּת:

טוֹב לְהֹדוֹת לַיהוָה. וּלְזַמֵּר לְשִׁמְךָ עֶלְיוֹן: לְהַגִּיד בַּבֹּקֶר חַסְדֶּךָ. וֶאֱמוּנָתְךָ בַּלֵּילוֹת: עֲלֵי עָשׂוֹר וַעֲלֵי־נָבֶל. עֲלֵי הִגָּיוֹן בְּכִנּוֹר: כִּי שִׂמַּחְתַּנִי יְהוָה בְּפָעֳלֶךָ. בְּמַעֲשֵׂי יָדֶיךָ אֲרַנֵּן: מַה־גָּדְלוּ מַעֲשֶׂיךָ יְהוָה. מְאֹד עָמְקוּ מַחְשְׁבֹתֶיךָ: אִישׁ בַּעַר לֹא יֵדָע. וּכְסִיל לֹא־יָבִין אֶת־זֹאת: בִּפְרֹחַ רְשָׁעִים כְּמוֹ עֵשֶׂב וַיָּצִיצוּ כָּל־פֹּעֲלֵי אָוֶן. לְהִשָּׁמְדָם עֲדֵי־עַד: וְאַתָּה מָרוֹם לְעֹלָם יְהוָה: כִּי הִנֵּה אֹיְבֶיךָ יְהוָה כִּי־הִנֵּה אֹיְבֶיךָ יֹאבֵדוּ. יִתְפָּרְדוּ כָּל־פֹּעֲלֵי אָוֶן: וַתָּרֶם כִּרְאֵים קַרְנִי. בַּלֹּתִי בְּשֶׁמֶן רַעֲנָן: וַתַּבֵּט עֵינִי בְּשׁוּרָי. בַּקָּמִים עָלַי מְרֵעִים תִּשְׁמַעְנָה אָזְנָי: צַדִּיק כַּתָּמָר יִפְרָח. כְּאֶרֶז בַּלְּבָנוֹן יִשְׂגֶּה: שְׁתוּלִים בְּבֵית יְהוָה. בְּחַצְרוֹת אֱלֹהֵינוּ יַפְרִיחוּ: עוֹד יְנוּבוּן בְּשֵׂיבָה. דְּשֵׁנִים וְרַעֲנַנִּים יִהְיוּ: לְהַגִּיד כִּי־יָשָׁר יְהוָה. צוּרִי וְלֹא־עַוְלָתָה בּוֹ:

לִשְׁלֹשׁ רְגָלִים

הָבוּ לַיהוָה בְּנֵי אֵלִים. הָבוּ לַיהוָה כָּבוֹד וָעֹז: הָבוּ לַיהוָה כְּבוֹד שְׁמוֹ. הִשְׁתַּחֲווּ לַיהוָה בְּהַדְרַת־קֹדֶשׁ: קוֹל יְהוָה עַל־הַמָּיִם. אֵל־הַכָּבוֹד הִרְעִים. יְהוָה עַל־מַיִם רַבִּים: קוֹל־יְהוָה בַּכֹּחַ. קוֹל יְהוָה בֶּהָדָר: קוֹל יְהוָה שֹׁבֵר אֲרָזִים. וַיְשַׁבֵּר יְהוָה אֶת־אַרְזֵי הַלְּבָנוֹן: וַיַּרְקִידֵם כְּמוֹ־עֵגֶל. לְבָנוֹן וְשִׂרְיֹן כְּמוֹ בֶן־רְאֵמִים: קוֹל־יְהוָה חֹצֵב לַהֲבוֹת אֵשׁ: קוֹל יְהוָה יָחִיל מִדְבָּר. יָחִיל יְהוָה מִדְבַּר קָדֵשׁ: קוֹל יְהוָה יְחוֹלֵל אַיָּלוֹת וַיֶּחֱשֹׂף יְעָרוֹת וּבְהֵיכָלוֹ כֻּלּוֹ אֹמֵר כָּבוֹד: יְהוָה לַמַּבּוּל יָשָׁב. וַיֵּשֶׁב יְהוָה מֶלֶךְ לְעוֹלָם: יְהוָה עֹז לְעַמּוֹ יִתֵּן. יְהוָה יְבָרֵךְ אֶת־עַמּוֹ בַשָּׁלוֹם:

MINISTER:

Borechu es Adonoy hammevoroch.
Praise ye the Lord to whom all praise is due!

CHOIR AND CONGREGATION:

Boruch Adonoy hammevoroch l'olom voëd.
Praised be the Lord, who is praised through all eternity.

Praise be to thee, O Lord our God, Ruler of the Universe, who by his word calls in the evening and in his wisdom opens the gates of the morning. He changes the times and the seasons by his understanding, and by his will he sets the stars in their heavenly watches. He alternates the light and the darkness; he leads out the day and brings in the night, the Lord of hosts is his name. May he rule over us forevermore. Praise be to thee, O God, who bringest in the evening.

With unchanging love thou hast guided thy people Israel; thou hast revealed to us thy law which will become a blessing to all mankind. Therefore we will ever think of thy word and rejoice in thy truth. It is our light and our life; we will cling to it day and night, and will proclaim thy name and thy unity before all the nations of the earth. Do thou, O God, never withold from us thy love and thy protection. Praise be to thee, O God, our Guardian and Keeper.

CHOIR: **Amen**.

MINISTER, THEN CHOIR AND CONGREGATION:

Sh'ma Yisroël, Adonoy Elohénu, Adonoy Echod.
HEAR, O ISRAEL, THE LORD OUR GOD, THE LORD IS ONE.

Boruch Shem kevod mal'chuso l'olom voëd.
Praised be the name of his glorious kingdom for evermore.

Thou shalt love the Eternal thy God with all thy heart, with all thy soul, and with all thy might. And these words, which I command thee to-day, shall be in thy heart. Thou shalt teach them diligently to thy children, and shalt talk of them when thou sittest in thy house, and when thou walkest by the way, and when thou liest down, and when thou risest up. And they shall be as a sign on thy hand and as an ornament

תפלת ערבית לשבת ויו״ט

בָּרְכוּ אֶת יְיָ הַמְבֹרָךְ:

בָּרוּךְ יְיָ הַמְבֹרָךְ לְעוֹלָם וָעֶד:

בָּרוּךְ אַתָּה יְיָ אֱלֹהֵינוּ מֶלֶךְ הָעוֹלָם. אֲשֶׁר בִּדְבָרוֹ מַעֲרִיב עֲרָבִים. בְּחָכְמָה פּוֹתֵחַ שְׁעָרִים. וּבִתְבוּנָה מְשַׁנֶּה עִתִּים וּמַחֲלִיף אֶת הַזְּמַנִּים. וּמְסַדֵּר אֶת הַכּוֹכָבִים בְּמִשְׁמְרוֹתֵיהֶם בָּרָקִיעַ כִּרְצוֹנוֹ. בּוֹרֵא יוֹם וָלָיְלָה. גּוֹלֵל אוֹר מִפְּנֵי חֹשֶׁךְ וְחֹשֶׁךְ מִפְּנֵי אוֹר. וּמַעֲבִיר יוֹם וּמֵבִיא לָיְלָה. יְיָ צְבָאוֹת שְׁמוֹ. אֵל חַי וְקַיָּם תָּמִיד יִמְלוֹךְ עָלֵינוּ לְעוֹלָם וָעֶד. בָּרוּךְ אַתָּה יְיָ הַמַּעֲרִיב עֲרָבִים:

אַהֲבַת עוֹלָם בֵּית יִשְׂרָאֵל עַמְּךָ אָהָבְתָּ. תּוֹרָה וּמִצְוֹת חֻקִּים וּמִשְׁפָּטִים אוֹתָנוּ לִמַּדְתָּ. עַל כֵּן יְיָ אֱלֹהֵינוּ בְּשָׁכְבֵנוּ וּבְקוּמֵנוּ נָשִׂיחַ בְּחֻקֶּיךָ. וְנִשְׂמַח בְּדִבְרֵי תוֹרָתֶךָ וּבְמִצְוֹתֶיךָ לְעוֹלָם וָעֶד. כִּי הֵם חַיֵּינוּ וְאֹרֶךְ יָמֵינוּ. וּבָהֶם נֶהְגֶּה יוֹמָם וָלָיְלָה. וְאַהֲבָתְךָ אַל־תָּסִיר מִמֶּנּוּ לְעוֹלָמִים. בָּרוּךְ אַתָּה יְיָ אוֹהֵב עַמּוֹ יִשְׂרָאֵל:

שְׁמַע יִשְׂרָאֵל יְהוָה אֱלֹהֵינוּ יְהוָה אֶחָד:

בָּרוּךְ שֵׁם כְּבוֹד מַלְכוּתוֹ לְעוֹלָם וָעֶד:

וְאָהַבְתָּ אֵת יְיָ אֱלֹהֶיךָ בְּכָל לְבָבְךָ וּבְכָל נַפְשְׁךָ וּבְכָל מְאֹדֶךָ: וְהָיוּ הַדְּבָרִים הָאֵלֶּה אֲשֶׁר אָנֹכִי מְצַוְּךָ הַיּוֹם עַל־לְבָבֶךָ: וְשִׁנַּנְתָּם לְבָנֶיךָ וְדִבַּרְתָּ בָּם. בְּשִׁבְתְּךָ בְּבֵיתֶךָ וּבְלֶכְתְּךָ בַדֶּרֶךְ וּבְשָׁכְבְּךָ וּבְקוּמֶךָ: וּקְשַׁרְתָּם לְאוֹת עַל־יָדֶךָ. וְהָיוּ לְטֹטָפֹת בֵּין עֵינֶיךָ: וּכְתַבְתָּם עַל־מְזֻזוֹת בֵּיתֶךָ וּבִשְׁעָרֶיךָ:

on thy brow. And thou shalt write them upon the doorposts of thy house and on thy gates. (DEUTER., CHAPT. 6, V. 4—9.)

CHOIR:

Unchangeable and immutable is this word with us: God is everlasting; his word is true unto all generations; his commandments stand for ever. He alone is our God and none besides him.

MINISTER:

Truly thou art our God, and we are thy people, whom thou hast delivered from the hand of mighty oppressors. Wonders without number thou hast wrought for us, and hast miraculously protected us during these many centuries. As thy arm saved us from the yoke of Egyptian slavery, so thou wast with us in all times of need and danger, when hatred and fanaticism threatened to destroy the remnant of Israel. Therefore we render thanks to thee, and praise thy name with the ancient song of our fathers:

MINISTER, THEN CHOIR AND CONGREGATION:

Mi chomocho boëlim Adonoy; mi komocho, neddor bakkodesh, noro sehillos, osé féleh.

Who is like thee among the mighty, O God, who is like thee glorified in Holiness, awe-inspiring, wonder-working!

MINISTER:

As thou hast revealed thy kingdom to our fathers, so manifest thy glorious help unto us, their children, who worship thee as their God and King, proclaiming:

Adonoy yimlôch l'olom voëd.
God will reign for ever and ever!

Continue to be with us, O God, and guard us from evil. Let our lying down and our rising up be in peace. O guide us with thy good counsel; protect us from grief and need, from sorrow and anxiety, from sickness and danger; for in thee, O God, we put our trust, our gracious and merciful father. Let our going out and coming in be in peace, henceforth and forevermore. Blessed art thou, O God, Redeemer and Keeper of Israel.

CHOIR: Amen.

תפלת ערבית לשבת ויו״ט

אֱמֶת וֶאֱמוּנָה כָּל זֹאת וְקַיָּם עָלֵינוּ. כִּי הוּא יְיָ אֱלֹהֵינוּ וְאֵין זוּלָתוֹ. וַאֲנַחְנוּ יִשְׂרָאֵל עַמּוֹ. הַפּוֹדֵנוּ מִיַּד מְלָכִים. מַלְכֵּנוּ הַגּוֹאֲלֵנוּ מִכַּף כָּל הֶעָרִיצִים. הָעוֹשֶׂה גְדוֹלוֹת עַד אֵין חֵקֶר. וְנִפְלָאוֹת עַד אֵין מִסְפָּר. הַשָּׂם נַפְשֵׁנוּ בַּחַיִּים. וְלֹא נָתַן לַמּוֹט רַגְלֵנוּ. הָעוֹשֶׂה לָּנוּ נִסִּים בְּמִצְרָיִם. אוֹתוֹת וּמוֹפְתִים בְּאַדְמַת בְּנֵי חָם. וְרָאוּ בָנָיו גְּבוּרָתוֹ. שִׁבְּחוּ וְהוֹדוּ לִשְׁמוֹ. וּמַלְכוּתוֹ בְּרָצוֹן קִבְּלוּ עֲלֵיהֶם. מֹשֶׁה וּבְנֵי יִשְׂרָאֵל לְךָ עָנוּ שִׁירָה בְּשִׂמְחָה רַבָּה וְאָמְרוּ כֻלָּם:

מִי כָמֹכָה בָּאֵלִם יְיָ מִי כָּמֹכָה נֶאְדָּר בַּקֹּדֶשׁ. נוֹרָא תְהִלֹּת עֹשֵׂה פֶלֶא:

מַלְכוּתְךָ רָאוּ בָנֶיךָ. בּוֹקֵעַ יָם לִפְנֵי מֹשֶׁה. זֶה אֵלִי עָנוּ וְאָמְרוּ:

יְיָ יִמְלֹךְ לְעֹלָם וָעֶד:

וְנֶאֱמַר כִּי פָדָה יְיָ אֶת יַעֲקֹב וּגְאָלוֹ מִיַּד חָזָק מִמֶּנּוּ. בָּרוּךְ אַתָּה יְיָ גָּאַל יִשְׂרָאֵל:

הַשְׁכִּיבֵנוּ יְיָ אֱלֹהֵינוּ לְשָׁלוֹם. וְהַעֲמִידֵנוּ מַלְכֵּנוּ לְחַיִּים. וּפְרֹשׂ עָלֵינוּ סֻכַּת שְׁלוֹמֶךָ. וְתַקְּנֵנוּ בְּעֵצָה טוֹבָה מִלְּפָנֶיךָ. וְהוֹשִׁיעֵנוּ לְמַעַן שְׁמֶךָ. וְהָגֵן בַּעֲדֵנוּ וְהָסֵר מֵעָלֵינוּ אוֹיֵב דֶּבֶר וְחֶרֶב וְרָעָב וְיָגוֹן. וּבְצֵל כְּנָפֶיךָ תַּסְתִּירֵנוּ. כִּי אֵל שׁוֹמְרֵנוּ וּמַצִּילֵנוּ אָתָּה. כִּי אֵל מֶלֶךְ חַנּוּן וְרַחוּם אָתָּה. וּשְׁמוֹר צֵאתֵנוּ וּבוֹאֵנוּ לְחַיִּים וּלְשָׁלוֹם מֵעַתָּה וְעַד עוֹלָם. בָּרוּךְ אַתָּה יְיָ שׁוֹמֵר עַמּוֹ יִשְׂרָאֵל לָעַד:

Praise be to thee, O Eternal, our God, God of our fathers, God of Abraham, Isaac and Jacob, Almighty and Supreme Being, Creator of heaven and earth! Shield of our ancestors, whose life-giving word sustains all things, O God of Holiness, who hast planted within us eternal life.

(ON SABBATH.)

Praise and thanks to thee, O merciful Father, for the precious gift of the Sabbath which thou hast ordained for us. Thou hast sanctified the seventh day and destined it to bring joy and comfort to man after the cares and struggles of the week; to offer to him the palm of peace as the heavenly reward for all his labors. Whatever we have and are is a gift from thy bountiful hand. Grant, O our Father, that all our work and undertaking may be good and pure in thy sight. May our inward strength be renewed through

(ON HOLIDAYS.)

We give thanks unto thee, O Eternal our God, for the unspeakeable love and mercy with which thou hast chosen our fathers from among all nations and hast appointed them to be the bearers of thy truth, to spread the knowledge of thy holy name and to consecrate their lives to thy service. In the abundance of thy grace thou hast given us Sabbaths for rest, festive days for joy and the return of seasons for gladness; even this (Sabbath-day and this) Day of the Feast of

Passover	Weeks	Tabernacles	Conclusion
the anniversary of our redemption from bondage	the anniversary of the revelation on Mount Sinai.	the time of thanksgiving for thy bountiful blessing.	the time of rejoicing over thy bountiful blessing.

a holy convocation, a memorial of our departure from Egypt.

O Eternal our God, God of our fathers, grant that our memorial, the memorial of our fathers, and of all thy people Israel, may come before thee for grace, favor and mercy, life and peace, on this Day of the Feast of

Passover, | Weeks, | Tabernacles, | Conclusion.

בָּרוּךְ אַתָּה יְיָ. אֱלֹהֵינוּ וֵאלֹהֵי אֲבוֹתֵינוּ. אֱלֹהֵי אַבְרָהָם אֱלֹהֵי יִצְחָק וֵאלֹהֵי יַעֲקֹב. הָאֵל הַגָּדוֹל הַגִּבּוֹר וְהַנּוֹרָא. אֵל עֶלְיוֹן קֹנֵה שָׁמַיִם וָאָרֶץ. מָגֵן אָבוֹת בִּדְבָרוֹ. מְחַיֵּה הַכֹּל בְּמַאֲמָרוֹ. הָאֵל הַקָּדוֹשׁ:

ל ש ב ת.

אַתָּה קִדַּשְׁתָּ אֶת יוֹם הַשְּׁבִיעִי לִשְׁמֶךָ. תַּכְלִית מַעֲשֵׂה שָׁמַיִם וָאָרֶץ. וּבֵרַכְתּוֹ מִכָּל־הַיָּמִים. וְקִדַּשְׁתּוֹ מִכָּל הַזְּמַנִּים. וְכֵן כָּתוּב בְּתוֹרָתֶךָ:

וַיְכֻלּוּ הַשָּׁמַיִם וְהָאָרֶץ וְכָל־צְבָאָם: וַיְכַל אֱלֹהִים בַּיּוֹם הַשְּׁבִיעִי מְלַאכְתּוֹ אֲשֶׁר עָשָׂה. וַיִּשְׁבֹּת בַּיּוֹם הַשְּׁבִיעִי מִכָּל־מְלַאכְתּוֹ אֲשֶׁר עָשָׂה: וַיְבָרֶךְ אֱלֹהִים אֶת־יוֹם הַשְּׁבִיעִי וַיְקַדֵּשׁ אֹתוֹ. כִּי בוֹ שָׁבַת מִכָּל־מְלַאכְתּוֹ אֲשֶׁר־בָּרָא אֱלֹהִים לַעֲשׂוֹת:

תפלה לשלש רגלים.

אַתָּה בְחַרְתָּנוּ מִכָּל הָעַמִּים. אָהַבְתָּ אוֹתָנוּ וְרָצִיתָ בָּנוּ. וְקִדַּשְׁתָּנוּ בְּמִצְוֹתֶיךָ. וְקֵרַבְתָּנוּ מַלְכֵּנוּ לַעֲבוֹדָתֶךָ. וְשִׁמְךָ הַגָּדוֹל וְהַקָּדוֹשׁ עָלֵינוּ קָרָאתָ. וַתִּתֶּן־לָנוּ יְיָ אֱלֹהֵינוּ בְּאַהֲבָה. שַׁבָּתוֹת לִמְנוּחָה. מוֹעֲדִים לְשִׂמְחָה. חַגִּים וּזְמַנִּים לְשָׂשׂוֹן. אֶת יוֹם (בְּשַׁבָּת וְאֶת יוֹם)

לפסח חַג הַמַּצּוֹת הַזֶּה. זְמַן חֵרוּתֵנוּ.

לשבועות חַג הַשָּׁבוּעוֹת הַזֶּה. זְמַן מַתַּן תּוֹרָתֵנוּ.

לסכות חַג הַסֻּכּוֹת הַזֶּה. זְמַן שִׂמְחָתֵנוּ.

לש״ע חַג הָעֲצֶרֶת הַזֶּה. זְמַן שִׂמְחָתֵנוּ.

מִקְרָא קֹדֶשׁ זֵכֶר לִיצִיאַת מִצְרָיִם:

(ON SABBATH.)

the blessing of the Sabbath, that we may become worthy to receive the light of thy wisdom, thy perfect holiness and unchanging love. Sanctify us, O God, through thy commandments, sustain us with thine infinite goodness, and gladden us by thy sure help. Purify our hearts to serve thee in love and truth; may we enjoy thy holy Sabbath with gladness of heart and peace of mind. Praise be to thee, O Lord, who hast hallowed the Sabbath-day.

(ON HOLIDAYS.)

Remember us, O Lord, for our good, bless us with happiness, and help us in the trials of life. Cause thy mercy to descend upon us and bring us salvation, according to the promise of of thy holy word; for to thee we look for aid, O our Heavenly father, who rulest all mankind in mercy and love.

Our God and Father, sanctify us through thy commandments and enlighten us by thy law. Sustain us from thine infinite goodness and gladden us by thy sure help. Purify our hearts to serve thee in truth and let us enjoy thy holy (Sabbaths and) festivals in love and gladness. Praise be to thee, O God, who sanctifiest Israel and the Festivals.

(ON SABBATH AND HOLIDAYS.)
In silent devotion.

O God, keep my tongue from evil, and my lips from uttering deceit, and grant that I may be meek and kind to those who bear ill-will against me. Implant humility in my heart and strengthen me with faith. Be my support when grief oppresses me and my comfort in affliction. Let thy truth illumine my path and guide me; for thou art my God and my aid; in thee I trust every day.

MINISTER, THEN CHOIR:

Let the words of my mouth and the meditation of my heart be acceptable in thy sight, O God, my Strength and my Redeemer. As thou preservest peace in the heavenly spheres, so preserve it to us and to all who invoke thy holy name. Amen.

לשבת.

אֱלֹהֵינוּ וֵאלֹהֵי אֲבוֹתֵינוּ. רְצֵה בִמְנוּחָתֵנוּ. קַדְּשֵׁנוּ בְּמִצְוֹתֶיךָ וְתֵן חֶלְקֵנוּ בְּתוֹרָתֶךָ. שַׂבְּעֵנוּ מִטּוּבֶךָ וְשַׂמְּחֵנוּ בִּישׁוּעָתֶךָ. וְטַהֵר לִבֵּנוּ לְעָבְדְּךָ בֶּאֱמֶת. וְהַנְחִילֵנוּ יְיָ אֱלֹהֵינוּ בְּאַהֲבָה וּבְרָצוֹן שַׁבַּת קָדְשֶׁךָ. וְיָנוּחוּ בָהּ יִשְׂרָאֵל מְקַדְּשֵׁי שְׁמֶךָ. בָּרוּךְ אַתָּה יְיָ מְקַדֵּשׁ הַשַּׁבָּת:

תפלה לשלש רגלים.

אֱלֹהֵינוּ וֵאלֹהֵי אֲבוֹתֵינוּ יַעֲלֶה וְיָבֹא זִכְרוֹנֵנוּ וְזִכְרוֹן אֲבוֹתֵינוּ. וְזִכְרוֹן כָּל עַמְּךָ בֵּית יִשְׂרָאֵל לְפָנֶיךָ. לְחֵן וּלְחֶסֶד וּלְרַחֲמִים לְחַיִּים וּלְשָׁלוֹם בְּיוֹם חַג הַמַּצּוֹת | חַג הַשָּׁבוּעוֹת | חַג הַסֻּכּוֹת | חַג הָעֲצֶרֶת הַזֶּה. זָכְרֵנוּ יְיָ אֱלֹהֵינוּ בּוֹ לְטוֹבָה. וּפָקְדֵנוּ בוֹ לִבְרָכָה. וְהוֹשִׁיעֵנוּ בוֹ לְחַיִּים. וּבִדְבַר יְשׁוּעָה וְרַחֲמִים חוּס וְחָנֵּנוּ. וְרַחֵם עָלֵינוּ וְהוֹשִׁיעֵנוּ. כִּי אֵלֶיךָ עֵינֵינוּ. כִּי אֵל מֶלֶךְ חַנּוּן וְרַחוּם אָתָּה:

אֱלֹהֵינוּ וֵאלֹהֵי אֲבוֹתֵינוּ (רְצֵה בִמְנוּחָתֵנוּ). קַדְּשֵׁנוּ בְּמִצְוֹתֶיךָ וְתֵן חֶלְקֵנוּ בְּתוֹרָתֶךָ. שַׂבְּעֵנוּ מִטּוּבֶךָ וְשַׂמְּחֵנוּ בִּישׁוּעָתֶךָ. וְטַהֵר לִבֵּנוּ לְעָבְדְּךָ בֶּאֱמֶת. וְהַנְחִילֵנוּ יְיָ אֱלֹהֵינוּ בְּאַהֲבָה וּבְרָצוֹן בְּשִׂמְחָה וּבְשָׂשׂוֹן (שַׁבָּת וּ)מוֹעֲדֵי קָדְשֶׁךָ. וְיִשְׂמְחוּ בְךָ יִשְׂרָאֵל מְקַדְּשֵׁי שְׁמֶךָ. בָּרוּךְ אַתָּה יְיָ מְקַדֵּשׁ (הַשַּׁבָּת וְ)יִשְׂרָאֵל וְהַזְּמַנִּים:

ADORATION.

Almighty God! Creator of heaven and earth! It behooves us to render praise and thanksgiving unto thee, who hast delivered us from the darkness of false belief and sent to us the light of thy truth. Thou art our God, there is no other.

We, therefore, bow the head and bend the knee before thee, Creator and Ruler of the world, and bless thy holy name!

MINISTER, THEN CHOIR AND CONGREGATION:

Vaanachnu, kór'im, umishtáchavim, umódim, lifné Mélech mal'ché hammelóchim, Hakkódosh boruch hu.

Thou art, in truth, our Father, our God, our Saviour, and there is none besides thee, as is written in thy law: Thou shalt know this day and reflect in thy heart that the Lord is God in heaven above as on earth below; and there is none else.

We fervently pray, O Lord our God, that we may speedily behold the glory of thy mighty power, banishing all impurities from the earth, destroying idolatry and wickedness, and establishing thy truth among mankind; that all the inhabitants of the earth may invoke thy name, acknowledge thy unity, and understand that to thee alone every knee must bend and every tongue swear fealty.

May all thy children, O God, soon be united in a common bond of brotherhood, may the time be hastened when no religious differences will separate them, but when they will all adore thee as the universal father, worship thee in the spirit of true religion, and unite in proclaiming the unity of thy holy name.

Thus, O God, do thou reign over them for ever and ever, for the kingdom is thine, and unto thee appertain power, glory and majesty from everlasting to everlasting. As it is written: The Lord will reign for ever and ever; the Lord will be king over all the earth; on that day shall God be acknowledged One and his name One.

MINISTER, THEN CHOIR AND CONGREGATION:

Veho-yoh Adonoy lemélech al kol hoórets, bayóm hahu yih'yéh Adonoy echod, u-shemo echad.

תפלת ערבית לשבת ויו״ט

עָלֵינוּ לְשַׁבֵּחַ לַאֲדוֹן הַכֹּל. לָתֵת גְּדֻלָּה לְיוֹצֵר בְּרֵאשִׁית. שֶׁהוּא נוֹטֶה שָׁמַיִם וְיוֹסֵד אָרֶץ. וּמוֹשַׁב יְקָרוֹ בַּשָּׁמַיִם מִמַּעַל. וּשְׁכִינַת עֻזּוֹ בְּגָבְהֵי מְרוֹמִים. הוּא אֱלֹהֵינוּ אֵין עוֹד.

וַאֲנַחְנוּ כֹּרְעִים וּמִשְׁתַּחֲוִים וּמוֹדִים

לִפְנֵי מֶלֶךְ מַלְכֵי הַמְּלָכִים. הַקָּדוֹשׁ בָּרוּךְ הוּא:

אֱמֶת מַלְכֵּנוּ אֶפֶס זוּלָתוֹ. כַּכָּתוּב בְּתוֹרָתוֹ. וְיָדַעְתָּ הַיּוֹם וַהֲשֵׁבֹתָ אֶל־לְבָבֶךָ. כִּי יְיָ הוּא הָאֱלֹהִים בַּשָּׁמַיִם מִמַּעַל וְעַל־הָאָרֶץ מִתָּחַת. אֵין עוֹד:

עַל כֵּן נְקַוֶּה לְךָ יְיָ אֱלֹהֵינוּ. לִרְאוֹת מְהֵרָה בְּתִפְאֶרֶת עֻזֶּךָ. לְהַעֲבִיר גִּלּוּלִים מִן הָאָרֶץ. וְהָאֱלִילִים כָּרוֹת יִכָּרֵתוּן. לְתַקֵּן עוֹלָם בְּמַלְכוּת שַׁדַּי. וְכָל־בְּנֵי בָשָׂר יִקְרְאוּ בִשְׁמֶךָ. לְהַפְנוֹת אֵלֶיךָ כָּל־רִשְׁעֵי אָרֶץ. יַכִּירוּ וְיֵדְעוּ כָּל־יוֹשְׁבֵי תֵבֵל. כִּי לְךָ תִּכְרַע כָּל־בֶּרֶךְ. תִּשָּׁבַע כָּל־לָשׁוֹן. לְפָנֶיךָ יְיָ אֱלֹהֵינוּ יִכְרְעוּ וְיִפֹּלוּ. וְלִכְבוֹד שִׁמְךָ יְקָר יִתֵּנוּ. וִיקַבְּלוּ כֻלָּם אֶת־עֹל מַלְכוּתֶךָ. וְתִמְלֹךְ עֲלֵיהֶם מְהֵרָה לְעוֹלָם וָעֶד. כִּי הַמַּלְכוּת שֶׁלְּךָ הִיא. וּלְעוֹלְמֵי עַד תִּמְלוֹךְ בְּכָבוֹד. כַּכָּתוּב בְּתוֹרָתֶךָ. יְיָ יִמְלֹךְ לְעֹלָם וָעֶד: וְנֶאֱמַר וְהָיָה יְיָ לְמֶלֶךְ עַל־כָּל־הָאָרֶץ בַּיּוֹם הַהוּא יִהְיֶה יְיָ אֶחָד וּשְׁמוֹ אֶחָד:

Address to the Mourners.

Brothers and sisters, who are mourning for dear lives departed, remember your beloved ones and honor their names in the midst of the congregation of Israel. May the memory of the righteous inspire you to noble deeds and works in their honor. Rise, and praise with me the name of the most High, according to the anscient custom of our fathers.

Mourners' Kaddish.

May thy great and ineffable name, O Lord of life and death, be exalted and sanctified throughout the world, which thou hast created according to thy will. May thy kingdom be established in our midst, in our lifetime and in our days, and in the days of the whole house of Israel. Amen.

The Congregation:

May his great and ineffable name be blessed and glorified for ever and ever.

Praised and hallowed be thy name who hast created man in thy image and planted within him eternal life. In thy hand is the soul of every living being and the spirit of all flesh. Blessed art thou, whose hymns, praises and benedictions are repeated throughout the world. Amen.

The Congregation:

Praised be he and his glorious name.

Unto Israel, unto all the righteous and unto all who departed this life according to the will of God, may there be granted abundance of peace, and a blissful portion in the life to come, grace and mercy by the Lord of heaven and earth.

May the fullness of peace from heaven, with life and health be granted unto us and unto all Israel. Amen.

May he who establisheth peace in his heavenly spheres grant happiness and peace unto us, unto all Israel and to all mankind. Amen.

Closing Song.
Benediction.

קדיש דאבלים.

יִתְגַּדַּל וְיִתְקַדַּשׁ שְׁמֵהּ רַבָּא. בְּעָלְמָא דִּי־בְרָא כִרְעוּתֵהּ. וְיַמְלִיךְ מַלְכוּתֵהּ. בְּחַיֵּיכוֹן וּבְיוֹמֵיכוֹן וּבְחַיֵּי דְכָל בֵּית יִשְׂרָאֵל. בַּעֲגָלָא וּבִזְמַן קָרִיב. וְאִמְרוּ אָמֵן.

יְהֵא שְׁמֵהּ רַבָּא מְבָרַךְ. לְעָלַם וּלְעָלְמֵי עָלְמַיָּא.

יִתְבָּרַךְ וְיִשְׁתַּבַּח וְיִתְפָּאַר וְיִתְרוֹמַם. וְיִתְנַשֵּׂא וְיִתְהַדָּר וְיִתְעַלֶּה וְיִתְהַלָּל שְׁמֵהּ דְּקוּדְשָׁא. בְּרִיךְ הוּא. לְעֵלָּא מִן כָּל בִּרְכָתָא וְשִׁירָתָא. תֻּשְׁבְּחָתָא וְנֶחֱמָתָא. דַּאֲמִירָן בְּעָלְמָא. וְאִמְרוּ אָמֵן:

עַל יִשְׂרָאֵל וְעַל צַדִּיקַיָּא. וְעַל־כָּל־מַן דְּאִתְפְּטַר מִן עָלְמָא הָדֵין בִּרְעוּתֵהּ דֶאֱלָהָא. יְהֵא לְהוֹן שְׁלָמָא רַבָּא וְחוּלָקָא־טָבָא לְחַיֵּי עָלְמָא דְּאָתֵי. וְחִסְדָּא וְרַחֲמֵי כָּן־קָדָם מָרֵא שְׁמַיָּא וְאַרְעָא. וְאִמְרוּ אָמֵן:

תִּתְקַבַּל צְלוֹתְהוֹן וּבָעוּתְהוֹן דְּכָל־יִשְׂרָאֵל קֳדָם אֲבוּהוֹן דִּי בִשְׁמַיָּא. וְאִמְרוּ אָמֵן:

יְהֵא שְׁלָמָא רַבָּא כִּן־שְׁמַיָּא וְחַיִּים. עָלֵינוּ וְעַל־כָּל־יִשְׂרָאֵל. וְאִמְרוּ אָמֵן:

עֹשֶׂה שָׁלוֹם בִּמְרוֹמָיו. הוּא יַעֲשֶׂה שָׁלוֹם עָלֵינוּ וְעַל כָּל יִשְׂרָאֵל. וְאִמְרוּ אָמֵן:

MORNING SERVICE

FOR

SABBATH AND HOLIDAYS.

Organ Prelude.

MINISTER:

מַה־טֹּבוּ אֹהָלֶיךָ יַעֲקֹב מִשְׁכְּנֹתֶיךָ יִשְׂרָאֵל: וַאֲנִי בְּרֹב
חַסְדְּךָ אָבֹא בֵיתֶךָ אֶשְׁתַּחֲוֶה אֶל־הֵיכַל קָדְשְׁךָ בְּיִרְאָתֶךָ:
יְיָ אָהַבְתִּי מְעוֹן בֵּיתֶךָ וּמְקוֹם מִשְׁכַּן כְּבוֹדֶךָ: וַאֲנִי
אֶשְׁתַּחֲוֶה וְאֶכְרָעָה אֶבְרְכָה לִפְנֵי־יְיָ עֹשִׂי: וַאֲנִי תְפִלָּתִי
לְךָ יְיָ עֵת רָצוֹן אֱלֹהִים בְּרָב־חַסְדֶּךָ עֲנֵנִי בֶּאֱמֶת יִשְׁעֶךָ:

How beautiful are thy tents, O Jacob, thy tabernacles, O Israel! With faith in thy loving kindness, O God, we enter thy house; with profound reverence we will worship thee in thy holy temple. We love thy dwelling-place, O Lord, the abode sanctified by thy holiness. We will bow down before thee, and offer up our supplication unto thee, O God our Creator. Accept our prayers at this hour in the fulness of thy grace. Hear us, O God, our stronghold and support.

CHOIR: (Either of the following sentences.)

Worship the Lord in the beauty of holiness;
Stand in awe before him all the earth.
Give unto the Lord glory and praise;
Worship the Lord in holy attire.
Serve the Lord with gladness;
Come before his presence with songs.

RESPONSIVE READING.

Select one or more Psalms from the following pages; for the Three Festivals, appropriate Psalms from the appended Collection, then begin Borechu on page 29.

Psalm 100. מזמור לתודה

Raise a voice of joy unto the Lord, all ye lands!

Serve the Lord with gladness; come before his presence with songs!

Know ye that the Lord is God; it is he that made us, and we are his, his people, and the flock of his pasture.

Enter into his gates with thanksgiving, and his courts with praise; be thankful to him, and bless his name!

For the Lord is good; his mercy is everlasting; and his truth endureth to all generations.

Psalm 19. השמים מספרים כבוד אל

The heavens declare the glory of God; the firmament showeth forth the work of his hands.

Day uttereth instruction unto day, and night showeth knowledge unto night.

They have no speech nor language, and their voice is not heard:

Yet their sound goeth forth to all the earth, and their words to the ends of the world.

In them hath he set tabernacle for the sun, which like a bridegroom he cometh forth from his chamber, and rejoiceth, like a hero, to run his course.

He goeth forth from the extremity of heaven, and maketh his circuit to the end of it; and nothing is hid from his heat.

The law of the Lord is perfect, reviving the soul; the precepts of the Lord are sure, making wise simple;

The statutes of the Lord are right, rejoicing the heart; the commandments of the Lord are pure, enlightening the eyes;

The fear of the Lord is clean, enduring for ever; the judgments of the Lord are true and righteous altogether.

More precious are they than gold; yea, than much fine gold; sweeter than honey and the honeycomb.

By them also is thy servant warned, and in keeping of them there is great reward.

Who knoweth his own offences? O, cleanse thou me from secret faults!

Keep back also thy servant from presumptuous sins; let them not have dominion over me!

Then shall I be upright, and free from gross transgression.

May the words of my mouth and the meditation of my heart be acceptable in thy sight, O Lord, my Strength and my Redeemer.

Psalm 34. אברכה את יי בכל עת

I will bless the Lord at all times; his praise shall continually be in my mouth.

In the Lord doth my soul boast; let the afflicted hear, and rejoice!

O magnify the Lord with me, and let us exalt his name together!

I sought the Lord, and he heard me, and delivered me from all my fears.

Look up to him, and ye shall have light; your faces shall never be ashamed.

This afflicted man cried, and the Lord heard, and saved him from all his troubles.

The angels of the Lord encamp around those who fear him, and deliver them.

O taste, and see how good is the Lord! happy the man who trusteth him!

O fear the Lord, ye his servants! for to those who fear him there shall be no want.

Young lions may want, and suffer hunger; but they who fear the Lord want no good thing.

Come, ye children, hearken to me! I will teach you the fear of the Lord.

Who is he that loveth life, and desireth many days, in which he may see good?

Guard well thy tongue from evil, and thy lips from speaking guile!

Depart from evil, and do good; seek peace, and pursue it!

The eyes of the Lord are upon the righteous, and his ears are open to their cry.

But the face of the Lord is against evil-doers, to cut off their remembrance from the earth.

The righteous cry, and the Lord heareth, and delivereth them from all their troubles.

The Lord is near to them that are of a broken heart, and saveth such as are of a contrite spirit.

Many are the afflictions of the righteous; but the Lord delivereth him from them all.

He guardeth all his bones; not one of them shall be broken.

Calamity destroyeth the wicked, and they who hate righteousness suffer for it.

The Lord redeemeth the life of his servants, and none that put their trust in him will suffer of it.

Psalm 33. רננו צדיקים בי״י

Rejoice, O ye righteous, in the Lord! for praise becometh the upright.

Praise the Lord with the harp; sing to him with the musical instruments!

Sing to him a new song; play skilfully amid the sound of trumpets!

For the word of the Lord is right, and all his acts are faithful.

He loveth justice and equity; the earth is full of the goodness of the Lord.

By the word of the Lord were the heavens made, and all the hosts of them by the breath of his mouth.

He gathereth the waters of the sea, as a heap; he layeth up the deep in storehouses.

Let all the earth fear the Lord; let all the inhabitants of the world stand in awe of him!

For he spake, and it was done; he commanded, and it stood fast.

The Lord bringeth the devices of the nations to nothing; he frustrateth the designs of kingdoms.

The purposes of the Lord stand for ever; the designs of his heart, to all generations.

Happy the nation whose God is the Lord; the people whom he hath chosen for his inheritance.
The Lord looketh down from heaven; he beholdeth all the children of men;
From his dwelling-place he beholdeth all the inhabitants of the earth, —
He that formed the hearts of all, and observeth all their works.
A king is not saved by the number of his forces, nor a hero by the greatness of his strength.
The horse is a vain thing for safety, nor can he deliver his master by his great strength.
Behold, the eye of the Lord is upon them that fear him,— upon them that trust in his goodness.
To save them from the power of death, and keep them alive in famine.
The hope of our souls is in the Lord; he is our help and our shield.
Yea, in him doth our heart rejoice; in his holy name we have confidence.
May thy goodness be upon us, O Lord! according as we trust in thee!

Psalm 145. ארוממך אלוה המלך

I will extol thee, my God, the King! I will praise thy name for ever and ever!
Great is the Lord, and greatly to be praised; yea, his greatness is unsearchable.
One generation shall praise thy works to another, and shall declare thy mighty deeds.
I will speak of the glorious honor of thy majesty, and of thy wonderful works.
Men shall speak of the might of thy wonderful deeds, and I will declare thy greatness;
They shall pour forth the praise of thy great goodness, and sing of thy righteousness.
The Lord is gracious, and full of compassion, slow to anger and rich in mercy.

The Lord is good to all, and his tender mercies are over all his works.

All thy works praise thee, O Lord! and thy holy ones bless thee!

They speak of the glory of thy kingdom, and talk of thy power;

To make known to the sons of men his mighty deeds, and the glorious majesty of his kingdom.

Thy kingdom is an everlasting kingdom, and thy dominion endureth throughout all generations.

The Lord upholdeth all that fall, and raiseth up all that are bowed down.

The eyes of all wait upon thee, and thou givest them their food in due season;

Thou openest thy hand, and satisfiest the desire of every living thing.

The Lord is righteous in all his ways, and merciful in all his works.

The Lord is nigh to all that call upon him, to all that call upon him in truth.

He fulfilleth the desire of them that fear him; he heareth their cry, and saveth them.

The Lord preserveth all that love him; but he will destroy the wicked.

My mouth shall speak the praise of the Lord; and let all flesh bless his holy name for ever and ever! Hallelujah!

MINISTER:

Borechu es Adonoy hammevoroch.
Praise ye the Lord to whom all praise is due!

Boruch Adonoy hammevoroch l'olom voëd.
Praised be the Lord through all eternity!

We praise thee, O Lord, our God, Ruler of the Universe, Creator of light and darkness, Source of all wisdom, Fountain of truth and peace. We praise thee, we thank thee, we magnify thee. In thy mercy thou causest light to radiate over the earth and all its inhabitants, and renewest daily in kindness the wonders of thy creation. Yea, how manifold are thy works, O Eternal, in wisdom thou hast made them all, the earth is full of thy treasures. O Lord of life, have compassion on us, be our defense, our shield, our protection. Praised be to thee, O God, Author of peace and light.

With infinite love, O Lord our God, thou hast guided our fathers, who trusted in thee, and hast taught them thy laws of life. O be gracious unto us; incline our hearts to thee, O merciful Father! May we love thy precepts, and be enabled to learn and to teach, to observe and to practice them in the spirit of love. Enlighten our minds in thy holy law, that we may learn to love and revere thy Name and so order our lives that we may never be put to shame for our deeds. In thy holy Name we put our trust; we rejoice and delight in thy help. For with thee alone is salvation. Thou hast appointed us, the children of Israel, to proclaim this truth, to acknowledge thee and thy unity before all nations of the earth. Praise be to thee, O Lord, who hast sanctified thy people Israel in love.

CHOIR: **Amen.**

MINISTER, THEN CHOIR AND CONGREGATION:

Sh'ma Yisroel, Adonoy Elohanu, Adonoy echod.
HEAR, O ISRAEL, GOD OUR LORD, GOD IS ONE.

Boruch Shem kevod mal'chuso l'olom voëd.
Praised be the name of his glorious Kingdom for evermore.

בָּרְכוּ אֶת יְיָ הַמְבֹרָךְ:
בָּרוּךְ יְיָ הַמְבֹרָךְ לְעוֹלָם וָעֶד:
בָּרוּךְ אַתָּה יְיָ אֱלֹהֵינוּ מֶלֶךְ הָעוֹלָם. יוֹצֵר אוֹר וּבוֹרֵא חֹשֶׁךְ. עֹשֶׂה שָׁלוֹם וּבוֹרֵא אֶת הַכֹּל:

הַמֵּאִיר לָאָרֶץ וְלַדָּרִים עָלֶיהָ בְּרַחֲמִים. וּבְטוּבוֹ מְחַדֵּשׁ בְּכָל יוֹם תָּמִיד מַעֲשֵׂה בְרֵאשִׁית. הַמֶּלֶךְ הַמְרוֹמָם לְבַדּוֹ מֵאָז. הַמְשֻׁבָּח וְהַמְפֹאָר וְהַמִּתְנַשֵּׂא מִימוֹת עוֹלָם: אֱלֹהֵי עוֹלָם בְּרַחֲמֶיךָ הָרַבִּים רַחֵם עָלֵינוּ. אֲדוֹן עֻזֵּנוּ צוּר מִשְׂגַּבֵּנוּ. מָגֵן יִשְׁעֵנוּ מִשְׂגָּב בַּעֲדֵנוּ: שִׁמְךָ יְיָ אֱלֹהֵינוּ יִתְקַדָּשׁ. וְזִכְרְךָ מַלְכֵּנוּ יִתְפָּאַר. בַּשָּׁמַיִם מִמַּעַל וְעַל הָאָרֶץ מִתָּחַת. תִּתְבָּרַךְ מוֹשִׁיעֵנוּ עַל שֶׁבַח מַעֲשֵׂה יָדֶיךָ. וְעַל מְאוֹרֵי אוֹר שֶׁעָשִׂיתָ יְפָאֲרוּךָ סֶּלָה: בָּרוּךְ אַתָּה יְיָ יוֹצֵר הַמְּאוֹרוֹת:

אַהֲבָה רַבָּה אֲהַבְתָּנוּ יְיָ אֱלֹהֵינוּ. חֶמְלָה גְדוֹלָה וִיתֵרָה חָמַלְתָּ עָלֵינוּ. אָבִינוּ מַלְכֵּנוּ. בַּעֲבוּר אֲבוֹתֵינוּ שֶׁבָּטְחוּ בְךָ. וַתְּלַמְּדֵם חֻקֵּי חַיִּים. כֵּן תְּחָנֵּנוּ וּתְלַמְּדֵנוּ: אָבִינוּ הָאָב הָרַחֲמָן. רַחֵם עָלֵינוּ. וְתֵן בְּלִבֵּנוּ לְהָבִין וּלְהַשְׂכִּיל. לִשְׁמֹעַ לִלְמֹד וּלְלַמֵּד. לִשְׁמֹר וְלַעֲשׂוֹת וּלְקַיֵּם אֶת כָּל דִּבְרֵי תַלְמוּד תּוֹרָתֶךָ בְּאַהֲבָה: וְהָאֵר עֵינֵינוּ בְּתוֹרָתֶךָ. וְדַבֵּק לִבֵּנוּ בְּמִצְוֹתֶיךָ. וְיַחֵד לְבָבֵנוּ לְאַהֲבָה וּלְיִרְאָה שְׁמֶךָ. וְלֹא נֵבוֹשׁ לְעוֹלָם וָעֶד: כִּי בְשֵׁם קָדְשְׁךָ בָּטָחְנוּ. נָגִילָה וְנִשְׂמְחָה בִּישׁוּעָתֶךָ. כִּי אֵל פּוֹעֵל יְשׁוּעוֹת אָתָּה. וּבָנוּ בָחַרְתָּ וְקֵרַבְתָּנוּ לְשִׁמְךָ הַגָּדוֹל סֶלָה בֶּאֱמֶת. לְהוֹדוֹת לְךָ וּלְיַחֶדְךָ בְּאַהֲבָה. בָּרוּךְ אַתָּה יְיָ הַבּוֹחֵר בְּעַמּוֹ יִשְׂרָאֵל בְּאַהֲבָה:

שְׁמַע יִשְׂרָאֵל יְהֹוָה אֱלֹהֵינוּ יְהֹוָה אֶחָד:
בָּרוּךְ שֵׁם כְּבוֹד מַלְכוּתוֹ לְעוֹלָם וָעֶד:

Thou shalt love the Eternal thy God with all thy heart, with all thy soul, and with all thy might. And these words, which I command thee to-day, shall be in thy heart. Thou shalt teach them diligently to thy children, and shalt talk of them when thou sittest in thy house, and when thou walkest by the way, and when thou liest down, and when thou risest. And they shall be as a sign on your hand and as an ornament on your brow. And thou shalt write them upon the door posts of thy house and on thy gates. (DEUTER., CHAPT. 6, V. 4—9.)

Unchangeable and immutable is this word with us: God is everlasting; his word is true unto all generations; his commandments stand for ever. He alone is our God and none besides him.

Thou hast been the protector of our fathers in time of distress, thou hast saved us from the hand of oppression; for thou art our Guide, Protector, and Redeemer, the Rock of our salvation, our Helper and Deliverer. Thou art the first and the last, and besides thee there is no power to help or redeem. Thou hast saved Israel from Egyptian bondage and to this day thou art our help and our refuge. Therefore we exalt thee, and praise thy name with the ancient song of our fathers:

MINISTER, THEN CHOIR AND CONGREGATION:

Mi chomocho boëlim Adonoy; mi komócho, neddor bakkódesh, nóro sehillos, osé féleh.

Who is like thee among the mighty, O God, who is like thee glorified through holiness, awe-inspiring, wonder-working!

The redeemed of the Lord sang a new song. They saw thy glorious help and worshipped thee as their God and King proclaiming:

Adonoy yimlóch l'olom voëd.

The Lord will reign for ever and ever.

O Rock of Israel, send redemption to those that are in bondage; for thou art the redeemer of the oppressed, as it is written: Our Redeemer is the Lord of Host, the Holy One of Israel is his name. Praise be to thee, O Lord, Redeemer of Israel. CHOIR: **Amen.**

תפלת שחרית לשבת ויו״ט

וְאָהַבְתָּ אֵת יְיָ אֱלֹהֶיךָ בְּכָל לְבָבְךָ וּבְכָל נַפְשְׁךָ וּבְכָל מְאֹדֶךָ: וְהָיוּ הַדְּבָרִים הָאֵלֶּה אֲשֶׁר אָנֹכִי מְצַוְּךָ הַיּוֹם עַל־לְבָבֶךָ: וְשִׁנַּנְתָּם לְבָנֶיךָ וְדִבַּרְתָּ בָּם. בְּשִׁבְתְּךָ בְּבֵיתֶךָ וּבְלֶכְתְּךָ בַדֶּרֶךְ וּבְשָׁכְבְּךָ וּבְקוּמֶךָ: וּקְשַׁרְתָּם לְאוֹת עַל־יָדֶךָ. וְהָיוּ לְטֹטָפֹת בֵּין עֵינֶיךָ: וּכְתַבְתָּם עַל־מְזֻזוֹת בֵּיתֶךָ וּבִשְׁעָרֶיךָ:

אֱמֶת. אֱלֹהֵי עוֹלָם מַלְכֵּנוּ. צוּר יַעֲקֹב מָגֵן יִשְׁעֵנוּ. לְדוֹר וָדוֹר הוּא קַיָּם וּשְׁמוֹ קַיָּם. וְכִסְאוֹ נָכוֹן וּמַלְכוּתוֹ וֶאֱמוּנָתוֹ לָעַד קַיֶּמֶת. וּדְבָרָיו חָיִים וְקַיָּמִים. נֶאֱמָנִים וְנֶחֱמָדִים לָעַד וּלְעוֹלְמֵי עוֹלָמִים. עַל אֲבוֹתֵינוּ וְעָלֵינוּ. עַל בָּנֵינוּ וְעַל דּוֹרוֹתֵינוּ. וְעַל כָּל דּוֹרוֹת זֶרַע יִשְׂרָאֵל עֲבָדֶיךָ: אֱמֶת. שָׁאַתָּה הוּא יְיָ אֱלֹהֵינוּ וֵאלֹהֵי אֲבוֹתֵינוּ. מַלְכֵּנוּ מֶלֶךְ אֲבוֹתֵינוּ. גּוֹאֲלֵנוּ גּוֹאֵל אֲבוֹתֵינוּ. יוֹצְרֵנוּ צוּר יְשׁוּעָתֵנוּ. פּוֹדֵנוּ וּמַצִּילֵנוּ מֵעוֹלָם שְׁמֶךָ. אֵין אֱלֹהִים זוּלָתֶךָ: אֱמֶת. אַתָּה הוּא רִאשׁוֹן וְאַתָּה הוּא אַחֲרוֹן. וּמִבַּלְעָדֶיךָ אֵין לָנוּ מֶלֶךְ גּוֹאֵל וּמוֹשִׁיעַ. מִמִּצְרַיִם גְּאַלְתָּנוּ יְיָ אֱלֹהֵינוּ. וּמִבֵּית עֲבָדִים פְּדִיתָנוּ. עַל זֹאת שִׁבְּחוּ אֲהוּבִים וְרוֹמְמוּ אֵל:

כִּי־כָמֹכָה בָּאֵלִם יְיָ מִי כָּמֹכָה נֶאְדָּר בַּקֹּדֶשׁ. נוֹרָא תְהִלֹּת עֹשֵׂה־פֶלֶא:

שִׁירָה חֲדָשָׁה שִׁבְּחוּ גְאוּלִים לְשִׁמְךָ. עַל שְׂפַת הַיָּם יַחַד כֻּלָּם הוֹדוּ וְהִמְלִיכוּ וְאָמְרוּ:

יְיָ יִמְלֹךְ לְעֹלָם וָעֶד:

צוּר יִשְׂרָאֵל. קוּמָה בְּעֶזְרַת יִשְׂרָאֵל. גּוֹאֲלֵנוּ יְיָ צְבָאוֹת שְׁמוֹ קְדוֹשׁ יִשְׂרָאֵל. בָּרוּךְ אַתָּה יְיָ גָּאַל יִשְׂרָאֵל:

Praise be to thee, O Eternal our God, God of our fathers, God of Abraham, Isaac, and Jacob, Almighty and Supreme Ruler of the world, who renderest just reward unto all. Thou rememberest the pious deeds of the fathers, and bringest redemption and love to their descendants; thou art our Father, our Protector, and Helper. Praise be to thee, O God, Shield of Abraham. *)

Thou art mighty, O Lord, thy help is ever near. Thou sustainest in kindness the living; thou upholdest the falling, healest the sick, loosest the bonds of captives, and keepest thy faith to those who sleep in the dust. Who is like unto thee, Almighty! Author of life and death, who givest salvation, and rememberest thy creatures unto life eternal! Praise be to thee, O God, who hast planted within us eternal life.

CHOIR: **Amen.**

Thou art holy, and thy name is holy, and thy worshippers daily praise thy holiness.

SANCTIFICATION.
(The Congregation will rise.)

Let us sanctify the Name of the Holy One of Israel, as it is sanctified throughout the universe, and in the solemn words of our prophets we exclaim:

Kodósh, Kodósh, Kodósh Adonoy Tsevoós, meló chol hoó·etz k'vodo.

Holy, holy, holy is the Lord of hosts, the whole earth is full of his glory.

CHOIR AND CONGREGATION: *Kodósh.*

---

*) On 1st Day of Passover.	*) On Atzereth.
Thou, O God, makest the wind blow and the dew descend:	Thou, O God, makest the wind blow and the rain descend.

O let it descend
To every one's blessing and the hurt of none!
CHOIR: **Amen.**
To every one's joy and the woe of none!
CHOIR: **Amen.**
To every one's life and the death of none!
CHOIR: **Amen.**

תפלת שחרית לשבת ויו״ט

בָּרוּךְ אַתָּה יְיָ אֱלֹהֵינוּ וֵאלֹהֵי אֲבוֹתֵינוּ. אֱלֹהֵי אַבְרָהָם אֱלֹהֵי יִצְחָק וֵאלֹהֵי יַעֲקֹב. הָאֵל הַגָּדֹל הַגִּבּוֹר וְהַנּוֹרָא. אֵל עֶלְיוֹן. גּוֹמֵל חֲסָדִים טוֹבִים. וְקֹנֶה הַכֹּל וְזוֹכֵר חַסְדֵי אָבוֹת. וּמֵבִיא גְאֻלָּה לִבְנֵי בְנֵיהֶם. לְמַעַן שְׁמוֹ בְּאַהֲבָה: מֶלֶךְ עוֹזֵר וּמוֹשִׁיעַ וּמָגֵן. בָּרוּךְ אַתָּה יְיָ מָגֵן אַבְרָהָם:

אַתָּה גִּבּוֹר לְעוֹלָם אֲדֹנָי. רַב לְהוֹשִׁיעַ: *) מְכַלְכֵּל חַיִּים בְּחֶסֶד. מְחַיֶּה הַכֹּל בְּרַחֲמִים רַבִּים. סוֹמֵךְ נוֹפְלִים וְרוֹפֵא חוֹלִים וּמַתִּיר אֲסוּרִים. וּמְקַיֵּם אֱמוּנָתוֹ לִישֵׁנֵי עָפָר. מִי כָמוֹךָ בַּעַל גְּבוּרוֹת. וּמִי דוֹמֶה לָּךְ. מֶלֶךְ מֵמִית וּמְחַיֶּה. וּמַצְמִיחַ יְשׁוּעָה. בָּרוּךְ אַתָּה יְיָ מְחַיֶּה הַכֹּל:

אַתָּה קָדוֹשׁ וְשִׁמְךָ קָדוֹשׁ. וּקְדוֹשִׁים בְּכָל יוֹם יְהַלְלוּךָ סֶּלָה:

קדושה:

נְקַדֵּשׁ אֶת שִׁמְךָ בָּעוֹלָם. כְּשֵׁם שֶׁמַּקְדִּישִׁים אוֹתוֹ בִּשְׁמֵי מָרוֹם. כַּכָּתוּב עַל יַד נְבִיאֶךָ. וְקָרָא זֶה אֶל זֶה וְאָמַר:

קָדוֹשׁ. קָדוֹשׁ. קָדוֹשׁ יְיָ צְבָאוֹת. מְלֹא כָל הָאָרֶץ כְּבוֹדוֹ:

כְּבוֹדוֹ מָלֵא עוֹלָם. מְשָׁרְתָיו שׁוֹאֲלִים זֶה לָזֶה. אַיֵּה מְקוֹם כְּבוֹדוֹ. לְעֻמָּתָם בָּרוּךְ יֹאמֵרוּ:

---

*)ביום א׳ דפסח *)ביום שמיני העצרת

מַשִּׁיב הָרוּחַ וּמוֹרִיד הַטָּל | מַשִּׁיב הָרוּחַ וּמוֹרִיד הַגֶּשֶׁם
אָנָּא הוֹרִידֵהוּ. לִבְרָכָה וְלֹא לִקְלָלָה:
לְשׂוֹבַע וְלֹא לְרָזוֹן. לְחַיִּים וְלֹא לְמָוֶת:

Yea, his glory fills the universe, everywhere is his throne of honor, and all creation sounds his praise continually, saying:

Boruch k'vód Adonoy mimmekomo.

Praised be the Glory of God which fills the universe!

May the glory of God appear to us; and in his mercy be gracious to those who twice daily, yea evening and morning, proclaim the unity of his Name in love and devotion:

Sh'ma Yisroel, Adonoy Elohénu, Adonoy Echud.

HEAR, O ISRAEL, THE LORD OUR GOD, THE LORD IS ONE.

The Lord is One; He is our Father, our King, our Saviour; He will grant our prayers and manifest himself before all mankind as the God of Israel.

CHOIR: *Ani Adonoy Elohéchem.*

I am the Lord your God.

The Lord is almighty, how excellent is his name throughout the world. And the Lord shall be King over all the earth, on that day shall the Lord be acknowledged one and his name one, as is written in Holy Scriptures:

Yimlóch Adonoy l'olom, Elohayich Zion l'dór, vodór Hallelujah.

The Lord shall reign for evermore, even thy God, O Zion, from generation to generation. Hallelujah!

For ever will we declare thy greatness and proclaim thy holiness, neither shall thy praise ever depart from our lips. Praise be to thee, Almighty and Holy God. Amen.

(The Congregation will be seated.)
(ON SABBATH.)

Accept our thanks, O Lord our God, for thy loving kindness to us in giving us this sacred day of rest. After six days of toil we hail this messenger of peace, that brings strength to the weary, courage to the despondent, freedom to the enslaved! May we wisely improve the precious opportunities which time offers, and never forget that thou blessest the fruit of our labor and providest us with all that we need; that man is sent into the world to live not by bread

בָּרוּךְ כְּבוֹד יְיָ מִמְּקוֹמוֹ:

מִמְּקוֹמוֹ הוּא יִפֶן בְּרַחֲמִים. וְיָחוֹן עַם הַמְיַחֲדִים שְׁמוֹ עֶרֶב וָבֹקֶר. בְּכָל יוֹם תָּמִיד פַּעֲמַיִם. בְּאַהֲבָה שְׁמַע אוֹמְרִים:

שְׁמַע יִשְׂרָאֵל יְהֹוָה אֱלֹהֵינוּ יְהֹוָה אֶחָד:

אֶחָד הוּא אֱלֹהֵינוּ. הוּא אָבִינוּ. הוּא מַלְכֵּנוּ. הוּא מוֹשִׁיעֵנוּ. וְהוּא יַשְׁמִיעֵנוּ בְּרַחֲמָיו שֵׁנִית. לְעֵינֵי כָּל חָי. לִהְיוֹת לָכֶם לֵאלֹהִים. אֲנִי יְיָ אֱלֹהֵיכֶם:

וְהָיָה יְיָ לְמֶלֶךְ עַל כָּל הָאָרֶץ. בַּיּוֹם הַהוּא יִהְיֶה יְיָ אֶחָד וּשְׁמוֹ אֶחָד:

יִמְלֹךְ יְיָ לְעוֹלָם. אֱלֹהַיִךְ צִיּוֹן לְדֹר וָדֹר. הַלְלוּיָהּ:

לְדוֹר וָדוֹר נַגִּיד גָּדְלֶךָ. וּלְנֵצַח נְצָחִים קְדֻשָּׁתְךָ נַקְדִּישׁ. וְשִׁבְחֲךָ אֱלֹהֵינוּ מִפִּינוּ לֹא יָמוּשׁ לְעוֹלָם וָעֶד. כִּי אֵל מֶלֶךְ גָּדוֹל וְקָדוֹשׁ אָתָּה. בָּרוּךְ אַתָּה יְיָ הָאֵל הַקָּדוֹשׁ:

לשבת.

יִשְׂמְחוּ בְמַלְכוּתְךָ שׁוֹמְרֵי שַׁבָּת וְקוֹרְאֵי עֹנֶג. עַם מְקַדְּשֵׁי שְׁבִיעִי. כֻּלָּם יִשְׂבְּעוּ וְיִתְעַנְּגוּ מִטּוּבֶךָ. וּבַשְּׁבִיעִי רָצִיתָ בּוֹ וְקִדַּשְׁתּוֹ. חֶמְדַּת יָמִים אוֹתוֹ קָרָאתָ. זֵכֶר לְמַעֲשֵׂה בְרֵאשִׁית. וְכֵן כָּתוּב בְּתוֹרָתֶךָ:

וְשָׁמְרוּ בְנֵי־יִשְׂרָאֵל אֶת־הַשַּׁבָּת. לַעֲשׂוֹת אֶת־הַשַּׁבָּת לְדֹרֹתָם. בְּרִית עוֹלָם: בֵּינִי וּבֵין בְּנֵי יִשְׂרָאֵל אוֹת הִוא לְעֹלָם. כִּי־שֵׁשֶׁת יָמִים עָשָׂה יְיָ אֶת־הַשָּׁמַיִם וְאֶת־הָאָרֶץ. וּבַיּוֹם הַשְּׁבִיעִי שָׁבַת וַיִּנָּפַשׁ:

(ON SABBATH.)

alone, but by thy word and by obedience to thy law. Bestow upon us a pure heart and a spirit quickened by thy holy word, that we may be steadfast in the duties and patient in the trials of life. Swiftly our years vanish, and soon there is an end to all our work and work-days on earth. Grant that when all the cares and anxieties of this life are passed away, we may look back with contentment upon our earthly career and enter upon the inheritance of the everlasting Sabbath-day, to enjoy eternal felicity in thy presence.

(ON HOLIDAYS.)

We give thanks unto thee, O Eternal our God, for the unspeakeable love and mercy with which thou hast chosen our fathers from among all nations and hast appointed them to be the bearers of thy truth, to spread the knowledge of thy holy name and to consecrate their lives to thy service. In the abundance of thy grace thou hast given us Sabbaths for rest, festive days for joy and the return of seasons for gladness; even this (Sabbath-day and this) Day of the Feast of

Passover	Weeks	Tabernacles	Conclusion
the anniversary of our redemption from bondage.	the anniversary of the revelation on Mount Sinai.	the time of thanksgiving for thy bountiful blessing.	the time of rejoicing over thy bountiful blessing.

a holy convocation, a memorial of our departure from Egypt.

O Eternal our God, God of our fathers, grant that our memorial, the memorial of our fathers, and of all thy people Israel, may come before thee for grace, favor and mercy, life and peace, on this Day of the Feast of

Passover, | Weeks, | Tabernacles, | Conclusion.

Remember us, O Lord, for our good, bless us with happiness, and help us in the trials of life. Cause thy mercy to descend upon us and bring us salvation, according to the promise of of thy holy word; for to thee we look for aid, O our Heavenly father, who rulest all mankind in mercy and love.

אֱלֹהֵינוּ וֵאלֹהֵי אֲבוֹתֵינוּ. רְצֵה בִמְנוּחָתֵנוּ. קַדְּשֵׁנוּ בְּמִצְוֹתֶיךָ. וְתֵן חֶלְקֵנוּ בְּתוֹרָתֶךָ. שַׂבְּעֵנוּ מִטּוּבֶךָ. וְשַׂמְּחֵנוּ בִּישׁוּעָתֶךָ. וְטַהֵר לִבֵּנוּ לְעָבְדְּךָ בֶּאֱמֶת. וְהַנְחִילֵנוּ יְיָ אֱלֹהֵינוּ בְּאַהֲבָה וּבְרָצוֹן שַׁבַּת קָדְשֶׁךָ. וְיָנוּחוּ בָה יִשְׂרָאֵל מְקַדְּשֵׁי שְׁמֶךָ. בָּרוּךְ אַתָּה יְיָ מְקַדֵּשׁ הַשַּׁבָּת:

לראש חדש וח״המ.

אֱלֹהֵינוּ וֵאלֹהֵי אֲבוֹתֵינוּ יַעֲלֶה וְיָבֹא זִכְרוֹנֵנוּ וְזִכְרוֹן אֲבוֹתֵינוּ. וְזִכְרוֹן כָּל עַמְּךָ בֵּית יִשְׂרָאֵל לְפָנֶיךָ. לְחֵן וּלְחֶסֶד וּלְרַחֲמִים לְחַיִּים וּלְשָׁלוֹם בְּיוֹם

רֹאשׁ הַחֹדֶשׁ | חַג הַמַּצּוֹת | חַג הַסֻּכּוֹת

הַזֶּה. זָכְרֵנוּ יְיָ אֱלֹהֵינוּ בּוֹ לְטוֹבָה. וּפָקְדֵנוּ בּוֹ לִבְרָכָה וְהוֹשִׁיעֵנוּ בּוֹ לְחַיִּים. וּבִדְבַר יְשׁוּעָה וְרַחֲמִים חוּס וְחָנֵּנוּ. וְרַחֵם עָלֵינוּ וְהוֹשִׁיעֵנוּ. כִּי אֵלֶיךָ עֵינֵינוּ. כִּי אֵל מֶלֶךְ חַנּוּן וְרַחוּם אָתָּה:

לשלש רגלים.

אַתָּה בְחַרְתָּנוּ מִכָּל הָעַמִּים. אָהַבְתָּ אוֹתָנוּ וְרָצִיתָ בָּנוּ. וְקִדַּשְׁתָּנוּ בְּמִצְוֹתֶיךָ. וְקֵרַבְתָּנוּ מַלְכֵּנוּ לַעֲבוֹדָתֶךָ. וְשִׁמְךָ הַגָּדוֹל וְהַקָּדוֹשׁ עָלֵינוּ קָרָאתָ. וַתִּתֶּן לָנוּ יְיָ אֱלֹהֵינוּ בְּאַהֲבָה. שַׁבָּתוֹת לִמְנוּחָה. מוֹעֲדִים לְשִׂמְחָה. חַגִּים וּזְמַנִּים לְשָׂשׂוֹן. אֶת יוֹם (בשבת וְאֶת יוֹם)

בפסח חַג הַמַּצּוֹת הַזֶּה. זְמַן חֵרוּתֵנוּ.
בשבועות חַג הַשָּׁבֻעוֹת הַזֶּה. זְמַן מַתַּן תּוֹרָתֵנוּ.
בסוכות חַג הַסֻּכּוֹת הַזֶּה. זְמַן שִׂמְחָתֵנוּ.
בש״ע חַג הָעֲצֶרֶת הַזֶּה. זְמַן שִׂמְחָתֵנוּ.

מִקְרָא קֹדֶשׁ זֵכֶר לִיצִיאַת מִצְרָיִם:

(ON SABBATH.)

Our God, God of our fathers, may our day of rest be acceptable to thee. O sanctify us with thy commandments, give us light by thy law, and grant us thy salvation. Purify us that we may serve thee in love and truth and enjoy thy holy Sabbath with gladness of heart and peace of mind. Praise be to thee, O Lord, who hast hallowed the Sabbath.

(ON HOLIDAYS.)

Our God and Father, sanctify us through thy commandments and enlighten us by thy law. Sustain us from thine infinite goodness and gladden us by thy sure help. Purify our hearts to serve thee in truth and let us enjoy thy holy (Sabbaths and) festivals in love and gladness. Praise be to thee, O God, who sanctifiest Israel and the Festivals.

CHOIR: **Amen.**

On 'Hanukkah.

We thank thee for the marvelous deliverance of our fathers and the glorious victory won by thy help in the days of Mattathias, the priest, and his sons, when the tyranny of the Syrians endeavored to make thy people, Israel, forsake thy law and renounce thy truth. Then in the fulness of thy mercy thou aidest them in their distress, foughtest their fight, and gavest victory to the feeble over the strong, to the few over the many, to the righteous over the wicked, to those who obeyed thy word over those who assailed truth and virtue with a high hand. And thus thy name became exalted and glorified over the world. And Israel, thy people, was saved and delivered and restored to freedom and independence. And thy children re-entered thy temple, cleansed its halls, purified the sanctuary and illuminated it, and instituted these days of dedication as days of thanksgiving and praise to thee. Amen.

On Purim.

We give thanks to thee, O Guardian of Israel, for the aid bestowed by thee on our people in the days of Mordecai, about this time of the year, when the malignity of Haman threatened with destruction all the Israelites of the Great Persian empire — men, women and children. Royal messengers had already spread throughout all its provinces, carrying the decree to exterminate all the children of thy people. The day had been fixed on which the cruel counselor was to still his revenge in a deluge of blood, when thy almighty hand broke through the bloody schemes of the enemy and thrust him into the snare which he had laid for the guiltless. And in the same way, O our loving Father, thy help has never been wanting to Israel whenever men arose against him and sought his destruction. Hasten the day, O God, when all hatred, malice and prejudice will have vanished from the earth, and all men be united by the bond of a common brotherhood and faith in thee our kind Guardian and Keeper. Amen.

תפלת שחרית לשבת ויו״ט

לשלש רגלים.

אֱלֹהֵינוּ וֵאלֹהֵי אֲבוֹתֵינוּ יַעֲלֶה וְיָבֹא זִכְרוֹנֵנוּ וְזִכְרוֹן אֲבוֹתֵינוּ. וְזִכְרוֹן כָּל עַמְּךָ בֵּית יִשְׂרָאֵל לְפָנֶיךָ. לְחֵן וּלְחֶסֶד וּלְרַחֲמִים לְחַיִּים וּלְשָׁלוֹם בְּיוֹם

חַג הַמַּצוֹת | חַג הַשָּׁבֻעוֹת | חַג הַסֻּכּוֹת | חַג הָעֲצֶרֶת

הַזֶּה, זָכְרֵנוּ יְיָ אֱלֹהֵינוּ בּוֹ לְטוֹבָה. וּפָקְדֵנוּ בוֹ לִבְרָכָה וְהוֹשִׁיעֵנוּ בּוֹ לְחַיִּים. וּבִדְבַר יְשׁוּעָה וְרַחֲמִים חוּס וְחָנֵּנוּ. וְרַחֵם עָלֵינוּ וְהוֹשִׁיעֵנוּ. כִּי אֵלֶיךָ עֵינֵינוּ. כִּי אֵל מֶלֶךְ חַנּוּן וְרַחוּם אָתָּה:

וְהַשִּׂיאֵנוּ יְיָ אֱלֹהֵינוּ אֶת בִּרְכַּת מוֹעֲדֶיךָ. כַּאֲשֶׁר רָצִיתָ וְאָמַרְתָּ לְבָרְכֵנוּ. קַדְּשֵׁנוּ בְּמִצְוֹתֶיךָ וְתֵן חֶלְקֵנוּ בְּתוֹרָתֶךָ. שַׂבְּעֵנוּ מִטּוּבֶךָ וְשַׂמְּחֵנוּ בִּישׁוּעָתֶךָ. וְטַהֵר לִבֵּנוּ לְעָבְדְּךָ בֶּאֱמֶת. וְהַנְחִילֵנוּ יְיָ אֱלֹהֵינוּ בְּאַהֲבָה וּבְרָצוֹן בְּשִׂמְחָה וּבְשָׂשׂוֹן "שַׁבָּת וּ" מוֹעֲדֵי קָדְשֶׁךָ. וְיִשְׂמְחוּ בְךָ יִשְׂרָאֵל מְקַדְּשֵׁי שְׁמֶךָ. בָּרוּךְ אַתָּה יְיָ מְקַדֵּשׁ "הַשַּׁבָּת וְ" יִשְׂרָאֵל וְהַזְּמַנִּים:

לחנוכה.

עַל הַנִּסִּים וְעַל הַפֻּרְקָן וְעַל הַגְּבוּרוֹת וְעַל הַתְּשׁוּעוֹת שֶׁעָשִׂיתָ לַאֲבוֹתֵינוּ בַּיָּמִים הָהֵם בַּזְּמַן הַזֶּה:

בִּימֵי מַתִּתְיָהוּ בֶּן יוֹחָנָן כֹּהֵן גָּדוֹל. חַשְׁמוֹנַאי וּבָנָיו. כְּשֶׁעָמְדָה מַלְכוּת יָוָן הָרְשָׁעָה עַל עַמְּךָ יִשְׂרָאֵל. לְהַשְׁכִּיחָם תּוֹרָתֶךָ. וּלְהַעֲבִירָם מֵחֻקֵּי רְצוֹנֶךָ. וְאַתָּה בְּרַחֲמֶיךָ הָרַבִּים עָמַדְתָּ לָהֶם בְּעֵת צָרָתָם. רַבְתָּ אֶת רִיבָם. דַּנְתָּ אֶת דִּינָם. מָסַרְתָּ גִבּוֹרִים בְּיַד חַלָּשִׁים. וְרַבִּים בְּיַד מְעַטִּים. וּרְשָׁעִים בְּיַד צַדִּיקִים. וְזֵדִים בְּיַד עוֹסְקֵי תוֹרָתֶךָ. וּלְךָ עָשִׂיתָ שֵׁם גָּדוֹל וְקָדוֹשׁ בְּעוֹלָמֶךָ. וּלְעַמְּךָ יִשְׂרָאֵל עָשִׂיתָ תְּשׁוּעָה גְדוֹלָה. וּפֻרְקָן כְּהַיּוֹם הַזֶּה. וְאַחַר כֵּן בָּאוּ בָנֶיךָ לִדְבִיר בֵּיתֶךָ. וּפִנּוּ אֶת הֵיכָלֶךָ. וְטִהֲרוּ אֶת מִקְדָּשֶׁךָ. וְהִדְלִיקוּ נֵרוֹת בְּחַצְרוֹת קָדְשֶׁךָ. וְקָבְעוּ שְׁמוֹנַת יְמֵי חֲנֻכָּה אֵלּוּ. לְהוֹדוֹת וּלְהַלֵּל לְשִׁמְךָ הַגָּדוֹל:

Look with kindness, O God, upon Israel, thy people: may their fervent prayers, and their worship, be always acceptable to thee. Praise be to thee, O God, whom alone we adore and worship.

From age to age we render thanks unto thee and recount thy praise, for our lives committed into thy hand, for our souls entrusted to thy care, for thy marvelous works, thy wonders which are manifested every day, and for thy boundless goodness in which thou enfoldest us at all times, evening, morning and noon. We bless thee, All-Good, whose mercies never cease, whose grace is infinite; our hopes are in thee forever.

Our God, God of our fathers! Bless us with the ancient priestly benediction:

Yevorechecho Adonoy v'yishmerecho.
May the Lord bless thee and guard thee.

CHOIR: **Amen.**

Yoër Adonoy ponov elecho vichunecko.
May the Lord let his countenance shine upon thee and be gracious unto thee.

CHOIR: **Amen.**

Yisso Adonoy ponov elecho v'yosaim locho sholom.
May the Lord lift up his countenance upon thee and give thee peace.

CHOIR: **Amen.**

Grant peace, happiness and blessing, grace and mercy to us, and to Israel thy people, and to all thy children. Bless us all, O our Father, with the light of thy countenance; as in the light of thy countenance thou hast given us the law of life, the love of virtue and justice, mercy and peace, so may it please thee to bless us with thy peace at all times and in all seasons. Praise be to thee, O Giver of peace.

(The Congregation in silent devotion.)

Our Heavenly Father, let thy blessing of peace rest upon us and give us strength. Help us to follow the voice of conscience and to cheerfully obey thy laws. May we love the

תפלת שחרית לשבת ויו״ט

רְצֵה יְיָ אֱלֹהֵינוּ בְּעַמְּךָ יִשְׂרָאֵל. וּתְפִלָּתָם בְּאַהֲבָה תְקַבֵּל. וּתְהִי לְרָצוֹן תָּמִיד עֲבוֹדַת יִשְׂרָאֵל עַמֶּךָ. בָּרוּךְ אַתָּה יְיָ שֶׁאוֹתְךָ לְבַדְּךָ בְּיִרְאָה נַעֲבוֹד:

מוֹדִים אֲנַחְנוּ לָךְ. שָׁאַתָּה הוּא יְיָ אֱלֹהֵינוּ וֵאלֹהֵי אֲבוֹתֵינוּ לְעוֹלָם וָעֶד. צוּר חַיֵּינוּ מָגֵן יִשְׁעֵנוּ אַתָּה הוּא לְדוֹר וָדוֹר. נוֹדֶה לְךָ וּנְסַפֵּר תְּהִלָּתֶךָ. עַל חַיֵּינוּ הַמְּסוּרִים בְּיָדֶךָ. וְעַל נִשְׁמוֹתֵינוּ הַפְּקוּדוֹת לָךְ. וְעַל נִסֶּיךָ שֶׁבְּכָל יוֹם עִמָּנוּ. וְעַל נִפְלְאוֹתֶיךָ וְטוֹבוֹתֶיךָ שֶׁבְּכָל עֵת. עֶרֶב וָבֹקֶר וְצָהֳרָיִם. הַטּוֹב כִּי לֹא כָלוּ רַחֲמֶיךָ. וְהַמְרַחֵם כִּי לֹא תַמּוּ חֲסָדֶיךָ. מֵעוֹלָם קִוִּינוּ לָךְ:

וְעַל כֻּלָּם יִתְבָּרֵךְ וְיִתְרוֹמַם שִׁמְךָ מַלְכֵּנוּ. תָּמִיד לְעוֹלָם וָעֶד. וְכֹל הַחַיִּים יוֹדוּךָ סֶּלָה וִיהַלְלוּ אֶת שִׁמְךָ בֶּאֱמֶת. הָאֵל יְשׁוּעָתֵנוּ וְעֶזְרָתֵנוּ סֶלָה. בָּרוּךְ אַתָּה יְיָ הַטּוֹב שִׁמְךָ וּלְךָ נָאֶה לְהוֹדוֹת:

אֱלֹהֵינוּ וֵאלֹהֵי אֲבוֹתֵינוּ. בָּרְכֵנוּ בַבְּרָכָה הַמְשֻׁלֶּשֶׁת בַּתּוֹרָה. הָאֲמוּרָה מִפִּי אַהֲרֹן וּבָנָיו כֹּהֲנִים עַם קְדוֹשֶׁךָ. כָּאָמוּר:

יְבָרֶכְךָ יְיָ וְיִשְׁמְרֶךָ:
יָאֵר יְיָ פָּנָיו אֵלֶיךָ וִיחֻנֶּךָּ:
יִשָּׂא יְיָ פָּנָיו אֵלֶיךָ וְיָשֵׂם לְךָ שָׁלוֹם:

שִׂים שָׁלוֹם טוֹבָה וּבְרָכָה. חֵן וָחֶסֶד וְרַחֲמִים. עָלֵינוּ וְעַל כָּל יִשְׂרָאֵל עַמֶּךָ. בָּרְכֵנוּ אָבִינוּ כֻּלָּנוּ כְּאֶחָד בְּאוֹר פָּנֶיךָ. כִּי בְאוֹר פָּנֶיךָ נָתַתָּ לָּנוּ יְיָ אֱלֹהֵינוּ. תּוֹרַת חַיִּים

truth and speak the truth. May we be kind to one another, tender-hearted and forgiving, holding no anger nor malice, nor speaking ill of any one. May the thought of thee keep us from evil. Inspire us with humility, with faith and trust in thee. Let the words of my mouth and the meditations of my heart be acceptable in thy sight, O God, my Strength and my Redeemer. CHOIR: **Amen.**

ORDER OF READING THE LAW.

CHOIR: *S'ú Sheórim roshéchem.*

Lift up your heads, O ye gates, and be lifted up, ye everlasting doors, for the King of glory shall come. Who is the King of glory? The Lord of hosts — he is the King of glory. Selah!

Or: *Vay'hi bin'soa hoóon.*

Arise, O Lord, let thy enemies be scattered and they who hate thy law flee before thee. For from Zion cometh forth the Law and the word of God from Jerusalem.

(ON HOLIDAYS.)

Adonoy, Adonoy, El rachum v'chanwn, erech appa-yim, v'rav chesed v'emés, notsér chesed lo-alofim, nosé ovón, vofésha, v'chattoóh.

The Eternal, the Eternal, is a merciful and gracious God, long-suffering and full of love and truth; keeping kindness unto thousands, forgiving iniquity, transgression and sin.

(Taking the Law out of the Ark.)

This Law is Israel's consecrated banner, inscribed with the glorious truth: Hear, O Israel, God our Lord, God is One!

CHOIR AND CONGREGATION:

Sh'ma Yisroel, Adonoy Elohénu, Adonoy echod.

MINISTER:

O magnify the Lord with me and let us exalt his Name together.

CHOIR: *L'chó Adonoy hagg'dulloh.*

Thine, O Lord, are greatness, power, and glory, victory, and majesty; thine is all that is in heaven and on earth; thine is the kingdom, O Lord, and thou art exalted, Supreme above all.

תפלת שחרית לשבת ויו״ט

וְאַהֲבַת חֶסֶד. וּצְדָקָה וּבְרָכָה. וְרַחֲמִים וְחַיִּים וְשָׁלוֹם. וְטוֹב בְּעֵינֶיךָ לְבָרֵךְ אֶת עַמְּךָ יִשְׂרָאֵל. בְּכָל עֵת וּבְכָל שָׁעָה בִּשְׁלוֹמֶךָ. בָּרוּךְ אַתָּה יְיָ עוֹשֵׂה הַשָּׁלוֹם:

סדר קריאת התורה.

שְׂאוּ שְׁעָרִים רָאשֵׁיכֶם. וּשְׂאוּ פִּתְחֵי עוֹלָם. וְיָבֹא מֶלֶךְ הַכָּבוֹד: מִי הוּא זֶה מֶלֶךְ הַכָּבוֹד. יְיָ צְבָאוֹת. הוּא מֶלֶךְ הַכָּבוֹד סֶלָה:

וַיְהִי בִּנְסֹעַ הָאָרֹן וַיֹּאמֶר מֹשֶׁה. קוּמָה יְיָ וְיָפֻצוּ אֹיְבֶיךָ וְיָנֻסוּ מְשַׂנְאֶיךָ מִפָּנֶיךָ: כִּי מִצִּיּוֹן תֵּצֵא תוֹרָה וּדְבַר יְיָ מִירוּשָׁלָיִם:

לשליש רגלים.

יְהֹוָה יְהֹוָה אֵל רַחוּם וְחַנּוּן אֶרֶךְ אַפַּיִם וְרַב־חֶסֶד וֶאֱמֶת. נֹצֵר חֶסֶד לָאֲלָפִים נֹשֵׂא עָוֹן וָפֶשַׁע וְחַטָּאָה:

מוציאין ס״ת.

וְזֹאת הַתּוֹרָה אֲשֶׁר שָׂם מֹשֶׁה לִפְנֵי בְּנֵי יִשְׂרָאֵל:

שְׁמַע יִשְׂרָאֵל יְהֹוָה אֱלֹהֵינוּ יְהֹוָה אֶחָד:

גַּדְּלוּ לַיְיָ אִתִּי. וּנְרוֹמְמָה שְׁמוֹ יַחְדָּו:

לְךָ יְיָ הַגְּדֻלָּה וְהַגְּבוּרָה. וְהַתִּפְאֶרֶת וְהַנֵּצַח וְהַהוֹד. כִּי כֹל בַּשָּׁמַיִם וּבָאָרֶץ. לְךָ יְיָ הַמַּמְלָכָה. וְהַמִּתְנַשֵּׂא לְכֹל לְרֹאשׁ:

MORNING SERVICE FOR SABBATH AND HOLIDAYS.

(Before the Reading of the Law.)

Praise be to thee, O Eternal, our God, Ruler of the universe, who hast called us unto thy service and hast given us thy law. Praise be to thee, O God, giver of the Law. Amen.

READING FROM THE PENTATEUCH.

(After the Reading of the Law.)

Praise be to thee, O Eternal, our God, Ruler of the universe, who hast given us a law of truth and implanted eternal life within us. Praise be to thee, O God, giver of the Law. Amen.

CHOIR:

God's law is perfect, inspiring the soul; God's testimony is true, making wise the simple; God's commandments are clear, cheering the heart; God's teachings are pure, giving light to the eye.

READING FROM THE PROPHETS.

(HERE MAY BE INTRODUCED ANY PRAYER FOR SPECIAL OCCASIONS.)

(Placing back the Law into the Ark.)

MINISTER:

Praise ye the Name of the Lord, for his Name alone is exalted!

CHOIR: *Hodo al eretz v'shomoyim.*

His glory is above heaven and earth. He will exalt the honor of his people, the children of Israel, his faithful worshippers. Hallelujah!

(Minister before the Ark.)

Return, O Lord, to the many thousands of Israel, thou and the ark of thy strength. A good instruction have given to you, forsake ye not my law. It is a tree of life to those who lay hold of it, and its supporters are happy. Its ways are ways of pleasantness and all its paths are peace.

CHOIR: *Hashivénu Adonoy.*

SERMON.

HYMN.

תפלת שחרית לשבת ויו״ט

ברכת התורה.

בָּרוּךְ אַתָּה יְיָ אֱלֹהֵינוּ מֶלֶךְ הָעוֹלָם. אֲשֶׁר בָּחַר בָּנוּ מִכָּל־הָעַמִּים וְנָתַן לָנוּ אֶת־תּוֹרָתוֹ. בָּרוּךְ אַתָּה יְיָ נוֹתֵן הַתּוֹרָה:

אחר הקריאה.

בָּרוּךְ אַתָּה יְיָ אֱלֹהֵינוּ מֶלֶךְ הָעוֹלָם. אֲשֶׁר נָתַן לָנוּ תּוֹרַת אֱמֶת וְחַיֵּי עוֹלָם נָטַע בְּתוֹכֵנוּ. בָּרוּךְ אַתָּה יְיָ נוֹתֵן הַתּוֹרָה:

בהגבהת התורה.

יְהַלְלוּ אֶת־שֵׁם יְיָ. כִּי נִשְׂגָּב שְׁמוֹ לְבַדּוֹ:

הוֹדוֹ עַל־אֶרֶץ וְשָׁמָיִם: וַיָּרֶם קֶרֶן לְעַמּוֹ תְּהִלָּה לְכָל־חֲסִידָיו לִבְנֵי יִשְׂרָאֵל עַם קְרֹבוֹ הַלְלוּיָהּ:

וּבְנֻחֹה יֹאמַר. שׁוּבָה יְיָ רִבֲבוֹת אַלְפֵי יִשְׂרָאֵל: קוּמָה יְיָ לִמְנוּחָתֶךָ אַתָּה וַאֲרוֹן עֻזֶּךָ: כֹּהֲנֶיךָ יִלְבְּשׁוּ־צֶדֶק וַחֲסִידֶיךָ יְרַנֵּנוּ: כִּי לֶקַח טוֹב נָתַתִּי לָכֶם תּוֹרָתִי אַל תַּעֲזֹבוּ: עֵץ־חַיִּים הִיא לַמַּחֲזִיקִים בָּהּ וְתֹמְכֶיהָ מְאֻשָּׁר: דְּרָכֶיהָ דַרְכֵי־נֹעַם וְכָל־נְתִיבוֹתֶיהָ שָׁלוֹם: הֲשִׁיבֵנוּ יְיָ אֵלֶיךָ וְנָשׁוּבָה חַדֵּשׁ יָמֵינוּ כְּקֶדֶם:

HALLEL.

(ON HOLIDAYS, SEMI-HOLIDAYS AND NEW MOON.)

Psalm 113.

Praise, ye servants of the Lord! praise the name of the Lord!
Blessed be the name of the Lord from this time forth, even for ever!
From the rising of the sun to its going down, may the name of the Lord be praised!
The Lord is high above all nations; his glory is above the heavens.
Who is like unto the Lord, our God, that dwelleth on high, that looketh down upon the heavens and the earth?
He raiseth the poor from the dust, the needy from his lowliness.
To set him among princes, the princes of his people.

Psalm 114.

When Israel wenth forth from Egypt, the house of Jacob from a strange people; Judah was his sanctuary, and Israel his dominion.
The sea beheld, and fled; the Jordan turned back; the mountains skipped like rams, and the hills like lambs.
What aileth thee, O sea! that thou fleest? thou Jordan, that turnest back? ye mountains, that ye skip like rams, and ye hills like lambs?
Tremble, O earth! at the presence of the Lord, at the presence of the God of Jacob!
Who turned the rock into a standing lake, and the flint into a fountain of water!

Psalm 115.

The Lord hath been mindful of us; he will bless us; he will bless the house of Israel.
He will bless them that fear the Lord, both small and great.
Blessed are ye of the Lord, who made heaven and earth.
The heaven is the Lord's heaven; but the earth he hath given to the sons of men.

תפלת שחרית לשבת ויו״ט

סדר הלל
לראש חדש, חנוכה, ולרגלים.

הַלְלוּיָהּ. הַלְלוּ עַבְדֵי יְיָ הַלְלוּ אֶת־שֵׁם יְיָ: יְהִי שֵׁם יְיָ מְבֹרָךְ מֵעַתָּה וְעַד־עוֹלָם: מִמִּזְרַח־שֶׁמֶשׁ עַד־מְבוֹאוֹ מְהֻלָּל שֵׁם יְיָ: רָם עַל־כָּל־גּוֹיִם יְיָ עַל־הַשָּׁמַיִם כְּבוֹדוֹ: מִי כַּיְיָ אֱלֹהֵינוּ הַמַּגְבִּיהִי לָשָׁבֶת: הַמַּשְׁפִּילִי לִרְאוֹת בַּשָּׁמַיִם וּבָאָרֶץ: מְקִימִי מֵעָפָר דָּל מֵאַשְׁפֹּת יָרִים אֶבְיוֹן: לְהוֹשִׁיבִי עִם־נְדִיבִים עִם נְדִיבֵי עַמּוֹ: מוֹשִׁיבִי עֲקֶרֶת הַבַּיִת אֵם־הַבָּנִים שְׂמֵחָה הַלְלוּיָהּ:

בְּצֵאת יִשְׂרָאֵל מִמִּצְרָיִם בֵּית יַעֲקֹב מֵעַם לֹעֵז: הָיְתָה יְהוּדָה לְקָדְשׁוֹ יִשְׂרָאֵל מַמְשְׁלוֹתָיו: הַיָּם רָאָה וַיָּנֹס הַיַּרְדֵּן יִסֹּב לְאָחוֹר: הֶהָרִים רָקְדוּ כְאֵילִים גְּבָעוֹת כִּבְנֵי־צֹאן: מַה־לְּךָ הַיָּם כִּי תָנוּס הַיַּרְדֵּן תִּסֹּב לְאָחוֹר: הֶהָרִים תִּרְקְדוּ כְאֵילִים גְּבָעוֹת כִּבְנֵי צֹאן: מִלִּפְנֵי אָדוֹן חוּלִי אָרֶץ מִלִּפְנֵי אֱלוֹהַּ יַעֲקֹב: הַהֹפְכִי הַצּוּר אֲגַם־מָיִם חַלָּמִישׁ לְמַעְיְנוֹ־מָיִם:

יְיָ זְכָרָנוּ יְבָרֵךְ יְבָרֵךְ אֶת בֵּית יִשְׂרָאֵל יְבָרֵךְ אֶת־בֵּית אַהֲרֹן: יְבָרֵךְ יִרְאֵי יְיָ הַקְּטַנִּים עִם הַגְּדוֹלִים: יֹסֵף יְיָ עֲלֵיכֶם עֲלֵיכֶם וְעַל־בְּנֵיכֶם: בְּרוּכִים אַתֶּם לַיְיָ עֹשֵׂה שָׁמַיִם וָאָרֶץ: הַשָּׁמַיִם שָׁמַיִם לַיְיָ וְהָאָרֶץ נָתַן לִבְנֵי־אָדָם: לֹא־הַמֵּתִים יְהַלְלוּ־יָהּ וְלֹא כָּל־יֹרְדֵי דוּמָה: וַאֲנַחְנוּ נְבָרֵךְ יָהּ מֵעַתָּה וְעַד־עוֹלָם הַלְלוּיָהּ:

The dead praise not the Lord, no one who goeth down into the silent grave.
But we will praise the Lord, from this time forth even for ever! Hallelujah!

Psalm 117.

Praise the Lord, all ye nations! praise him, all ye people!
For great toward us hath been his kindness, and the faithfulness of the Lord endureth for ever. Hallelujah!

Psalm 118.   MINISTER, THEN CHOIR:

Hólu Ladonoy ki tó:, ki l'olom chasdo.

O give thanks to the Lord for he is good, his kindness endureth for ever!

Yómar no Yisroël, ki l'olom chasdo.

Let Israel now say, his kindness endureth for ever.

Yómar no bés Aharón, ki l'olom chasdo.

Let the House of Aaron now say, his kindness endureth for ever.

Yómar no Yir'éh Adonoy, ki l'olom chasdo.

Let all who fear the Lord now say, his kindness endureth for ever.

I called upon the Lord in distress; the Lord heard me and delivered me.

The Lord is with me, I will not fear: what can man do to me?

It is better to trust in the Lord than to put confidence in man;

It is better to trust in the Lord than to put confidence in princes.

All the nations beset me around, but in the name of the Lord I triumphed over them.

They did assail me with violence to bring me down! but the Lord was my support.

The Lord is my strength and my song; for to him I owe my salvation.

תפלת שחרית לשבת ויו״ט

מָה אָשִׁיב לַיְיָ כָּל־תַּגְמוּלוֹהִי עָלָי: כּוֹס־יְשׁוּעוֹת אֶשָּׂא וּבְשֵׁם יְיָ אֶקְרָא: נְדָרַי לַיְיָ אֲשַׁלֵּם נֶגְדָה־נָּא לְכָל־עַמּוֹ: יָקָר בְּעֵינֵי יְיָ הַמָּוְתָה לַחֲסִידָיו: אָנָּא יְיָ כִּי־אֲנִי עַבְדֶּךָ אֲנִי עַבְדְּךָ בֶּן־אֲמָתֶךָ פִּתַּחְתָּ לְמוֹסֵרָי: לְךָ אֶזְבַּח זֶבַח תּוֹדָה וּבְשֵׁם יְיָ אֶקְרָא: נְדָרַי לַיְיָ אֲשַׁלֵּם נֶגְדָה־נָּא לְכָל־עַמּוֹ: בְּחַצְרוֹת בֵּית יְיָ בְּתוֹכֵכִי יְרוּשָׁלָיִם הַלְלוּיָהּ:

הַלְלוּ אֶת־יְיָ כָּל־גּוֹיִם שַׁבְּחוּהוּ כָּל־הָאֻמִּים: כִּי גָבַר עָלֵינוּ חַסְדּוֹ וֶאֱמֶת־יְיָ לְעוֹלָם הַלְלוּיָהּ:

הוֹדוּ לַיְיָ כִּי טוֹב   כִּי לְעוֹלָם חַסְדּוֹ:
יֹאמַר־נָא יִשְׂרָאֵל   כִּי לְעוֹלָם חַסְדּוֹ:
יֹאמְרוּ נָא בֵית אַהֲרֹן   כִּי לְעוֹלָם חַסְדּוֹ:
יֹאמְרוּ נָא יִרְאֵי יְיָ   כִּי לְעוֹלָם חַסְדּוֹ:

מִן־הַמֵּצַר קָרָאתִי יָּהּ עָנָנִי בַמֶּרְחָב יָהּ: יְיָ לִי לֹא אִירָא מַה־יַּעֲשֶׂה לִי אָדָם: יְיָ לִי בְּעֹזְרָי וַאֲנִי אֶרְאֶה בְשֹׂנְאָי: טוֹב לַחֲסוֹת בַּיְיָ מִבְּטֹחַ בָּאָדָם: טוֹב לַחֲסוֹת בַּיְיָ מִבְּטֹחַ בִּנְדִיבִים: כָּל־גּוֹיִם סְבָבוּנִי בְּשֵׁם יְיָ כִּי אֲמִילַם: סַבּוּנִי גַם־סְבָבוּנִי בְּשֵׁם יְיָ כִּי אֲמִילַם: סַבּוּנִי כִדְבֹרִים הֹעֲכוּ כְּאֵשׁ קוֹצִים בְּשֵׁם יְיָ כִּי אֲמִילַם: דָּחֹה דְחִיתַנִי לִנְפֹּל וַיְיָ עֲזָרָנִי: עָזִּי וְזִמְרָת יָהּ וַיְהִי־לִי לִישׁוּעָה: קוֹל רִנָּה

The voice of joy and salvation is in the habitations of the righteous.

"The right hand of the Lord doeth valiantly; the right hand of the Lord is exalted."

I shall not die, but live, and declare the deeds of the Lord.

The Lord hath chastened and corrected me, but he hath not given me over to death.

Open to me the gates of righteousness, that I may go in, and praise the Lord!

This is the gate of the Lord, through which the righteous enter.

I praise thee that thou hast afflicted me, it has been my salvation.

The stone which the builders rejected hath become the chief corner-stone.

This is the Lord's doing; it is marvellous in our eyes!

This is the day which the Lord hath made; let us rejoice and be glad in it!

MINISTER, THEN CHOIR:

Onnu Adonoy hóshioh no.
Hear, O Lord, and bless us!

Onnu Adonoy hatselichoh no.
Hear, O Lord, and send us prosperity!

Blessed be he that cometh in the name of the Lord! we bless you from the house of the Lord.

The Eternal is God, he hath shone upon us!

Thou art my God, and I will praise thee; thou art my God, and I will exalt thee!

O give thanks to the Lord, for he is good; for his kindness endureth for ever!

MINISTER, THEN CHOIR:

Hódu Ladonoy ki tóv, ki l'olom chasdo.

תפלת שחרית לשבת ויו״ט

וִישׁוּעָה בְּאָהֳלֵי צַדִּיקִים יְמִין יְיָ עֹשָׂה חָיִל: יְמִין יְיָ רוֹמֵמָה יְמִין יְיָ עֹשָׂה חָיִל: לֹא־אָמוּת כִּי־אֶחְיֶה וַאֲסַפֵּר מַעֲשֵׂה־יָהּ: יַסֹּר יִסְּרַנִּי יָהּ וְלַמָּוֶת לֹא נְתָנָנִי: פִּתְחוּ־לִי שַׁעֲרֵי־צֶדֶק אָבֹא בָם אוֹדֶה יָהּ: זֶה־הַשַּׁעַר לַיְיָ צַדִּיקִים יָבֹאוּ בוֹ: אוֹדְךָ כִּי עֲנִיתָנִי וַתְּהִי־לִי לִישׁוּעָה: אֶבֶן מָאֲסוּ הַבּוֹנִים הָיְתָה לְרֹאשׁ פִּנָּה: מֵאֵת יְיָ הָיְתָה זֹּאת הִיא נִפְלָאת בְּעֵינֵינוּ: זֶה הַיּוֹם עָשָׂה יְיָ נָגִילָה וְנִשְׂמְחָה בוֹ:

אָנָּא יְיָ הוֹשִׁיעָה נָּא: אָנָּא יְיָ הוֹשִׁיעָה נָּא:
אָנָּא יְיָ הַצְלִיחָה נָּא: אָנָּא יְיָ הַצְלִיחָה נָּא:

בָּרוּךְ הַבָּא בְּשֵׁם יְיָ בֵּרַכְנוּכֶם מִבֵּית יְיָ: אֵל ׀ יְיָ וַיָּאֶר לָנוּ אִסְרוּ־חַג בַּעֲבֹתִים עַד קַרְנוֹת הַמִּזְבֵּחַ: אֵלִי אַתָּה וְאוֹדֶךָּ אֱלֹהַי אֲרוֹמְמֶךָּ:

הוֹדוּ לַיְיָ כִּי־טוֹב כִּי לְעוֹלָם חַסְדּוֹ:

ADORATION.

Almighty God! Creator of heaven and earth! It behoves us to render praise and thanksgiving unto thee, who hast delivered us from the darkness of false belief and sent to us the light of thy truth. Thou art our God, there is no other.

We, therefore, bow the head and bend the knee before thee, Creator and Ruler of the world, and bless thy holy name!

MINISTER, THEN CHOIR AND CONGREGATION:

Vaanachnu, kór'im, umishtáchavim, umódim, lifné Mélech mal'ché hammelóchim, Hakkódosh boruch hu.

Thou art, in truth, our Father, our God, our Saviour, and there is none besides thee, as is written in thy law: Thou shalt know this day and reflect in thy heart that the Lord is God in heaven above as on earth below; and there is none else.

We fervently pray, O Lord our God, that we may speedily behold the glory of thy mighty power, banishing all impurities from the earth, destroying idolatry and wickedness, and establishing thy truth among mankind; that all the inhabitants of the earth may invoke thy name, acknowledge thy unity, and understand that to thee alone every knee must bend and every tongue swear fealty.

May all thy children, O God, soon be united in a common bond of brotherhood, may the time be hastened when no religious differences will separate them, but when they will all adore thee as the universal father, worship thee in the spirit of true religion, and unite in proclaiming the unity of thy holy name.

Thus, O God, do thou reign over them for ever and ever, for the kingdom is thine, and unto thee appertain power, glory and majesty from everlasting to everlasting. As it is written: The Lord will reign for ever and ever; the Lord will be king over all the earth; on that day shall God be acknowledged One and his name One.

MINISTER, THEN CHOIR AND CONGREGATION:

V'iho-yoh Adonoy lemélech al kol hoórets, bayóm hahu yih'yéh Adonoy echod, u-shemo echod.

תפלת שחרית לשבת ויו״ט

עָלֵינוּ לְשַׁבֵּחַ לַאֲדוֹן הַכֹּל. לָתֵת גְּדֻלָּה לְיוֹצֵר בְּרֵאשִׁית. שֶׁהוּא נוֹטֶה שָׁמַיִם וְיוֹסֵד אָרֶץ. וּמוֹשַׁב יְקָרוֹ בַּשָּׁמַיִם מִמַּעַל. וּשְׁכִינַת עֻזּוֹ בְּגָבְהֵי מְרוֹמִים. הוּא אֱלֹהֵינוּ אֵין עוֹד.

וַאֲנַחְנוּ כּוֹרְעִים וּמִשְׁתַּחֲוִים וּמוֹדִים לִפְנֵי מֶלֶךְ מַלְכֵי הַמְּלָכִים. הַקָּדוֹשׁ בָּרוּךְ הוּא:

אֱמֶת מַלְכֵּנוּ אֶפֶס זוּלָתוֹ. כַּכָּתוּב בְּתוֹרָתוֹ. וְיָדַעְתָּ הַיּוֹם וַהֲשֵׁבֹתָ אֶל-לְבָבֶךָ. כִּי יְיָ הוּא הָאֱלֹהִים בַּשָּׁמַיִם מִמַּעַל וְעַל-הָאָרֶץ מִתָּחַת. אֵין עוֹד:

עַל כֵּן נְקַוֶּה לְךָ יְיָ אֱלֹהֵינוּ. לִרְאוֹת מְהֵרָה בְּתִפְאֶרֶת עֻזֶּךָ לְהַעֲבִיר גִּלּוּלִים מִן הָאָרֶץ. וְהָאֱלִילִים כָּרוֹת יִכָּרֵתוּן. לְתַקֵּן עוֹלָם בְּמַלְכוּת שַׁדַּי. וְכָל-בְּנֵי בָשָׂר יִקְרְאוּ בִשְׁמֶךָ. לְהַפְנוֹת אֵלֶיךָ כָּל-רִשְׁעֵי אָרֶץ. יַכִּירוּ וְיֵדְעוּ כָּל-יוֹשְׁבֵי תֵבֵל. כִּי לְךָ תִּכְרַע כָּל-בֶּרֶךְ. תִּשָּׁבַע כָּל-לָשׁוֹן. לְפָנֶיךָ יְיָ אֱלֹהֵינוּ יִכְרְעוּ וְיִפּוֹלוּ. וְלִכְבוֹד שִׁמְךָ יְקָר יִתֵּנוּ. וִיקַבְּלוּ כֻלָּם אֶת-עֹל מַלְכוּתֶךָ. וְתִמְלוֹךְ עֲלֵיהֶם מְהֵרָה לְעוֹלָם וָעֶד. כִּי הַמַּלְכוּת שֶׁלְּךָ הִיא. וּלְעוֹלְמֵי עַד תִּמְלוֹךְ בְּכָבוֹד. כַּכָּתוּב בְּתוֹרָתֶךָ. יְיָ יִמְלוֹךְ לְעוֹלָם וָעֶד: וְנֶאֱמַר וְהָיָה יְיָ לְמֶלֶךְ עַל-כָּל-הָאָרֶץ. בַּיּוֹם הַהוּא יִהְיֶה יְיָ אֶחָד וּשְׁמוֹ אֶחָד:

Address to the Mourners.

Brothers and sisters, who are mourning for dear lives departed, remember your beloved ones and honor their names in the midst of the congregation of Israel. May the memory of the righteous inspire you to noble deeds and works in their honor. Rise, and praise with me the name of the most High, according to the anscient custom of our fathers.

MOURNERS' KADDISH.

May thy great and ineffable name, O Lord of life and death, be exalted and sanctified throughout the world, which thou hast created according to thy will. May thy kingdom be established in our midst, in our lifetime and in our days, and in the days of the whole house of Israel. Amen.

THE CONGREGATION:

May his great and ineffable name be blessed and glorified for ever and ever.

Praised and hallowed be thy name who hast created man in thy image and planted within him eternal life. In thy hand is the soul of every living being and the spirit of all flesh. Blessed art thou, whose hymns, praises and benedictions are repeated throughout the world. Amen.

THE CONGREGATION:

Praised be he and his glorious name.

Unto Israel, unto all the righteous and unto all who departed this life according to the will of God, may there be granted abundance of peace, and a blissful portion in the life to come, grace and mercy by the Lord of heaven and earth. Amen.

THE CONGREGATION:

May the fullness of peace from heaven, with life and health be granted unto us and unto all Israel. Amen.

May he who establisheth peace in his heavenly spheres grant happiness and peace unto us, unto all Israel and to all mankind. Amen.

קדיש דאבלים.

יִתְגַּדַּל וְיִתְקַדַּשׁ שְׁמֵהּ רַבָּא. בְּעָלְמָא דִי־בְרָא כִרְעוּתֵהּ. וְיַמְלִיךְ מַלְכוּתֵהּ. בְּחַיֵּיכוֹן וּבְיוֹמֵיכוֹן וּבְחַיֵּי דְכָל בֵּית יִשְׂרָאֵל. בַּעֲגָלָא וּבִזְמַן קָרִיב. וְאִמְרוּ אָמֵן.

יְהֵא שְׁמֵהּ רַבָּא מְבָרַךְ. לְעָלַם וּלְעָלְמֵי עָלְמַיָּא.

יִתְבָּרַךְ וְיִשְׁתַּבַּח וְיִתְפָּאַר וְיִתְרוֹמַם. וְיִתְנַשֵּׂא וְיִתְהַדָּר וְיִתְעַלֶּה וְיִתְהַלָּל שְׁמֵהּ דְּקוּדְשָׁא. בְּרִיךְ הוּא. לְעֵלָּא מִן כָּל בִּרְכָתָא וְשִׁירָתָא. תֻּשְׁבְּחָתָא וְנֶחֱמָתָא. דַּאֲמִירָן בְּעָלְמָא. וְאִמְרוּ אָמֵן:

עַל יִשְׂרָאֵל וְעַל צַדִּיקַיָּא. וְעַל־כָּל־מַן דְּאִתְפְּטַר מִן עָלְמָא הָדֵין בִּרְעוּתֵהּ דֶאֱלָהָא. יְהֵא לְהוֹן שְׁלָמָא רַבָּא וְחוּלָקָא טָבָא לְחַיֵּי עָלְמָא דְּאָתֵי. וְחִסְדָּא וְרַחֲמֵי מִן־קֳדָם מָרֵא שְׁמַיָּא וְאַרְעָא. וְאִמְרוּ אָמֵן:

תִּתְקַבַּל צְלוֹתְהוֹן וּבָעוּתְהוֹן דְּכָל־יִשְׂרָאֵל קֳדָם אֲבוּהוֹן דִּי בִשְׁמַיָּא. וְאִמְרוּ אָמֵן:

יְהֵא שְׁלָמָא רַבָּא מִן־שְׁמַיָּא וְחַיִּים. עָלֵינוּ וְעַל־כָּל־יִשְׂרָאֵל. וְאִמְרוּ אָמֵן:

עֹשֶׂה שָׁלוֹם בִּמְרוֹמָיו. הוּא יַעֲשֶׂה שָׁלוֹם עָלֵינוּ וְעַל כָּל יִשְׂרָאֵל. וְאִמְרוּ אָמֵן:

אֲדוֹן עוֹלָם אֲשֶׁר מָלַךְ. בְּטֶרֶם כָּל־יְצִיר נִבְרָא:
לְעֵת נַעֲשָׂה בְחֶפְצוֹ כֹּל. אֲזַי מֶלֶךְ שְׁמוֹ נִקְרָא:
וְאַחֲרֵי כִּכְלוֹת הַכֹּל. לְבַדּוֹ יִמְלוֹךְ נוֹרָא:
וְהוּא הָיָה וְהוּא הֹוֶה. וְהוּא יִהְיֶה בְּתִפְאָרָה:
וְהוּא אֶחָד וְאֵין שֵׁנִי. לְהַמְשִׁיל לוֹ לְהַחְבִּירָה:
בְּלִי רֵאשִׁית בְּלִי תַכְלִית. וְלוֹ הָעֹז וְהַמִּשְׂרָה:
וְהוּא אֵלִי וְחַי גּוֹאֲלִי. וְצוּר חֶבְלִי בְּעֵת צָרָה:
וְהוּא נִסִּי וּמָנוֹס לִי. מְנָת כּוֹסִי בְּיוֹם אֶקְרָא:
בְּיָדוֹ אַפְקִיד רוּחִי. בְּעֵת אִישַׁן וְאָעִירָה:
וְעִם רוּחִי גְּוִיָּתִי. יְיָ לִי וְלֹא אִירָא:

אֵין כֵּאלֹהֵינוּ. אֵין כַּאדוֹנֵינוּ.
אֵין כְּמַלְכֵּנוּ. אֵין כְּמוֹשִׁיעֵנוּ:

מִי כֵאלֹהֵינוּ. מִי כַאדוֹנֵינוּ.
מִי כְמַלְכֵּנוּ. מִי כְמוֹשִׁיעֵנוּ:

נוֹדֶה לֵאלֹהֵינוּ. נוֹדֶה לַאדוֹנֵינוּ.
נוֹדֶה לְמַלְכֵּנוּ. נוֹדֶה לְמוֹשִׁיעֵנוּ:

בָּרוּךְ אֱלֹהֵינוּ. בָּרוּךְ אֲדוֹנֵינוּ.
בָּרוּךְ מַלְכֵּנוּ. בָּרוּךְ מוֹשִׁיעֵנוּ:

אַתָּה הוּא אֱלֹהֵינוּ. אַתָּה הוּא אֲדוֹנֵינוּ.
אַתָּה הוּא מַלְכֵּנוּ. אַתָּה הוּא מוֹשִׁיעֵנוּ:

HYMNS.

SOVEREIGN LORD.
ADON OLOM.

(From Temple Emanu-El Hymn-book.)

Sovereign Lord, whose sceptre reigned
    Ere yet time its course began ;
Since creation was ordained,
    It is guided by his plan.

When all things fade and decline,
    He abides in majesty;
As he was in power divine,
    Is and will he ever be.

No beginning and no end —
    His is rule and victory ;
My redeemer, rock and friend,
    My salvation's guaranty.

When my lips the Lord extol,
    I feel safe in ev'ry sphere,
Safe in body and in soul :
    God with me — I have no fear.

'NONE IS LIKE GOD.
EN KELOHENU.

Who is like thee, O universal Lord !
Who dare thy praise and glory share ?
Who is in heav'n, most high, like thee adored ?
Who can on earth with thee compare ?
Thou art the one true God alone,
And firmly founded is thy throne.

Thy tender love embraces all mankind,
As children all by thee are blest ;
Repentant sinners with thee mercy find,
Thy hand upholdeth the opprest ;
All worlds attest thy power sublime,
Thy glory shines in every clime.

THE SABBATH.

Holy Sabbath-rest !
Pious lips hail thy advent ;
With thee God his love hath sent,
Mind and heart of man to guard,
And to lead him heavenward.

Holy Sabbath-jóy !
O ! our yearning soul inspire :
Warm us with thy heavenly fire,
That in sacred hymns of praise
We to God our hearts upraise.

Father Everlasting !
From thy holy throne of grace
To thy children turn thy face ;
Bless this day — preferred by thee —
Emblem of eternity.

ISRAEL'S MISSION.

Sing to the Sovereign of the skies,
  To his great name alone,
Let winged words of praise arise
  To the Almighty's throne.
For he has given his law of light
  A radiant star to be,
To guide our erring steps aright,
  For all eternity.

Praise be to thee, who didst command,
  Thy first-born Israel,
In every clime, in every land,
  Thy living truths to tell.
O may they ever be our guide,
  And bear us safely o'er
Life's dark and swiftly flowing tide,
  Until it flows no more.

THANKSGIVING.

Loud let the swelling anthems rise,
    Let all the nations sing,
To him who rules above the skies,
    Unto the Lord, our King!
The sun, at his command,
    Renewed the barren ground —
Rich harvest decks the land,
    And plenty smiles around.

Praise ye the Lord, proclaim his might,
    Who made our fathers free,
Who gave to us a heavenly light,
    The sun of liberty.
A prosperous people hails
    Its bright and genial ray,
And golden peace prevails
    Wide o'er the land to-day.

Then let your hymns of thanks ascend,
    To the Almighty's throne,
To whom in gratitude we bend,
    Who reigns supreme alone.
Of his great mercies tell,
    Whom earth and heaven adore,
Let hallelujahs swell
    His praise for-evermore!

ORDER OF SERVICE
FOR
NEW YEAR'S EVE.

Organ Prelude.

MINISTER:

מַה־טֹּבוּ אֹהָלֶיךָ יַעֲקֹב מִשְׁכְּנֹתֶיךָ יִשְׂרָאֵל: וַאֲנִי בְּרֹב
חַסְדְּךָ אָבֹא בֵיתֶךָ אֶשְׁתַּחֲוֶה אֶל־הֵיכַל קָדְשְׁךָ בְּיִרְאָתֶךָ:
יְיָ אָהַבְתִּי מְעוֹן בֵּיתֶךָ וּמְקוֹם מִשְׁכַּן כְּבוֹדֶךָ: וַאֲנִי
אֶשְׁתַּחֲוֶה וְאֶכְרָעָה אֶבְרְכָה לִפְנֵי־יְיָ עֹשִׂי: וַאֲנִי תְפִלָּתִי
לְךָ יְיָ עֵת רָצוֹן אֱלֹהִים בְּרָב־חַסְדֶּךָ עֲנֵנִי בֶּאֱמֶת יִשְׁעֶךָ:

How beautiful are thy tents, O Jacob, thy tabernacles, O Israel! With faith in thy loving kindness, O God, we enter thy house; with profound reverence we will worship thee in thy holy temple. We love thy dwelling-place, O Lord, the abode sanctified by thy holiness. We will bow down before thee, and offer up our supplication unto thee, O God our Creator. Accept our prayers at this hour in the fulness of thy grace. Hear us, O God, our stronghold and support.

CHOIR: (Either of the following sentences.)

Worship the Lord in the beauty of holiness;
Stand in awe before him all the earth.

Give unto the Lord glory and praise;
Worship the Lord in holy attire.

Serve the Lord with gladness;
Come before his presence with songs.

RESPONSIVE READING.

Select one or more Psalms from the following pages; for the Three Festivals, appropriate Psalms from the appended Collection, then begin Borechu on page 65.

Psalm 121.   אשא עיני אל ההרים

I lift up my eyes unto the hills: whence cometh my help?
My help cometh from the Lord, who made heaven and earth.
He will not suffer thy foot to stumble; thy guardian doth not slumber.
Behold, the guardian of Israel doth neither slumber nor sleep.
The Lord is thy guardian; the Lord is thy shade at thy right hand.
The sun shall not smite thee by day, nor the moon by night.
The Lord will preserve thee from all evil; he will preserve thy life.
The Lord will preserve thy going out and thy coming in, from this time forth and for ever.

Psalm 91.   יושב בסתר עליון

He who dwelleth under the shelter of the Most High will abide in the shadow of the Almighty.
I say to the Lord, thou art my refuge and my fortress; my God, in whom I trust.
Surely he will deliver thee from the snare of the fowler, and from the wasting pestilence;
He will cover thee with his pinions, and under his wings shalt thou find refuge; his faithfulness shall be thy shield and buckler.
Thou shalt not be afraid of the terror of the night, nor of the arrow that flieth by day;
Nor of the pestilence that walketh in darkness, nor of the plague that destroyeth at noonday.
A thousand may fall by thy side, and ten thousand at thy right hand; but thee it shall not touch.
Thou shalt only behold with thy eyes, and see the recompense of the wicked.
Because thou hast made the Lord thy refuge, and the Most High thy habitation,
No evil shall befall thee, nor any plague come near thy dwelling.

SERVICE FOR NEW YEAR'S EVE.

For he will give his angels charge over thee, to guard thee in all thy ways.

They shall bear thee up in their hands, lest thou dash thy foot against a stone.

Thou shalt tread upon the lion and the adder; the young lion and the dragon shalt thou trample under foot.

"Because he loveth me, I will deliver him; I will set him on high, because he knoweth my name.

When he calleth upon me, I will answer him; I will be with him in trouble; I will deliver him, and bring him to honor.

With long life will I satisfy him, and show him my salvation."

Hymn.

Lo, our Father's tender care
Slumber's not, nor sleepeth,
Gracious gifts his lavish hand
Daily on us heapeth.
Through fierce storms, through perils lower —
Is not God our sheltering tower?
  Tremble not!
At his word the storm is still,
Perils vanish at his will —
And his love ordains our lot.
Lo, our Guardian slumbers not.

Lo, our Father's gracious love
Slumbers not, nor sleepeth.
Trust with all thy heart in him,
Who thy portion keepeth;
Who till now protection granted
All thy fortune wisely planted.
  Fear thou not!
God, who life and being grants
Kindly, too, supplies your wants.
Let but duty guide our lot.
Lo, our Guardian slumbers not.

MINISTER:

Borechu es Adonoy hammevoroch.

Praise ye the Lord to whom all praise is due!

CHOIR AND CONGREGATION:

Boruch Adonoy hammevoroch l'olom voëd.

Praised be the Lord, who is praised through all eternity.

Praise be to thee, O Lord our God, Ruler of the Universe, who by his word calls in the evening and in his wisdom opens the gates of the morning. He changes the times and the seasons by his understanding, and by his will he sets the stars in their heavenly watches. He alternates the light and the darkness; he leads out the day and brings in the night, the Lord of hosts is his name. May he rule over us forevermore. Praise be to thee, O God, who bringest in the evening.

With unchanging love thou hast guided thy people Israel; thou hast revealed to us thy law which will become a blessing to all mankind. Therefore we will ever think of thy word and rejoice in thy truth. It is our light and our life; we will cling to it day and night, and will proclaim thy name and thy unity before all the nations of the earth. Do thou, O God, never withold from us thy love and thy protection. Praise be to thee, O God, our Guardian and Keeper.

CHOIR: **Amen.**

MINISTER, THEN CHOIR AND CONGREGATION:

Sh'ma Yisroel, Adonoy Elohanu, Adonoy Echod.

HEAR, O ISRAEL, THE LORD OUR GOD, THE LORD IS ONE.

Boruch Shem kevod mal'chuso l'olom voëd.

Praised be the name of his glorious kingdom for evermore.

Thou shalt love the Eternal thy God with all thy heart, with all thy soul, and with all thy might. And these words, which I command thee to-day, shall be in thy heart. Thou shalt teach them diligently to thy children, and shalt talk of them when thou sittest in thy house, and when thou walkest by the way, and when thou liest down, and when thou risest up. And they shall be as a sign on thy hand and as an ornament

תפלת ערבית לראש השנה

בָּרְכוּ אֶת יְיָ הַמְבֹרָךְ:

בָּרוּךְ יְיָ הַמְבֹרָךְ לְעוֹלָם וָעֶד:

בָּרוּךְ אַתָּה יְיָ אֱלֹהֵינוּ מֶלֶךְ הָעוֹלָם. אֲשֶׁר בִּדְבָרוֹ מַעֲרִיב עֲרָבִים. בְּחָכְמָה פּוֹתֵחַ שְׁעָרִים. וּבִתְבוּנָה מְשַׁנֶּה עִתִּים וּמַחֲלִיף אֶת הַזְּמַנִּים. וּמְסַדֵּר אֶת הַכּוֹכָבִים בְּמִשְׁמְרוֹתֵיהֶם בָּרָקִיעַ כִּרְצוֹנוֹ. בּוֹרֵא יוֹם וָלָיְלָה. גּוֹלֵל אוֹר מִפְּנֵי חֹשֶׁךְ וְחֹשֶׁךְ מִפְּנֵי אוֹר. וּמַעֲבִיר יוֹם וּמֵבִיא לָיְלָה. יְיָ צְבָאוֹת שְׁמוֹ. אֵל חַי וְקַיָּם תָּמִיד יִמְלוֹךְ עָלֵינוּ לְעוֹלָם וָעֶד. בָּרוּךְ אַתָּה יְיָ הַמַּעֲרִיב עֲרָבִים:

אַהֲבַת עוֹלָם בֵּית יִשְׂרָאֵל עַמְּךָ אָהָבְתָּ. תּוֹרָה וּמִצְוֹת חֻקִּים וּמִשְׁפָּטִים אוֹתָנוּ לִמַּדְתָּ. עַל כֵּן יְיָ אֱלֹהֵינוּ בְּשָׁכְבֵנוּ וּבְקוּמֵנוּ נָשִׂיחַ בְּחֻקֶּיךָ. וְנִשְׂמַח בְּדִבְרֵי תוֹרָתֶךָ וּבְמִצְוֹתֶיךָ לְעוֹלָם וָעֶד. כִּי הֵם חַיֵּינוּ וְאֹרֶךְ יָמֵינוּ. וּבָהֶם נֶהְגֶּה יוֹמָם וָלָיְלָה. וְאַהֲבָתְךָ אַל תָּסִיר מִמֶּנּוּ לְעוֹלָמִים. בָּרוּךְ אַתָּה יְיָ אוֹהֵב עַמּוֹ יִשְׂרָאֵל:

שְׁמַע יִשְׂרָאֵל יְהֹוָה אֱלֹהֵינוּ יְהֹוָה אֶחָד:

בָּרוּךְ שֵׁם כְּבוֹד מַלְכוּתוֹ לְעוֹלָם וָעֶד:

וְאָהַבְתָּ אֵת יְיָ אֱלֹהֶיךָ בְּכָל לְבָבְךָ וּבְכָל נַפְשְׁךָ וּבְכָל מְאֹדֶךָ: וְהָיוּ הַדְּבָרִים הָאֵלֶּה אֲשֶׁר אָנֹכִי מְצַוְּךָ הַיּוֹם עַל־לְבָבֶךָ: וְשִׁנַּנְתָּם לְבָנֶיךָ וְדִבַּרְתָּ בָּם. בְּשִׁבְתְּךָ בְּבֵיתֶךָ וּבְלֶכְתְּךָ בַדֶּרֶךְ וּבְשָׁכְבְּךָ וּבְקוּמֶךָ: וּקְשַׁרְתָּם לְאוֹת עַל־יָדֶךָ. וְהָיוּ לְטֹטָפֹת בֵּין עֵינֶיךָ: וּכְתַבְתָּם עַל־מְזֻזוֹת בֵּיתֶךָ וּבִשְׁעָרֶיךָ:

on thy brow. And thou shalt write them upon the doorposts of thy house and on thy gates. (DEUTER., CHAPT. 6, V. 4—9.)

CHOIR:

Unchangeable and immutable is this word with us: God is everlasting; his word is true unto all generations; his commandments stand for ever. He alone is our God and none besides him.

MINISTER:

Truly thou art our God, and we are thy people, whom thou hast delivered from the hand of mighty oppressors. Wonders without number thou hast wrought for us, and hast miraculously protected us during these many centuries. As thy arm saved us from the yoke of Egyptian slavery, so thou wast with us in all times of need and danger, when hatred and fanaticism threatened to destroy the remnant of Israel. Therefore we render thanks to thee, and praise thy name with the ancient song of our fathers:

MINISTER, THEN CHOIR AND CONGREGATION:

Mi chomocho boëlim Adonoy; mi komocho, neddor bakkodesh, noro sehillos, ové féleh.

Who is like thee among the mighty, O God, who is like thee glorified in Holiness, awe-inspiring, wonder-working!

MINISTER:

As thou hast revealed thy kingdom to our fathers, so manifest thy glorious help unto us, their children, who worship thee as their God and King, proclaiming:

Adonoy yim'óch l'olom voëd.
God will reign for ever and ever!

Continue to be with us, O God, and guard us from evil. Let our lying down and our rising up be in peace. O guide us with thy good counsel; protect us from grief and need, from sorrow and anxiety, from sickness and danger; for in thee, O God, we put our trust, our gracious and merciful father. Let our going out and coming in be in peace, henceforth and forevermore. Blessed art thou, O God, Redeemer and Keeper of Israel.

CHOIR: **Amen.**

תפלת ערבית לראש השנה

אֱמֶת וֶאֱמוּנָה כָּל זֹאת וְקַיָּם עָלֵינוּ. כִּי הוּא יְיָ אֱלֹהֵינוּ וְאֵין זוּלָתוֹ. וַאֲנַחְנוּ יִשְׂרָאֵל עַמּוֹ. הַפּוֹדֵנוּ מִיַּד מְלָכִים. מַלְכֵּנוּ הַגּוֹאֲלֵנוּ מִכַּף כָּל־הֶעָרִיצִים. הָעוֹשֶׂה גְדוֹלוֹת עַד אֵין חֵקֶר. וְנִפְלָאוֹת עַד אֵין מִסְפָּר. הַשָּׂם נַפְשֵׁנוּ בַּחַיִּים. וְלֹא נָתַן לַמּוֹט רַגְלֵנוּ. הָעוֹשֶׂה לָּנוּ נִסִּים בְּמִצְרָיִם. אוֹתוֹת וּמוֹפְתִים בְּאַדְמַת בְּנֵי חָם. וְרָאוּ בָנָיו גְּבוּרָתוֹ. שִׁבְּחוּ וְהוֹדוּ לִשְׁמוֹ. וּמַלְכוּתוֹ בְּרָצוֹן קִבְּלוּ עֲלֵיהֶם. מֹשֶׁה וּבְנֵי יִשְׂרָאֵל לְךָ עָנוּ שִׁירָה בְּשִׂמְחָה רַבָּה וְאָמְרוּ כֻלָּם:

מִי־כָמֹכָה בָּאֵלִים יְיָ מִי כָּמֹכָה נֶאְדָּר בַּקֹּדֶשׁ. נוֹרָא תְהִלֹּת עֹשֵׂה־פֶלֶא:

מַלְכוּתְךָ רָאוּ בָנֶיךָ. בּוֹקֵעַ יָם לִפְנֵי מֹשֶׁה. זֶה אֵלִי עָנוּ וְאָמְרוּ:

יְיָ יִמְלֹךְ לְעֹלָם וָעֶד:

וְנֶאֱמַר כִּי־פָדָה יְיָ אֶת־יַעֲקֹב וּגְאָלוֹ מִיַּד חָזָק מִמֶּנּוּ. בָּרוּךְ אַתָּה יְיָ גָּאַל יִשְׂרָאֵל:

הַשְׁכִּיבֵנוּ יְיָ אֱלֹהֵינוּ לְשָׁלוֹם. וְהַעֲמִידֵנוּ מַלְכֵּנוּ לְחַיִּים. וּפְרֹשׂ עָלֵינוּ סֻכַּת שְׁלוֹמֶךָ. וְתַקְּנֵנוּ בְּעֵצָה טוֹבָה מִלְּפָנֶיךָ. וְהוֹשִׁיעֵנוּ לְמַעַן שְׁמֶךָ. וְהָגֵן בַּעֲדֵנוּ וְהָסֵר מֵעָלֵינוּ אוֹיֵב דֶּבֶר וְחֶרֶב וְרָעָב וְיָגוֹן. וּבְצֵל כְּנָפֶיךָ תַּסְתִּירֵנוּ. כִּי אֵל שׁוֹמְרֵנוּ וּמַצִּילֵנוּ אָתָּה. כִּי אֵל מֶלֶךְ חַנּוּן וְרַחוּם אָתָּה. וּשְׁמֹר צֵאתֵנוּ וּבוֹאֵנוּ לְחַיִּים וּלְשָׁלוֹם מֵעַתָּה וְעַד עוֹלָם. בָּרוּךְ אַתָּה יְיָ שׁוֹמֵר עַמּוֹ יִשְׂרָאֵל לָעַד:

Praise be to thee, O Eternal our God, God of our fathers, God of Abraham, Isaac, and Jacob, Almighty and Supreme Ruler of the world, who renderest just reward unto all. Thou rememberest the pious deeds of the fathers, and bringest redemption and love to their descendants. Remember us unto life, O Sovereign who ordainest life, and inscribe us in the book of life, for thy sake, O God of life; for thou art our Father, our Protector, and Helper. Praise be to thee, O God, Shield of Abraham.

Thou art mighty, O Lord, thy help is ever near. Thou sustainest in kindness the living; thou upholdest the falling, healest the sick, loosest the bonds of captives, and keepest thy faith to those who sleep in the dust. Who is like unto thee, Merciful Father! Author of life and death, who givest salvation, and rememberest thy creatures unto life eternal! Praise be to thee, O God, who hast planted within us eternal life.

CHOIR: **Amen.**

We give thanks unto thee, O Eternal, our God, for the unspeakable love and mercy with which thou hast chosen our fathers to recognize thee before all the nations of the earth; thou hast guided us, and called us to thy service. In thy grace thou hast given us, O Lord our God, (this day of the Sabbath and) this Day of Memorial, that we may remember that thou guidest our destinies and that before thy throne of judgment every son of man is accountable for his acts.

Our God, God of our fathers, grant that our memorial and the memorial of our fathers, and the memorial of Israel, thy people, may ascend and come before thee for grace, favor and mercy, life and peace, on this Day of Memorial.

Remember us, O Lord, for our good; bless us with happiness, and help us in the trials of life.

Cause thy mercy to descend upon us, and bring us salvation, according to the promise of thy holy word; for unto thee we look for aid, O our Heavenly Father, who in loving mercy rulest all mankind.

תפלת ערבית לראש השנה

בָּרוּךְ אַתָּה יְיָ אֱלֹהֵינוּ וֵאלֹהֵי אֲבוֹתֵינוּ. אֱלֹהֵי אַבְרָהָם אֱלֹהֵי יִצְחָק וֵאלֹהֵי יַעֲקֹב. הָאֵל הַגָּדֹל הַגִּבּוֹר וְהַנּוֹרָא. אֵל עֶלְיוֹן. גּוֹמֵל חֲסָדִים טוֹבִים. וְקֹנֵה הַכֹּל וְזוֹכֵר חַסְדֵי אָבוֹת. וּמֵבִיא גְאֻלָּה לִבְנֵי בְנֵיהֶם. לְמַעַן שְׁמוֹ בְּאַהֲבָה:

זָכְרֵנוּ לַחַיִּים. מֶלֶךְ חָפֵץ בַּחַיִּים. וְכָתְבֵנוּ בְּסֵפֶר הַחַיִּים. לְמַעַנְךָ אֱלֹהִים חַיִּים:

מֶלֶךְ עוֹזֵר וּמוֹשִׁיעַ וּמָגֵן. בָּרוּךְ אַתָּה יְיָ מָגֵן אַבְרָהָם:

אַתָּה גִּבּוֹר לְעוֹלָם אֲדֹנָי. רַב לְהוֹשִׁיעַ. מְכַלְכֵּל חַיִּים בְּחֶסֶד. מְחַיֵּה הַכֹּל בְּרַחֲמִים רַבִּים. סוֹמֵךְ נוֹפְלִים וְרוֹפֵא חוֹלִים וּמַתִּיר אֲסוּרִים. וּמְקַיֵּם אֱמוּנָתוֹ לִישֵׁנֵי עָפָר. מִי כָמוֹךָ בַּעַל גְּבוּרוֹת. וּמִי דוֹמֶה לָּךְ. מֶלֶךְ מֵמִית וּמְחַיֶּה. וּמַצְמִיחַ יְשׁוּעָה:

מִי כָמוֹךָ אַב הָרַחֲמִים. זוֹכֵר יְצוּרָיו לְחַיִּים בְּרַחֲמִים:

בָּרוּךְ אַתָּה יְיָ מְחַיֵּה הַכֹּל:

אַתָּה קָדוֹשׁ וְשִׁמְךָ קָדוֹשׁ. וּקְדוֹשִׁים בְּכָל יוֹם יְהַלְלוּךָ סֶּלָה: בָּרוּךְ אַתָּה יְיָ הַמֶּלֶךְ הַקָּדוֹשׁ:

אַתָּה בְחַרְתָּנוּ מִכָּל הָעַמִּים. אָהַבְתָּ אוֹתָנוּ וְרָצִיתָ בָּנוּ. וְקִדַּשְׁתָּנוּ בְּמִצְוֹתֶיךָ. וְקֵרַבְתָּנוּ מַלְכֵּנוּ לַעֲבוֹדָתֶךָ. וְשִׁמְךָ הַגָּדוֹל וְהַקָּדוֹשׁ עָלֵינוּ קָרָאתָ. וַתִּתֶּן לָנוּ יְיָ אֱלֹהֵינוּ בְּאַהֲבָה אֶת יוֹם (שַׁבָּת וְאֶת יוֹם) הַזִּכָּרוֹן הַזֶּה. יוֹם תְּרוּעָה. מִקְרָא קֹדֶשׁ. זֵכֶר לִיצִיאַת מִצְרָיִם:

אֱלֹהֵינוּ וֵאלֹהֵי אֲבוֹתֵינוּ יַעֲלֶה וְיָבֹא זִכְרוֹנֵנוּ וְזִכְרוֹן אֲבוֹתֵינוּ. וְזִכְרוֹן כָּל עַמְּךָ בֵּית יִשְׂרָאֵל לְפָנֶיךָ. לְחֵן

Our God, God of our fathers, reign thou over the whole world in thy glory, and be exalted in thy majesty; let truth and justice triumphantly shine forth upon all mankind, that every creature may know that thou hast created it, and every being understand that thou hast formed it, and all in whom there is the breath of life exclaim: The Eternal, the God of Israel reigneth, and his supreme power ruleth over all!

Grant, therefore, O Lord our God, that all thy works may reverence thee, and the fear of thee fill all created beings; that all may bow before thee in awe and humility, and unite with one accord to do thy will with an upright heart; for we know and acknowledge, O Lord our God, that thou art the Supreme Ruler of the universe, that thy power, thy might, and thy awe-inspiring name are manifested in all thy works.

Grant also that thy people Israel may everywhere be given the honor due their sacred mission; that the doctrines of universal freedom and righteousness may everywhere be realized. Then shall the righteous be glad and rejoice. For truth shall triumph over error and falsehood; inquity shall be silenced in shame, all manner of wickedness vanish like smoke, and tyranny and oppression be removed from the face of the earth. To thee alone shall all thy creatures then pay homage, verifying the words of holy writ: The Lord shall reign for ever and for ever, even thy God, O Zion, from generation to generation. Hallelujah!

Thou art holy and thy name is awe-inspiring, for there is no God besides thee; and thus we read: The Lord of Hosts is exalted in judgment, and God, the Holy-One is sanctified through righteousness.

Sanctify us, O God, through thy commandments, and give us light through thy law. Satisfy us with thy goodness and gladden us by thy help. Purify our hearts that we may serve thee in truth, for thou, O God, art Truth, and thy word is true and endureth for ever. Blessed be thou, O Lord, Sovereign of the universe, who sanctifiest (the Sabbath), Israel, and the Day of Memorial.

CHOIR: **Amen.**

תפלת ערבית לראש השנה

וּלְחֶסֶד וּלְרַחֲמִים. לְחַיִּים וּלְשָׁלוֹם. בְּיוֹם הַזִּכָּרוֹן הַזֶּה. זָכְרֵנוּ יְיָ אֱלֹהֵינוּ בּוֹ לְטוֹבָה. וּפָקְדֵנוּ בוֹ לִבְרָכָה. וְהוֹשִׁיעֵנוּ בוֹ לְחַיִּים. וּבִדְבַר יְשׁוּעָה וְרַחֲמִים חוּס וְחָנֵּנוּ. וְרַחֵם עָלֵינוּ וְהוֹשִׁיעֵנוּ. כִּי אֵלֶיךָ עֵינֵינוּ. כִּי אֵל מֶלֶךְ חַנּוּן וְרַחוּם אָתָּה:

אֱלֹהֵינוּ וֵאלֹהֵי אֲבוֹתֵינוּ. מְלוֹךְ עַל כָּל הָעוֹלָם כֻּלּוֹ בִּכְבוֹדֶךָ. וְהִנָּשֵׂא עַל כָּל הָאָרֶץ בִּיקָרֶךָ. וְהוֹפַע בַּהֲדַר גְּאוֹן עֻזֶּךָ עַל כָּל יוֹשְׁבֵי תֵבֵל אַרְצֶךָ. וְיֵדַע כָּל פָּעוּל כִּי אַתָּה פְעַלְתּוֹ. וְיָבִין כָּל יָצוּר כִּי אַתָּה יְצַרְתּוֹ. וְיֹאמַר כֹּל אֲשֶׁר נְשָׁמָה בְאַפּוֹ. יְיָ אֱלֹהֵי יִשְׂרָאֵל מֶלֶךְ. וּמַלְכוּתוֹ בַּכֹּל מָשָׁלָה:

וּבְכֵן תֵּן פַּחְדְּךָ יְיָ אֱלֹהֵינוּ עַל־כָּל־מַעֲשֶׂיךָ. וְאֵימָתְךָ עַל כָּל־מַה־שֶּׁבָּרָאתָ. וְיִירָאוּךָ כָּל־הַמַּעֲשִׂים. וְיִשְׁתַּחֲווּ לְפָנֶיךָ כָּל הַבְּרוּאִים. וְיֵעָשׂוּ כֻלָּם אֲגֻדָּה אֶחָת. לַעֲשׂוֹת רְצוֹנְךָ בְּלֵבָב שָׁלֵם. כְּמוֹ שֶׁיָּדַעְנוּ יְיָ אֱלֹהֵינוּ שֶׁהַשִּׁלְטוֹן לְפָנֶיךָ. עֹז בְּיָדְךָ וּגְבוּרָה בִּימִינֶךָ. וְשִׁמְךָ נוֹרָא עַל־כָּל־מַה־שֶּׁבָּרָאתָ:

וּבְכֵן צַדִּיקִים יִרְאוּ וְיִשְׂמָחוּ. וִישָׁרִים יַעֲלֹזוּ. וַחֲסִידִים בְּרִנָּה יָגִילוּ. וְעוֹלָתָה תִּקְפָּץ פִּיהָ. וְכָל הָרִשְׁעָה כֻּלָּהּ כְּעָשָׁן תִּכְלֶה. כִּי תַעֲבִיר מֶמְשֶׁלֶת זָדוֹן מִן הָאָרֶץ:

וְתִמְלוֹךְ אַתָּה יְיָ לְבַדֶּךָ עַל כָּל מַעֲשֶׂיךָ. כַּכָּתוּב בְּדִבְרֵי קָדְשֶׁךָ. יִמְלֹךְ יְיָ לְעוֹלָם. אֱלֹהַיִךְ צִיּוֹן לְדֹר וָדֹר. הַלְלוּיָהּ:

קָדוֹשׁ אַתָּה וְנוֹרָא שְׁמֶךָ: וְאֵין אֱלוֹהַּ מִבַּלְעָדֶיךָ. כַּכָּתוּב. וַיִּגְבַּהּ יְיָ צְבָאוֹת בַּמִּשְׁפָּט. וְהָאֵל הַקָּדוֹשׁ נִקְדַּשׁ בִּצְדָקָה. בָּרוּךְ אַתָּה יְיָ הַמֶּלֶךְ הַקָּדוֹשׁ:

(The Congregation in silent devotion.)

O God, keep my tongue from evil, and my lips from uttering deceit, and grant that I may be meek and kind to those who bear ill-will against me. Implant humility in my heart and strengthen me with faith. Be my support when grief oppresses me and my comfort in affliction. Let thy truth illumine my path and guide me; for thou art my God and my aid; in thee I trust every day.

Let the words of my mouth and the meditation of my heart be acceptable in thy sight, O God, my Strength and my Redeemer. As thou preservest peace in the heavenly spheres, so preserve it to us and to all who invoke thy holy name. Amen.

HYMN.

On wings of wind roll swiftly by
    The hours, the days, the year;
We cannot check, howe'er we try,
    The march of time's career.
A fleeting shadow is our life,
    A brief and passing dream;
Its labors are but empty strife,
    Its aims not what they seem.

We step, O God, with awe and fears
    Before thy holy throne —
Our thoughts, our deeds, our joys, our tears
    To thee, O Lord, are known.
The angels e'en, so pure and bright,
    Cannot endure thy test —
How, then, can we approach thy sight,
    Who are by sin opprest.

We cannot hide our trespasses
    And not our deeds rescind;
With contrite heart we do confess:
    'Our Father, we have sinned!'
O God, thy pardon we implore,
    Remember we are frail;
Refresh us from thy mercy's store,
    Assist us, when we fail.

SERMON.
HYMN.

תפלת ערבית לראש השנה

אֱלֹהֵינוּ וֵאלֹהֵי אֲבוֹתֵינוּ (רְצֵה בִמְנוּחָתֵנוּ). קַדְּשֵׁנוּ בְּמִצְוֹתֶיךָ. וְתֵן חֶלְקֵנוּ בְּתוֹרָתֶךָ. שַׂבְּעֵנוּ מִטּוּבֶךָ. וְשַׂמְּחֵנוּ בִּישׁוּעָתֶךָ. וְטַהֵר לִבֵּנוּ לְעָבְדְּךָ בֶּאֱמֶת. כִּי אַתָּה אֱלֹהִים אֱמֶת. וּדְבָרְךָ אֱמֶת וְקַיָּם לָעַד. בָּרוּךְ אַתָּה יְיָ מֶלֶךְ עַל כָּל הָאָרֶץ. מְקַדֵּשׁ (בַּשַּׁבָּת וְ) יִשְׂרָאֵל וְיוֹם הַזִּכָּרוֹן:

אֱלֹהַי נְצוֹר לְשׁוֹנִי מֵרָע וּשְׂפָתַי מִדַּבֵּר מִרְמָה וְלִמְקַלְלַי נַפְשִׁי תִדּוֹם וְנַפְשִׁי כֶּעָפָר לַכֹּל תִּהְיֶה: פְּתַח לִבִּי בְּתוֹרָתֶךָ וּבְמִצְוֹתֶיךָ תִּרְדּוֹף נַפְשִׁי. וְכֹל הַחוֹשְׁבִים עָלַי רָעָה מְהֵרָה הָפֵר עֲצָתָם וְקַלְקֵל מַחֲשַׁבְתָּם. עֲשֵׂה לְמַעַן שְׁמֶךָ. עֲשֵׂה לְמַעַן יְמִינֶךָ. עֲשֵׂה לְמַעַן קְדֻשָּׁתֶךָ. עֲשֵׂה לְמַעַן תּוֹרָתֶךָ. לְמַעַן יֵחָלְצוּן יְדִידֶיךָ. הוֹשִׁיעָה יְמִינְךָ וַעֲנֵנִי: יִהְיוּ לְרָצוֹן אִמְרֵי פִי וְהֶגְיוֹן לִבִּי לְפָנֶיךָ יְיָ צוּרִי וְגוֹאֲלִי: עֹשֶׂה שָׁלוֹם בִּמְרוֹמָיו הוּא יַעֲשֶׂה שָׁלוֹם עָלֵינוּ וְעַל כָּל יִשְׂרָאֵל וְאִמְרוּ אָמֵן:

ADORATION.

Almighty God! Creator of heaven and earth! It behooves us to render praise and thanksgiving unto thee, who hast delivered us from the darkness of false belief and sent to us the light of thy truth. Thou art our God, there is no other.

We, therefore, bow the head and bend the knee before thee, Creator and Ruler of the world, and bless thy holy name!

MINISTER, THEN CHOIR AND CONGREGATION:

Vaanachnu, kór'im, umishtáchavim, umódim, lifné Mélech mal'ché hammelóchim, Hakkódosh boruch hu.

Thou art, in truth, our Father, our God, our Saviour, and there is none besides thee, as is written in thy law: Thou shalt know this day and reflect in thy heart that the Lord is God in heaven above as on earth below; and there is none else.

We fervently pray, O Lord our God, that we may speedily behold the glory of thy mighty power, banishing all impurities from the earth, destroying idolatry and wickedness, and establishing thy truth among mankind; that all the inhabitants of the earth may invoke thy name, acknowledge thy unity, and understand that to thee alone every knee must bend and every tongue swear fealty.

May all thy children, O God, soon be united in a common bond of brotherhood, may the time be hastened when no religious differences will separate them, but when they will all adore thee as the universal father, worship thee in the spirit of true religion, and unite in proclaiming the unity of thy holy name.

Thus, O God, do thou reign over them for ever and ever, for the kingdom is thine, and unto thee appertain power, glory and majesty from everlasting to everlasting. As it is written: The Lord will reign for ever and ever; the Lord will be king over all the earth; on that day shall God be acknowledged One and his name One.

MINISTER, THEN CHOIR AND CONGREGATION:

Veho-yoh Adonoy lemélech al kol hoórets, bayóm hahu yih'yéh Adonoy echod, u-shemo echod.

תפלת ערבית לראש השנה

עָלֵינוּ לְשַׁבֵּחַ לַאֲדוֹן הַכֹּל. לָתֵת גְּדֻלָּה לְיוֹצֵר בְּרֵאשִׁית. שֶׁהוּא נוֹטֶה שָׁמַיִם וְיוֹסֵד אָרֶץ. וּמוֹשַׁב יְקָרוֹ בַּשָּׁמַיִם מִמַּעַל. וּשְׁכִינַת עֻזּוֹ בְּגָבְהֵי מְרוֹמִים. הוּא אֱלֹהֵינוּ אֵין עוֹד.

וַאֲנַחְנוּ כֹּרְעִים וּמִשְׁתַּחֲוִים וּמוֹדִים

לִפְנֵי מֶלֶךְ מַלְכֵי הַמְּלָכִים. הַקָּדוֹשׁ בָּרוּךְ הוּא:

אֱמֶת מַלְכֵּנוּ אֶפֶס זוּלָתוֹ. כַּכָּתוּב בְּתוֹרָתוֹ. וְיָדַעְתָּ הַיּוֹם וַהֲשֵׁבֹתָ אֶל־לְבָבֶךָ. כִּי יְיָ הוּא הָאֱלֹהִים בַּשָּׁמַיִם מִמַּעַל וְעַל־הָאָרֶץ מִתָּחַת. אֵין עוֹד:

עַל כֵּן נְקַוֶּה לְךָ יְיָ אֱלֹהֵינוּ. לִרְאוֹת מְהֵרָה בְּתִפְאֶרֶת עֻזֶּךָ. לְהַעֲבִיר גִּלּוּלִים מִן הָאָרֶץ. וְהָאֱלִילִים כָּרוֹת יִכָּרֵתוּן. לְתַקֵּן עוֹלָם בְּמַלְכוּת שַׁדַּי. וְכָל־בְּנֵי בָשָׂר יִקְרְאוּ בִשְׁמֶךָ. לְהַפְנוֹת אֵלֶיךָ כָּל־רִשְׁעֵי אָרֶץ. יַכִּירוּ וְיֵדְעוּ כָּל־יוֹשְׁבֵי תֵבֵל. כִּי לְךָ תִּכְרַע כָּל־בֶּרֶךְ. תִּשָּׁבַע כָּל־לָשׁוֹן. לְפָנֶיךָ יְיָ אֱלֹהֵינוּ יִכְרְעוּ וְיִפֹּלוּ. וְלִכְבוֹד שִׁמְךָ יְקָר יִתֵּנוּ. וִיקַבְּלוּ כֻלָּם אֶת־עֹל מַלְכוּתֶךָ. וְתִמְלוֹךְ עֲלֵיהֶם מְהֵרָה לְעוֹלָם וָעֶד. כִּי הַמַּלְכוּת שֶׁלְּךָ הִיא. וּלְעוֹלְמֵי עַד תִּמְלוֹךְ בְּכָבוֹד. כַּכָּתוּב בְּתוֹרָתֶךָ. יְיָ יִמְלֹךְ לְעֹלָם וָעֶד: וְנֶאֱמַר וְהָיָה יְיָ לְמֶלֶךְ עַל־כָּל־הָאָרֶץ. בַּיּוֹם הַהוּא יִהְיֶה יְיָ אֶחָד וּשְׁמוֹ אֶחָד:

Address to the Mourners.

Brothers and sisters, who are mourning for dear lives departed, remember your beloved ones and honor their names in the midst of the congregation of Israel. May the memory of the righteous inspire you to noble deeds and works in their honor. Rise, and praise with me the name of the most High, according to the anscient custom of our fathers.

MOURNERS' KADDISH.

May thy great and ineffable name, O Lord of life and death, be exalted and sanctified throughout the world, which thou hast created according to thy will. May thy kingdom be established in our midst, in our lifetime and in our days, and in the days of the whole house of Israel. Amen.

The Congregation:

May his great and ineffable name be blessed and glorified for ever and ever.

Praised and hallowed be thy name who hast created man in thy image and planted within him eternal life. In thy hand is the soul of every living being and the spirit of all flesh. Blessed art thou, whose hymns, praises and benedictions are repeated throughout the world. Amen.

The Congregation:

Praised be he and his glorious name.

Unto Israel, unto all the righteous and unto all who departed this life according to the will of God, may there be granted abundance of peace, and a blissful portion in the life to come, grace and mercy by the Lord of heaven and earth. Amen.

The Congregation:

May the fullness of peace from heaven, with life and health be granted unto us and unto all Israel. Amen.

May he who establisheth peace in his heavenly spheres grant happiness and peace unto us, unto all Israel and to all mankind. Amen.

קדיש דאבלים.

יִתְגַּדַּל וְיִתְקַדַּשׁ שְׁמֵהּ רַבָּא. בְּעָלְמָא דִּי־בְרָא כִרְעוּתֵהּ. וְיַמְלִיךְ מַלְכוּתֵהּ. בְּחַיֵּיכוֹן וּבְיוֹמֵיכוֹן וּבְחַיֵּי דְכָל בֵּית יִשְׂרָאֵל. בַּעֲגָלָא וּבִזְמַן קָרִיב. וְאִמְרוּ אָמֵן.

יְהֵא שְׁמֵהּ רַבָּא מְבָרַךְ. לְעָלַם וּלְעָלְמֵי עָלְמַיָּא.

יִתְבָּרַךְ וְיִשְׁתַּבַּח וְיִתְפָּאַר וְיִתְרוֹמַם. וְיִתְנַשֵּׂא וְיִתְהַדָּר וְיִתְעַלֶּה וְיִתְהַלָּל שְׁמֵהּ דְּקוּדְשָׁא. בְּרִיךְ הוּא. לְעֵלָּא מִן כָּל בִּרְכָתָא וְשִׁירָתָא. תֻּשְׁבְּחָתָא וְנֶחָמָתָא. דַּאֲמִירָן בְּעָלְמָא. וְאִמְרוּ אָמֵן:

עַל יִשְׂרָאֵל וְעַל צַדִּיקַיָּא. וְעַל־כָּל־מַן דְּאִתְפְּטַר מִן עָלְמָא הָדֵין בִּרְעוּתֵהּ דֶּאֱלָהָא. יְהֵא לְהוֹן שְׁלָמָא רַבָּא וְחוּלָקָא־טָבָא לְחַיֵּי עָלְמָא דְאָתֵי. וְחִסְדָּא וְרַחֲמֵי מִן־קֳדָם מָרֵא שְׁמַיָּא וְאַרְעָא. וְאִמְרוּ אָמֵן:

תִּתְקַבַּל צְלוֹתְהוֹן וּבָעוּתְהוֹן דְּכָל־יִשְׂרָאֵל. קֳדָם אֲבוּהוֹן דִּי בִשְׁמַיָּא. וְאִמְרוּ אָמֵן:

יְהֵא שְׁלָמָא רַבָּא מִן־שְׁמַיָּא וְחַיִּים. עָלֵינוּ וְעַל־כָּל־יִשְׂרָאֵל. וְאִמְרוּ אָמֵן:

עֹשֶׂה שָׁלוֹם בִּמְרוֹמָיו. הוּא יַעֲשֶׂה שָׁלוֹם עָלֵינוּ וְעַל כָּל יִשְׂרָאֵל. וְאִמְרוּ אָמֵן:

RESOLVE.

BY PENINA MOSES.

(From Dr. G. Gottheil's Hymn-book)

Into the tomb of ages past
Another year hath now been cast;
Shall time unheeded take its flight,
Nor leave one ray of higher light,
That on man's pilgrimage may shine
And lead his soul to spheres divine?

With firm resolve your bosoms nerve,
The God of right alone to serve;
Speech, thought, and act to regulate,
By what his perfect laws dictate;
Nor from his holy precepts stray
By worldly idols lured away.

Peace to the house of Israel!
May joy within it ever dwell!
May sorrow on the opening year,
Forgetting its accustomed tear,
With smiles again fond kindred meet,
With hopes revived the festal greet!

MORNING SERVICE
FOR
NEW YEAR'S DAY.

Organ Prelude.

MINISTER:

מַה־טֹּבוּ אֹהָלֶיךָ יַעֲקֹב מִשְׁכְּנֹתֶיךָ יִשְׂרָאֵל: וַאֲנִי בְּרֹב
חַסְדְּךָ אָבֹא בֵיתֶךָ אֶשְׁתַּחֲוֶה אֶל־הֵיכַל קָדְשְׁךָ בְּיִרְאָתֶךָ:
יְיָ אָהַבְתִּי מְעוֹן בֵּיתֶךָ וּמְקוֹם מִשְׁכַּן כְּבוֹדֶךָ: וַאֲנִי
אֶשְׁתַּחֲוֶה וְאֶכְרָעָה אֶבְרְכָה לִפְנֵי־יְיָ עֹשִׂי: וַאֲנִי תְפִלָּתִי
לְךָ יְיָ עֵת רָצוֹן אֱלֹהִים בְּרָב־חַסְדֶּךָ עֲנֵנִי בֶּאֱמֶת יִשְׁעֶךָ:

How beautiful are thy tents, O Jacob, thy tabernacles, O Israel! With faith in thy loving kindness, O God, we enter thy house; with profound reverence we will worship thee in thy holy temple. We love thy dwelling-place, O Lord, the abode sanctified by thy holiness. We will bow down before thee, and offer up our supplication unto thee, O God our Creator. Accept our prayers at this hour in the fulness of thy grace. Hear us, O God, our stronghold and support.

CHOIR: (Either of the following sentences.

Worship the Lord in the beauty of holiness;
Stand in awe before him all the earth.

Give unto the Lord glory and praise;
Worship the Lord in holy attire.

Serve the Lord with gladness;
Come before his presence with songs.

RESPONSIVE READING.

Select one or more Psalms from the following pages; for the Three Festivals, appropriate Psalms from the appended Collection, then begin Borechu on page 83.

Psalm 90. תפלה למשה

Lord! thou hast been our refuge in all generations!

Before the mountains were brought forth, or ever thou hadst formed the earth and the world, even from everlasting to everlasting thou art God!

But man thou turnest again to dust, and sayst, "Return, ye children of men!"

For a thousand years are, in thy sight, as yesterday when it is past, and as a watch in the night.

Thou carriest him away as with a flood; he is a dream; in the morning he springeth up like grass,

Which flourisheth and shooteth up in the morning, and in the evening is cut down, and withered.

For we are consumed by thy anger, and by thy wrath are we destroyed.

If thou settest our iniquities before thee, our secret sins in the the light of thy countenance:

Then in thine anger all our days vanish away; we spend our years like a thought.

The days of our life are threescore years and ten, and by reason of strength may be fourscore years:

Yet is the pride of them weariness and sorrow; for it vanisheth swiftly, and we fly away.

Yet who attendeth to the power of thy anger? who with due reverence regardeth thy indignation?

Teach us so to number our days, that we may apply our hearts to wisdom!

Desist, O Lord! How long —? have compassion upon thy servants!

Satisfy us speedily with thy mercy, that we may rejoice and be glad all our days!

Make us glad according to the time in which thou hast afflicted us; according to the years in which we have seen adversity!

Let thy deeds be known to thy servants, and thy glory to their children!

Let the favor of the Lord our God be upon us, and establish for us the work of our hands; yea, the work of our hands, establish thou it!

Hymn.

Tho' faint, yet pursuing, we go on our way,
The Lord is our leader, his word is our stay;
Tho' suffering and sorrow and trial be near,
The Lord is our refuge, and whom can we fear?

He raiseth the fallen, he cheereth the faint,
The weak and oppress'd, he will hear their complaint;
The way may be weary and thorny the road,
But how can we falter? our help is in God.

Tho' clouds may surround us, our God is our light;
Tho' storms rage around us, our God is our might;
So, faint, yet pursuing, still onward we go,
The Lord is our leader, no fear can we know.

MINISTER:

Borechu es Adonoy hammevoroch.
Praise ye the Lord to whom all praise is due ·

Boruch Adonoy hammevoroch l'olom voëd.
Praised be the Lord through all eternity!

We praise thee, O Lord, our God, Ruler of the Universe, Creator of light and darkness, Source of all wisdom, Fountain of truth and peace. We praise thee, we thank thee, we magnify thee. In thy mercy thou causest light to radiate over the earth and all its inhabitants, and renewest daily in kindness the wonders of thy creation. Yea, how manifold are thy works, O Eternal, in wisdom thou hast made them all, the earth is full of thy treasures. O Lord of life, have compassion on us, be our defense, our shield, our protection. Praised be to thee, O God, Author of peace and light.

With infinite love, O Lord our God, thou hast guided our fathers, who trusted in thee, and hast taught them thy laws of life. O be gracious unto us; incline our hearts to thee, O merciful Father! May we love thy precepts, and be enabled to learn and to teach, to observe and to practice them in the spirit of love. Enlighten our minds in thy holy law, that we may learn to love and revere thy Name and so order our lives that we may never be put to shame for our deeds. In thy holy Name we put our trust; we rejoice and delight in thy help. For with thee alone is salvation. Thou hast appointed us, the children of Israel, to proclaim this truth, to acknowledge thee and thy unity before all nations of the earth. Praise be to thee, O Lord, who hast sanctified thy people Israel in love.

CHOIR: **Amen.**

MINISTER, THEN CHOIR AND CONGREGATION:

Sh'ma Yisroel, Adonoy Elohanu, Adonoy echod.
HEAR, O ISRAEL, THE LORD OUR GOD, THE LORD IS ONE.

Boruch Shem kevod mal'chuso l'olom voëd.
Praised be the name of his glorious Kingdom for evermore.

תפלת שחרית לראש השנה

בָּרְכוּ אֶת יְיָ הַמְבֹרָךְ:
בָּרוּךְ יְיָ הַמְבֹרָךְ לְעוֹלָם וָעֶד:
בָּרוּךְ אַתָּה יְיָ אֱלֹהֵינוּ מֶלֶךְ הָעוֹלָם. יוֹצֵר אוֹר וּבוֹרֵא חֹשֶׁךְ. עֹשֶׂה שָׁלוֹם וּבוֹרֵא אֶת הַכֹּל:

הַמֵּאִיר לָאָרֶץ וְלַדָּרִים עָלֶיהָ בְּרַחֲמִים. וּבְטוּבוֹ מְחַדֵּשׁ בְּכָל יוֹם תָּמִיד מַעֲשֵׂה בְרֵאשִׁית. הַמֶּלֶךְ הַמְרוֹמָם לְבַדּוֹ מֵאָז. הַמְשֻׁבָּח וְהַמְפֹאָר וְהַמִּתְנַשֵּׂא מִימוֹת עוֹלָם: אֱלֹהֵי עוֹלָם בְּרַחֲמֶיךָ הָרַבִּים רַחֵם עָלֵינוּ. אֲדוֹן עֻזֵּנוּ צוּר מִשְׂגַּבֵּנוּ. מָגֵן יִשְׁעֵנוּ מִשְׂגָּב בַּעֲדֵנוּ: שִׁמְךָ יְיָ אֱלֹהֵינוּ יִתְקַדָּשׁ. וְזִכְרְךָ מַלְכֵּנוּ יִתְפָּאַר. בַּשָּׁמַיִם מִמַּעַל וְעַל הָאָרֶץ מִתָּחַת. תִּתְבָּרַךְ מוֹשִׁיעֵנוּ עַל שֶׁבַח מַעֲשֵׂה יָדֶיךָ. וְעַל מְאוֹרֵי אוֹר שֶׁעָשִׂיתָ יְפָאֲרוּךָ סֶּלָה: בָּרוּךְ אַתָּה יְיָ יוֹצֵר הַמְּאוֹרוֹת:

אַהֲבָה רַבָּה אֲהַבְתָּנוּ יְיָ אֱלֹהֵינוּ. חֶמְלָה גְדוֹלָה וִיתֵרָה חָמַלְתָּ עָלֵינוּ. אָבִינוּ מַלְכֵּנוּ. בַּעֲבוּר אֲבוֹתֵינוּ שֶׁבָּטְחוּ בְךָ. וַתְּלַמְּדֵם חֻקֵּי חַיִּים. כֵּן תְּחָנֵּנוּ וּתְלַמְּדֵנוּ: אָבִינוּ הָאָב הָרַחֲמָן. רַחֵם עָלֵינוּ. וְתֵן בְּלִבֵּנוּ לְהָבִין וּלְהַשְׂכִּיל. לִשְׁמֹעַ לִלְמֹד וּלְלַמֵּד. לִשְׁמֹר וְלַעֲשׂוֹת וּלְקַיֵּם אֶת כָּל דִּבְרֵי תַלְמוּד תּוֹרָתֶךָ בְּאַהֲבָה: וְהָאֵר עֵינֵינוּ בְּתוֹרָתֶךָ. וְדַבֵּק לִבֵּנוּ בְּמִצְוֹתֶיךָ. וְיַחֵד לְבָבֵנוּ לְאַהֲבָה וּלְיִרְאָה שְׁמֶךָ. וְלֹא נֵבוֹשׁ לְעוֹלָם וָעֶד: כִּי בְשֵׁם קָדְשְׁךָ בָּטָחְנוּ. נָגִילָה וְנִשְׂמְחָה בִּישׁוּעָתֶךָ. כִּי אֵל פּוֹעֵל יְשׁוּעוֹת אָתָּה. וּבָנוּ בָחַרְתָּ וְקֵרַבְתָּנוּ לְשִׁמְךָ הַגָּדוֹל סֶלָה בֶּאֱמֶת. לְהוֹדוֹת לְךָ וּלְיַחֶדְךָ בְּאַהֲבָה. בָּרוּךְ אַתָּה יְיָ הַבּוֹחֵר בְּעַמּוֹ יִשְׂרָאֵל בְּאַהֲבָה:

שְׁמַע יִשְׂרָאֵל יְהוָה אֱלֹהֵינוּ יְהוָה אֶחָד:
בָּרוּךְ שֵׁם כְּבוֹד מַלְכוּתוֹ לְעוֹלָם וָעֶד:

Thou shalt love the Eternal thy God with all thy heart, with all thy soul, and with all thy might. And these words, which I command thee to-day, shall be in thy heart. Thou shalt teach them diligently to thy children, and shalt talk of them when thou sittest in thy house, and when thou walkest by the way, and when thou liest down, and when thou risest. And they shall be as a sign on your hand and as an ornament on your brow. And thou shalt write them upon the door posts of thy house and on thy gates. (DEUTER., CHAPT. 6, V. 4—9.)

Unchangeable and immutable is this word with us: God is everlasting; his word is true unto all generations; his commandments stand for ever. He alone is our God and none besides him.

Thou hast been the protector of our fathers in time of distress, thou hast saved us from the hand of oppression; for thou art our Guide, Protector, and Redeemer, the Rock of our salvation, our Helper and Deliverer. Thou art the first and the last, and besides thee there is no power to help or redeem. Thou hast saved Israel from Egyptian bondage and to this day thou art our help and our refuge. Therefore we exalt thee, and praise thy name with the ancient song of our fathers:

MINISTER, THEN CHOIR AND CONGREGATION:

Mi chomocho boëlim Adonoy; mi komócho, neddor bakkódesh, nóro sehillos, osé féleh.

Who is like thee among the mighty, O God, who is like thee glorified through holiness, awe-inspiring, wonder-working!

The redeemed of the Lord sang a new song. They saw thy glorious help and worshipped thee as their God and King proclaiming:

Adonoy yimlóch l'olom voëd.

The Lord will reign for ever and ever.

O Rock of Israel, send redemption to those that are in bondage; for thou art the redeemer of the oppressed, as it is written: Our Redeemer is the Lord of Host, the Holy One of Israel is his name. Praise be to thee, O Lord, Redeemer of Israel.   CHOIR: **Amen.**

תפלת שחרית לראש השנה

וְאָהַבְתָּ אֵת יְיָ אֱלֹהֶיךָ בְּכָל לְבָבְךָ וּבְכָל נַפְשְׁךָ וּבְכָל מְאֹדֶךָ: וְהָיוּ הַדְּבָרִים הָאֵלֶּה אֲשֶׁר אָנֹכִי מְצַוְּךָ הַיּוֹם עַל־לְבָבֶךָ: וְשִׁנַּנְתָּם לְבָנֶיךָ וְדִבַּרְתָּ בָּם. בְּשִׁבְתְּךָ בְּבֵיתֶךָ וּבְלֶכְתְּךָ בַדֶּרֶךְ וּבְשָׁכְבְּךָ וּבְקוּמֶךָ: וּקְשַׁרְתָּם לְאוֹת עַל־יָדֶךָ. וְהָיוּ לְטֹטָפֹת בֵּין עֵינֶיךָ: וּכְתַבְתָּם עַל־מְזֻזוֹת בֵּיתֶךָ וּבִשְׁעָרֶיךָ:

אֱמֶת. אֱלֹהֵי עוֹלָם מַלְכֵּנוּ. צוּר יַעֲקֹב מָגֵן יִשְׁעֵנוּ. לְדוֹר וָדוֹר הוּא קַיָּם וּשְׁמוֹ קַיָּם. וְכִסְאוֹ נָכוֹן וּמַלְכוּתוֹ וֶאֱמוּנָתוֹ לָעַד קַיֶּמֶת. וּדְבָרָיו חָיִים וְקַיָּמִים. נֶאֱמָנִים וְנֶחֱמָדִים לָעַד וּלְעוֹלְמֵי עוֹלָמִים. עַל אֲבוֹתֵינוּ וְעָלֵינוּ. עַל בָּנֵינוּ וְעַל דּוֹרוֹתֵינוּ. וְעַל כָּל דּוֹרוֹת זֶרַע יִשְׂרָאֵל עֲבָדֶיךָ: אֱמֶת. שָׁאַתָּה הוּא יְיָ אֱלֹהֵינוּ וֵאלֹהֵי אֲבוֹתֵינוּ. מַלְכֵּנוּ מֶלֶךְ אֲבוֹתֵינוּ. גּוֹאֲלֵנוּ גּוֹאֵל אֲבוֹתֵינוּ. יוֹצְרֵנוּ צוּר יְשׁוּעָתֵנוּ. פּוֹדֵנוּ וּמַצִּילֵנוּ מֵעוֹלָם שְׁמֶךָ. אֵין אֱלֹהִים זוּלָתֶךָ: אֱמֶת. אַתָּה הוּא רִאשׁוֹן וְאַתָּה הוּא אַחֲרוֹן. וּמִבַּלְעָדֶיךָ אֵין לָנוּ מֶלֶךְ גּוֹאֵל וּמוֹשִׁיעַ. מִמִּצְרַיִם גְּאַלְתָּנוּ יְיָ אֱלֹהֵינוּ. וּמִבֵּית עֲבָדִים פְּדִיתָנוּ. עַל זֹאת שִׁבְּחוּ אֲהוּבִים וְרוֹמְמוּ אֵל:

מִי־כָמֹכָה בָּאֵלִים יְיָ מִי כָּמֹכָה נֶאְדָּר בַּקֹּדֶשׁ. נוֹרָא תְהִלֹּת עֹשֵׂה־פֶלֶא:

שִׁירָה חֲדָשָׁה שִׁבְּחוּ גְאוּלִים לְשִׁמְךָ. עַל שְׂפַת הַיָּם יַחַד כֻּלָּם הוֹדוּ וְהִמְלִיכוּ וְאָמְרוּ:

יְיָ יִמְלֹךְ לְעֹלָם וָעֶד:

צוּר יִשְׂרָאֵל. קוּמָה בְּעֶזְרַת יִשְׂרָאֵל. גּוֹאֲלֵנוּ יְיָ צְבָאוֹת שְׁמוֹ קְדוֹשׁ יִשְׂרָאֵל. בָּרוּךְ אַתָּה יְיָ גָּאַל יִשְׂרָאֵל:

May the glory of God appear to us; and in his mercy be gracious to those who twice daily, yea evening and morning, proclaim the unity of his Name in love and devotion:

Sh'ma Yisroel, Adonoy Elohénu, Adonoy Echod.

HEAR, O ISRAEL, THE LORD OUR GOD, THE LORD IS ONE.

The Lord is One; He is our Father, our King, our Saviour; He will grant our prayers and manifest himself before all mankind as the God of Israel.

CHOIR: *Ani Adonoy Elohéchem.*

I am the Lord your God.

The Lord is almighty, how excellent is his name throughout the world. And the Lord shall be King over all the earth, on that day shall the Lord be acknowledged One and his name One, as is written in Holy Scriptures:

Yimlóch Adonoy l'olom, Elohayich Zion l'dór, vodór Hallelujah.

The Lord shall reign for evermore, even thy God, O Zion, from generation to generation. Hallelujah!

For ever will we declare thy greatness and proclaim thy holiness, neither shall thy praise ever depart from our lips. Praise be to thee, Almighty and Holy God. Amen.

(The Congregation will be seated.)

We give thanks unto thee, O Eternal, our God, for the unspeakable love and mercy with which thou hast chosen our fathers to recognize thee before all the nations of the earth; thou hast guided us, and called us to thy service. In thy grace thou hast given us, O Lord our God, (this day of the Sabbath and) this Day of Memorial, that we may remember that thou guidest our destinies and that before thy throne of judgment every son of man is accountable for his acts.

Our God, God of our fathers, grant that our memorial and the memorial of our fathers, and the memorial of Israel, thy people, may ascend and come before thee for grace, favor and mercy, life and peace, on this Day of Memorial.

תפלת שחרית לראש השנה

בָּרוּךְ כְּבוֹד יְיָ מִמְּקוֹמוֹ:

מִמְּקוֹמוֹ הוּא יִפֶן בְּרַחֲמִים. וְיָחוֹן עַם הַמְיַחֲדִים שְׁמוֹ עֶרֶב וָבֹקֶר. בְּכָל יוֹם תָּמִיד פַּעֲמַיִם. בְּאַהֲבָה שְׁמַע אוֹמְרִים:

שְׁמַע יִשְׂרָאֵל יְהֹוָה אֱלֹהֵינוּ יְהֹוָה אֶחָד:

אֶחָד הוּא אֱלֹהֵינוּ. הוּא אָבִינוּ. הוּא מַלְכֵּנוּ. הוּא מוֹשִׁיעֵנוּ. וְהוּא יַשְׁמִיעֵנוּ בְּרַחֲמָיו שֵׁנִית. לְעֵינֵי כָּל חָי. לִהְיוֹת לָכֶם לֵאלֹהִים. אֲנִי יְיָ אֱלֹהֵיכֶם:

וְהָיָה יְיָ לְמֶלֶךְ עַל כָּל הָאָרֶץ. בַּיּוֹם הַהוּא יִהְיֶה יְיָ אֶחָד וּשְׁמוֹ אֶחָד:

יִמְלֹךְ יְיָ לְעוֹלָם. אֱלֹהַיִךְ צִיּוֹן לְדֹר וָדֹר. הַלְלוּיָהּ:

לְדוֹר וָדוֹר נַגִּיד גָּדְלֶךָ. וּלְנֵצַח נְצָחִים קְדֻשָּׁתְךָ נַקְדִּישׁ. וְשִׁבְחֲךָ אֱלֹהֵינוּ מִפִּינוּ לֹא יָמוּשׁ לְעוֹלָם וָעֶד. כִּי אֵל מֶלֶךְ גָּדוֹל וְקָדוֹשׁ אָתָּה. בָּרוּךְ אַתָּה יְיָ הַמֶּלֶךְ הַקָּדוֹשׁ:

אַתָּה בְחַרְתָּנוּ מִכָּל הָעַמִּים. אָהַבְתָּ אוֹתָנוּ וְרָצִיתָ בָּנוּ. וְקִדַּשְׁתָּנוּ בְּמִצְוֹתֶיךָ. וְקֵרַבְתָּנוּ מַלְכֵּנוּ לַעֲבוֹדָתֶךָ. וְשִׁמְךָ הַגָּדוֹל וְהַקָּדוֹשׁ עָלֵינוּ קָרָאתָ. וַתִּתֶּן לָנוּ יְיָ אֱלֹהֵינוּ בְּאַהֲבָה אֶת יוֹם (בְּשַׁבָּת וְאֶת יוֹם) הַזִּכָּרוֹן הַזֶּה. יוֹם תְּרוּעָה. מִקְרָא קֹדֶשׁ. זֵכֶר לִיצִיאַת מִצְרָיִם:

אֱלֹהֵינוּ וֵאלֹהֵי אֲבוֹתֵינוּ יַעֲלֶה וְיָבֹא זִכְרוֹנֵנוּ וְזִכְרוֹן אֲבוֹתֵינוּ. וְזִכְרוֹן כָּל עַמְּךָ בֵּית יִשְׂרָאֵל לְפָנֶיךָ. לְחֵן וּלְחֶסֶד וּלְרַחֲמִים. לְחַיִּים וּלְשָׁלוֹם. בְּיוֹם הַזִּכָּרוֹן הַזֶּה. זָכְרֵנוּ יְיָ אֱלֹהֵינוּ בּוֹ לְטוֹבָה. וּפָקְדֵנוּ בוֹ לִבְרָכָה.

Remember us, O Lord, for our good; bless us with happiness, and help us in the trials of life.

Cause thy mercy to descend upon us, and bring us salvation, according to the promise of thy holy word; for unto thee we look for aid, O our Heavenly Father, who in loving mercy rulest all mankind.

Our God, God of our fathers, reign thou over the whole world in thy glory, and be exalted in thy majesty; let truth and justice triumphantly shine forth upon all mankind, that every creature may know that thou hast created it, and every being understand that thou hast formed it, and all in whom there is the breath of life exclaim: The Eternal, the God of Israel reigneth, and his supreme power ruleth over all!

Grant, therefore, O Lord our God, that all thy works may reverence thee, and the fear of thee fill all created beings; that all may bow before thee in awe and humility, and unite with one accord to do thy will with an upright heart; for we know and acknowledge, O Lord our God, that thou art the Supreme Ruler of the universe, that thy power, thy might, and thy awe-inspiring name are manifested in all thy works.

Grant also that thy people Israel may everywhere be given the honor due their sacred mission; that the doctrines of universal freedom and righteousness may everywhere be realized. Then shall the righteous be glad and rejoice. For truth shall triumph over error and falsehood; inquity shall be silenced in shame, all manner of wickedness vanish like smoke, and tyranny and oppression be removed from the face of the earth. To thee alone shall all thy creatures then pay homage, verifying the words of holy writ: The Lord shall reign for ever and for ever, even thy God, O Zion, from generation to generation. Hallelujah!

Thou art holy and thy name is awe-inspiring, for there is no God besides thee; and thus we read: The Lord of Hosts is exalted in judgment, and God, the Holy-One is sanctified through righteousness.

וְהוֹשִׁיעֵנוּ בּוֹ לְחַיִּים. וּבִדְבַר יְשׁוּעָה וְרַחֲמִים חוּס וְחָנֵּנוּ. וְרַחֵם עָלֵינוּ וְהוֹשִׁיעֵנוּ. כִּי אֵלֶיךָ עֵינֵינוּ. כִּי אֵל מֶלֶךְ חַנּוּן וְרַחוּם אָתָּה:

אֱלֹהֵינוּ וֵאלֹהֵי אֲבוֹתֵינוּ. מְלוֹךְ עַל כָּל הָעוֹלָם כֻּלּוֹ בִּכְבוֹדֶךָ. וְהִנָּשֵׂא עַל כָּל הָאָרֶץ בִּיקָרֶךָ. וְהוֹפַע בַּהֲדַר גְּאוֹן עֻזֶּךָ עַל כָּל יוֹשְׁבֵי תֵבֵל אַרְצֶךָ. וְיֵדַע כָּל פָּעוּל כִּי אַתָּה פְעַלְתּוֹ. וְיָבִין כָּל יְצוּר כִּי אַתָּה יְצַרְתּוֹ. וְיֹאמַר כֹּל אֲשֶׁר נְשָׁמָה בְאַפּוֹ. יְיָ אֱלֹהֵי יִשְׂרָאֵל מֶלֶךְ. וּמַלְכוּתוֹ בַּכֹּל מָשָׁלָה:

וּבְכֵן תֵּן פַּחְדְּךָ יְיָ אֱלֹהֵינוּ עַל־כָּל־מַעֲשֶׂיךָ. וְאֵימָתְךָ עַל כָּל־מַה־שֶּׁבָּרָאתָ. וְיִירָאוּךָ כָּל־הַמַּעֲשִׂים. וְיִשְׁתַּחֲווּ לְפָנֶיךָ כָּל הַבְּרוּאִים. וְיֵעָשׂוּ כֻלָּם אֲגֻדָּה אֶחָת. לַעֲשׂוֹת רְצוֹנְךָ בְּלֵבָב שָׁלֵם. כְּמוֹ שֶׁיָּדַעְנוּ יְיָ אֱלֹהֵינוּ שֶׁהַשִּׁלְטוֹן לְפָנֶיךָ. עֹז בְּיָדְךָ וּגְבוּרָה בִּימִינֶךָ. וְשִׁמְךָ נוֹרָא עַל־כָּל־מַה־שֶּׁבָּרָאתָ:

וּבְכֵן צַדִּיקִים יִרְאוּ וְיִשְׂמָחוּ. וִישָׁרִים יַעֲלֹזוּ. וַחֲסִידִים בְּרִנָּה יָגִילוּ. וְעוֹלָתָה תִּקְפָּץ פִּיהָ. וְכָל הָרִשְׁעָה כֻּלָּהּ כֶּעָשָׁן תִּכְלֶה. כִּי תַעֲבִיר מֶמְשֶׁלֶת זָדוֹן מִן הָאָרֶץ:

וְתִמְלוֹךְ אַתָּה יְיָ לְבַדֶּךָ עַל כָּל מַעֲשֶׂיךָ. כַּכָּתוּב בְּדִבְרֵי קָדְשֶׁךָ. יִמְלֹךְ יְיָ לְעוֹלָם. אֱלֹהַיִךְ צִיּוֹן לְדֹר וָדֹר. הַלְלוּיָהּ:

קָדוֹשׁ אַתָּה וְנוֹרָא שְׁמֶךָ. וְאֵין אֱלוֹהַּ מִבַּלְעָדֶיךָ. כַּכָּתוּב. וַיִּגְבַּהּ יְיָ צְבָאוֹת בַּמִּשְׁפָּט. וְהָאֵל הַקָּדוֹשׁ נִקְדָּשׁ בִּצְדָקָה. בָּרוּךְ אַתָּה יְיָ הַמֶּלֶךְ הַקָּדוֹשׁ:

אֱלֹהֵינוּ וֵאלֹהֵי אֲבוֹתֵינוּ (רְצֵה בִּמְנוּחָתֵנוּ). קַדְּשֵׁנוּ בְּמִצְוֹתֶיךָ. וְתֵן חֶלְקֵנוּ בְּתוֹרָתֶךָ. שַׂבְּעֵנוּ מִטּוּבֶךָ.

Omniscient Father and Judge, thou rememberest all events and seest all things, both of the past and of the future. Nothing is forgotten before the throne of thy glory, nothing is concealed from thy all-seeing eye. No creature escapes thee; thou knowest the thoughts of man from afar; before thee are revealed the innermost emotions of the human heart. Ere the mountains were born, and the foundations laid of the earth and the world, thou didst determine the destinies of all men and ordain the lives of all the numberless myriads of thy creatures. As from the beginning of time thou hast established the immutable laws by which the heavenly hosts roll in their orbits, even so thou hast revealed the laws of truth and virtue to man who, in obedience or disobedience, works out his own fate according to thy just decrees. For every action of man is unfailingly recorded before thee; all his doings and meditations, his schemes and designs are noticed by thee; thou weighest the most secret motives, the faintest impulses of his soul.

Generations come and go; they all pass before thee as the flock before the shepherd's eye, and thou allotest to each individual man thy decree:

CHOIR: *Mi Yichyeh umi yomus.*

Whether life or death, length of days or a premature end, nature's fury, creeping disease and ravaging pestilence; a quiet, tranquil existence, or one tossed on the waves of trouble; ease and prosperity, or trials and vicissitudes, riches and affluence, or poverty and want, love and honor, or misery and degredation.

From thy aweful throne of justice thou guidest the destinies of nations, even as of every individual man. War and peace, victory or defeat, want or abundance, thou dispensest all in thy supreme wisdom. Happy the man who forgets not thee; happy the dust-born who clings to thee; for they who seek thee will never stumble; they who trust in thee will never be put to shame, in the hour when thou summonest thy creatures before thy judgment seat and searchest all their doings.

תפלת שחרית לראש השנה

וְשַׂמְּחֵנוּ בִּישׁוּעָתֶךָ. וְטַהֵר לִבֵּנוּ לְעָבְדְּךָ בֶּאֱמֶת. כִּי אַתָּה אֱלֹהִים אֱמֶת. וּדְבָרְךָ אֱמֶת וְקַיָּם לָעַד. בָּרוּךְ אַתָּה יְיָ מֶלֶךְ עַל כָּל הָאָרֶץ. מְקַדֵּשׁ (בשבת הַשַּׁבָּת וְ) יִשְׂרָאֵל וְיוֹם הַזִּכָּרוֹן:

אַתָּה זוֹכֵר מַעֲשֵׂה עוֹלָם. וּפוֹקֵד כָּל־יְצוּרֵי קֶדֶם. לְפָנֶיךָ נִגְלוּ כָּל־תַּעֲלוּמוֹת וַהֲמוֹן נִסְתָּרוֹת שֶׁמִּבְּרֵאשִׁית. אֵין שִׁכְחָה לִפְנֵי כִסֵּא כְבוֹדֶךָ. וְאֵין נִסְתָּר מִנֶּגֶד עֵינֶיךָ: אַתָּה זוֹכֵר אֶת־כָּל־הַמִּפְעָל. וְגַם כָּל־הַיְצוּר לֹא נִכְחָד מִמֶּךָּ. הַכֹּל גָּלוּי וְיָדוּעַ לְפָנֶיךָ יְיָ אֱלֹהֵינוּ. צוֹפֶה וּמַבִּיט עַד סוֹף כָּל־הַדּוֹרוֹת. כִּי תָבִיא חֹק זִכָּרוֹן לְהִפָּקֵד כָּל־רוּחַ וָנָפֶשׁ. לְהִזָּכֵר מַעֲשִׂים רַבִּים וַהֲמוֹן בְּרִיּוֹת לְאֵין תַּכְלִית. מֵרֵאשִׁית כָּזֹאת הוֹדַעְתָּ. וּמִלְּפָנִים אוֹתָהּ גִּלִּיתָ. זֶה הַיּוֹם תְּחִלַּת מַעֲשֶׂיךָ. זִכָּרוֹן לְיוֹם רִאשׁוֹן. כִּי חֹק לְיִשְׂרָאֵל הִיא מִשְׁפָּט לֵאלֹהֵי יַעֲקֹב:

כְּבַקָּרַת רוֹעֶה עֶדְרוֹ. מַעֲבִיר צֹאנוֹ תַּחַת שִׁבְטוֹ. כֵּן תַּעֲבִיר וְתִסְפֹּר וְתִמְנֶה. וְתִפְקֹד נֶפֶשׁ כָּל חָי. וְתַחְתֹּךְ קִצְבָה לְכָל בְּרִיּוֹתֶיךָ. וְתִכְתֹּב אֶת גְּזַר דִּינָם:

מִי יִחְיֶה. וּמִי יָמוּת. מִי בְקִצּוֹ. וּמִי לֹא בְקִצּוֹ. מִי בַמַּיִם. וּמִי בָאֵשׁ. מִי בַחֶרֶב. וּמִי בַחַיָּה. מִי בָרָעָב ' וּמִי בַצָּמָא. מִי בָרַעַשׁ. וּמִי בַמַּגֵּפָה. מִי יָנוּחַ. וּמִי יָנוּעַ. מִי יִשָּׁקֵט. וּמִי יִטָּרֵף. מִי יִשָּׁלֵו. וּמִי יִתְיַסָּר. מִי יֵעָנִי. וּמִי יֵעָשֵׁר. מִי יִשָּׁפֵל. וּמִי יָרוּם:

Our God, God of our fathers, Remember us in thy love, grant us thy salvation and visit us with thy blessing and peace. Help us to become worthy of the covenant of mercy which thou didst make with Abraham, our ancestor, assuring him on Mount Moriah that through his children all the families of the earth shall be blessed. May thy kindness which has led us in the past, be with us evermore, O Heavenly Father. Grant us life and health, and guard us against the numberless perils which constantly beset our life. Satisfy us from thy rich and bountiful hand, by giving us food, raiment and shelter, and bless the fruit of our labor, that we may never need the gift of man. Grant joy to dwell in our hearts, happiness in our homes, and peace in our surroundings. Bless our country, that it may remain for ever the rock of freedom and the refuge of the down-trodden. Let peace and prosperity reign within her borders, righteousness and justice within her gates. Bless Israel, thy people, strengthen it in its sacred mission to proclaim thy truth and thy salvation to all the children of man. Let thy promises of grace be fulfilled in us, as thou hast assured us through thy servant Moses: I will remember unto them the covenant with their ancestors whom I brought forth from the land of Egypt, to be their God; I am the Eternal your God.

Blessed art thou, O Omniscient Ruler and Judge, before whose throne of Majesty there is no oblivion, who rememberest and fulfillest thy covenant.

Sanctify us, O God, through thy commandments, and give us light through thy law. Satisfy us with thy goodness and gladden us by thy help. Purify our hearts that we may serve thee in truth, for thou, O God, art Truth, and thy word is true and endureth for ever. Blessed be thou, O Lord, Sovereign of the universe, who sanctifiest (the Sabbath), Israel, and the Day of Memorial.

CHOIR: **Amen.**

תפלת שחרית לראש השנה

וְעַל הַמְּדִינוֹת בּוֹ יֵאָמֵר. אֵיזוֹ לַחֶרֶב. וְאֵיזוֹ לַשָּׁלוֹם. אֵיזוֹ לָרָעָב. וְאֵיזוֹ לַשּׂבַע. וּבְרִיּוֹת בּוֹ יִפָּקֵדוּ. לְהַזְכִּירָם לַחַיִּים וְלַמָּוֶת. מִי לֹא נִפְקַד כְּהַיּוֹם הַזֶּה. כִּי זֵכֶר כָּל הַיְצוּר לְפָנֶיךָ בָּא. מַעֲשֵׂה אִישׁ וּפְקֻדָּתוֹ. וַעֲלִילוֹת מִצְעֲדֵי גָבֶר. מַחְשְׁבוֹת אָדָם וְתַחְבּוּלוֹתָיו. וְיִצְרֵי מַעַלְלֵי אִישׁ: אַשְׁרֵי אִישׁ שֶׁלֹּא יִשְׁכָּחֶךָ. וּבֶן אָדָם יִתְאַמֶּץ בָּךְ. כִּי דוֹרְשֶׁיךָ לְעוֹלָם לֹא יִכָּשֵׁלוּ. וְלֹא יִכָּלְמוּ לָנֶצַח כָּל הַחוֹסִים בָּךְ: כִּי זֵכֶר כָּל הַמַּעֲשִׂים לְפָנֶיךָ בָּא. וְאַתָּה דוֹרֵשׁ מַעֲשֵׂה כֻלָּם:

אֱלֹהֵינוּ וֵאלֹהֵי אֲבוֹתֵינוּ. זָכְרֵנוּ בְּזִכָּרוֹן טוֹב לְפָנֶיךָ. וּפָקְדֵנוּ בִּפְקֻדַּת יְשׁוּעָה וְרַחֲמִים. וּזְכָר לָנוּ אֶת-הַבְּרִית וְאֶת-הַחֶסֶד וְאֶת-הַשְּׁבוּעָה. אֲשֶׁר נִשְׁבַּעְתָּ לְאַבְרָהָם אָבִינוּ בְּהַר הַמּוֹרִיָּה. וְקַיֶּם-לָנוּ אֶת-הַדָּבָר שֶׁהִבְטַחְתָּנוּ בְתוֹרָתֶךָ עַל יְדֵי מֹשֶׁה עַבְדֶּךָ כְּפִי כְבוֹדֶךָ כָּאָמוּר: וְזָכַרְתִּי לָהֶם בְּרִית רִאשֹׁנִים אֲשֶׁר הוֹצֵאתִי-אוֹתָם מֵאֶרֶץ מִצְרַיִם לְעֵינֵי הַגּוֹיִם לִהְיוֹת לָהֶם לֵאלֹהִים אֲנִי יְיָ: כִּי זוֹכֵר כָּל-הַנִּשְׁכָּחוֹת אַתָּה הוּא מֵעוֹלָם. וְאֵין שִׁכְחָה לִפְנֵי כִסֵּא כְבוֹדֶךָ. בָּרוּךְ אַתָּה יְיָ זוֹכֵר הַבְּרִית:

Look with kindness, O God, upon Israel, thy people: may their fervent prayers, and their worship, be always acceptable to thee. Praise be to thee, O God, whom alone we adore and worship.

From age to age we render thanks unto thee and recount thy praise, for our lives committed into thy hand, for our souls entrusted to thy care, for thy marvelous works, thy wonders which are manifested every day, and for thy boundless goodness in which thou enfoldest us at all times, evening, morning and noon. We bless thee, All-Good, whose mercies never cease, whose grace is infinite; our hopes are in thee forever.

Our God, God of our fathers! Bless us with the ancient priestly benediction :

Yevorechecho Adonoy v'yishmerecho.
May the Lord bless thee and guard thee.

CHOIR: **Amen.**

Yoër Adonoy ponov elecho vichunecko.
May the Lord let his countenance shine upon thee and be gracious unto thee.

CHOIR: **Amen.**

Yisso Adonoy ponov elecho v'yosaim locho sholóm.
May the Lord lift up his countenance upon thee and give thee peace.

CHOIR: **Amen.**

Grant peace, happiness and blessing, grace and mercy to us, and to Israel thy people, and to all thy children. Bless us all, O our Father, with the light of thy countenance; as in the light of thy countenance thou hast given us the law of life, the love of virtue and justice, mercy and peace, so may it please thee to bless us with thy peace at all times and in all seasons. Praise be to thee, O Giver of peace.

(The Congregation in silent devotion.)

Our Heavenly Father, let thy blessing of peace rest upon us and give us strength. Help us to follow the voice of conscience and to cheerfully obey thy laws. May we love the

תפלת שחרית לראש השנה

רְצֵה יְיָ אֱלֹהֵינוּ בְּעַמְּךָ יִשְׂרָאֵל. וְתִפְלָּתָם בְּאַהֲבָה תְקַבֵּל. וּתְהִי לְרָצוֹן תָּמִיד עֲבוֹדַת יִשְׂרָאֵל עַמֶּךָ. בָּרוּךְ אַתָּה יְיָ שֶׁאוֹתְךָ לְבַדְּךָ בְּיִרְאָה נַעֲבוֹד:

מוֹדִים אֲנַחְנוּ לָךְ. שָׁאַתָּה הוּא יְיָ אֱלֹהֵינוּ וֵאלֹהֵי אֲבוֹתֵינוּ לְעוֹלָם וָעֶד. צוּר חַיֵּינוּ מָגֵן יִשְׁעֵנוּ אַתָּה הוּא לְדוֹר וָדוֹר. נוֹדֶה לְךָ וּנְסַפֵּר תְּהִלָּתֶךָ. עַל חַיֵּינוּ הַמְּסוּרִים בְּיָדֶךָ. וְעַל נִשְׁמוֹתֵינוּ הַפְּקוּדוֹת לָךְ. וְעַל נִסֶּיךָ שֶׁבְּכָל יוֹם עִמָּנוּ. וְעַל נִפְלְאוֹתֶיךָ וְטוֹבוֹתֶיךָ שֶׁבְּכָל עֵת. עֶרֶב וָבֹקֶר וְצָהֳרָיִם. הַטּוֹב כִּי לֹא כָלוּ רַחֲמֶיךָ. וְהַמְרַחֵם כִּי לֹא תַמּוּ חֲסָדֶיךָ. מֵעוֹלָם קִוִּינוּ לָךְ:

וְעַל כֻּלָּם יִתְבָּרַךְ וְיִתְרוֹמַם שִׁמְךָ מַלְכֵּנוּ. תָּמִיד לְעוֹלָם וָעֶד. וּכְתוֹב לְחַיִּים טוֹבִים כָּל־בְּנֵי בְרִיתֶךָ. וְכֹל הַחַיִּים יוֹדוּךָ סֶּלָה וִיהַלְלוּ אֶת שִׁמְךָ בֶּאֱמֶת. הָאֵל יְשׁוּעָתֵנוּ וְעֶזְרָתֵנוּ סֶלָה. בָּרוּךְ אַתָּה יְיָ הַטּוֹב שִׁמְךָ וּלְךָ נָאֶה לְהוֹדוֹת:

אֱלֹהֵינוּ וֵאלֹהֵי אֲבוֹתֵינוּ. בָּרְכֵנוּ בַּבְּרָכָה הַמְשֻׁלֶּשֶׁת בַּתּוֹרָה. הָאֲמוּרָה מִפִּי אַהֲרֹן וּבָנָיו כֹּהֲנִים עַם קְדוֹשֶׁךָ. כָּאָמוּר:

יְבָרֶכְךָ יְיָ וְיִשְׁמְרֶךָ: יָאֵר יְיָ פָּנָיו אֵלֶיךָ וִיחֻנֶּךָּ: יִשָּׂא יְיָ פָּנָיו אֵלֶיךָ וְיָשֵׂם לְךָ שָׁלוֹם:

truth and speak the truth. May we be kind to one another, tender-hearted and forgiving, holding no anger nor malice, nor speaking ill of any one. May the thought of thee keep us from evil. Inspire us with humility, with faith and trust in thee. Let the words of my mouth and the meditations of my heart be acceptable in thy sight, O God, my Strength and my Redeemer. As thou preservest peace in the heavenly spheres, so preserve it to us and to all who invoke thy holy name. Amen.

CHOIR: **Amen.**

(MINISTER; CONGREGATION REPEATING EACH SENTENCE.)

Our Heavenly Father, we have sinned before thee.
Our Heavenly Father, we pay homage to none but thee.
Our Heavenly Father, grant us thy favor for the sake of thy name.
Our Heavenly Father, grant us a year of happiness.
Our Heavenly Father, keep far from us sickness, war and famine.
Our Heavenly Father, grant perfect health to the feeble and the sick.
Our Heavenly Father, have pity on us and our innocent children.
Our Heavenly Father, inscribe us in the book of a happy life.
Our Heavenly Father, inscribe us in the book of redemption and salvation.
Our Heavenly Father, inscribe us in the book of pardon and forgiveness.
Our Heavenly Father, inscribe us in the book of ample sustainance.
Our Heavenly Father, accept favorably our prayers and supplications.
Our Heavenly Father, dismiss us not empty from thy presence.
Our Heavenly Father, graciously answer us; though we deserve not thy love, yet deal thou kindly with us and save us. Amen.

CHOIR: **Amen.**

תפלת שחרית לראש השנה

שִׂים שָׁלוֹם טוֹבָה וּבְרָכָה. חֵן וָחֶסֶד וְרַחֲמִים. עָלֵינוּ וְעַל כָּל יִשְׂרָאֵל עַמֶּךָ. בָּרְכֵנוּ אָבִינוּ כֻּלָּנוּ כְּאֶחָד בְּאוֹר פָּנֶיךָ. כִּי בְאוֹר פָּנֶיךָ נָתַתָּ לָּנוּ יְיָ אֱלֹהֵינוּ. תּוֹרַת חַיִּים וְאַהֲבַת חֶסֶד. וּצְדָקָה וּבְרָכָה. וְרַחֲמִים וְחַיִּים וְשָׁלוֹם. וְטוֹב בְּעֵינֶיךָ לְבָרֵךְ אֶת עַמְּךָ יִשְׂרָאֵל. בְּכָל עֵת וּבְכָל שָׁעָה בִּשְׁלוֹמֶךָ. בְּסֵפֶר חַיִּים בְּרָכָה וְשָׁלוֹם וּפַרְנָסָה טוֹבָה נִזָּכֵר וְנִכָּתֵב לְפָנֶיךָ אֲנַחְנוּ וְכָל עַמְּךָ בֵּית יִשְׂרָאֵל. לְחַיִּים טוֹבִים וּלְשָׁלוֹם: בָּרוּךְ אַתָּה יְיָ עוֹשֵׂה הַשָּׁלוֹם:

אָבִינוּ מַלְכֵּנוּ חָטָאנוּ לְפָנֶיךָ:
אָבִינוּ מַלְכֵּנוּ אֵין לָנוּ מֶלֶךְ אֶלָּא אָתָּה:
אָבִינוּ מַלְכֵּנוּ עֲשֵׂה עִמָּנוּ לְמַעַן שְׁמֶךָ:
אָבִינוּ מַלְכֵּנוּ חַדֵּשׁ עָלֵינוּ שָׁנָה טוֹבָה:
אָבִינוּ מַלְכֵּנוּ כַּלֵּה דֶּבֶר וְחֶרֶב וְרָעָב מֵאַרְצֵנוּ:
אָבִינוּ מַלְכֵּנוּ מְנַע מַגֵּפָה מִבָּחֲתֵנוּ:
אָבִינוּ מַלְכֵּנוּ שְׁלַח רְפוּאָה שְׁלֵמָה לְחוֹלֵי עַמֶּךָ:
אָבִינוּ מַלְכֵּנוּ חֲמוֹל עָלֵינוּ וְעַל עוֹלָלֵינוּ וְטַפֵּנוּ:
אָבִינוּ מַלְכֵּנוּ זָכְרֵנוּ בְּזִכָּרוֹן טוֹב לְפָנֶיךָ:
אָבִינוּ מַלְכֵּנוּ כָּתְבֵנוּ בְּסֵפֶר חַיִּים טוֹבִים:
אָבִינוּ מַלְכֵּנוּ כָּתְבֵנוּ בְּסֵפֶר גְּאֻלָּה וִישׁוּעָה:
אָבִינוּ מַלְכֵּנוּ קַבֵּל בְּרַחֲמִים וּבְרָצוֹן אֶת תְּפִלָּתֵנוּ:
אָבִינוּ מַלְכֵּנוּ נָא אַל תְּשִׁיבֵנוּ רֵיקָם מִלְּפָנֶיךָ:
אָבִינוּ מַלְכֵּנוּ חָנֵּנוּ וַעֲנֵנוּ כִּי אֵין בָּנוּ מַעֲשִׂים עֲשֵׂה עִמָּנוּ צְדָקָה וָחֶסֶד וְהוֹשִׁיעֵנוּ: אמן

ORDER OF READING THE LAW.

CHOIR: *S'u Sheórim roshéchem.*

Lift up your heads, O ye gates, and be lifted up, ye everlasting doors, for the King of glory shall come. Who is the King of glory? The Lord of hosts — he is the King of glory. Selah!

Or: Vay'hi bin'soa hoóron.

Arise, O Lord, let thy enemies be scattered and they who hate thy law flee before thee. For from Zion cometh forth the Law and the word of God from Jerusalem.

MINISTER, THEN CHOIR AND CONGREGATION:

Adonoy, Adonoy, El rachum v'channun, erech appa-yim, v'rav chesed v'emés, notsér chesed lo-alofim, nosé ovón, vofésha, v'chattoóh.

The Eternal, the Eternal, is a merciful and gracious God, long-suffering and full of love and truth; keeping kindness unto thousands, forgiving iniquity, transgression and sin.

(Taking the Law out of the Ark.)

This Law is Israel's consecrated banner, inscribed with the glorious truth: Hear, O Israel, God our Lord, God is One!

CHOIR AND CONGREGATION:

Sh'ma Yisroel, Adonoy Elohénu, Adonoy echod.

MINISTER:

O magnify the Lord with me and let us exalt his Name together.

CHOIR: *L'chó Adonoy hagg'dulloh.*

Thine, O Lord, are greatness, power, and glory, victory, and majesty; thine is all that is in heaven and on earth; thine is the kingdom, O Lord, and thou art exalted, Supreme above all.

(Before the Reading of the Law.)

Praise be to thee, O Eternal, our God, Ruler of the universe, who hast called us unto thy service and hast given us thy law. Praise be to thee, O God, giver of the Law. Amen.

תפלה שחרית לראש השנה

סדר קריאת התורה

שְׂאוּ שְׁעָרִים רָאשֵׁיכֶם. וּשְׂאוּ פִּתְחֵי עוֹלָם. וְיָבֹא מֶלֶךְ הַכָּבוֹד: מִי הוּא זֶה מֶלֶךְ הַכָּבוֹד. יְיָ צְבָאוֹת. הוּא מֶלֶךְ הַכָּבוֹד סֶלָה:

וַיְהִי בִּנְסֹעַ הָאָרֹן וַיֹּאמֶר מֹשֶׁה. קוּמָה יְיָ וְיָפֻצוּ אֹיְבֶיךָ וְיָנֻסוּ מְשַׂנְאֶיךָ מִפָּנֶיךָ: כִּי מִצִּיּוֹן תֵּצֵא תוֹרָה וּדְבַר יְיָ מִירוּשָׁלָיִם:

יְהֹוָה יְהֹוָה אֵל רַחוּם וְחַנּוּן אֶרֶךְ אַפַּיִם וְרַב־חֶסֶד וֶאֱמֶת. נֹצֵר חֶסֶד לָאֲלָפִים נֹשֵׂא עָוֹן וָפֶשַׁע וְחַטָּאָה:

מוציאין ס״ת.

וְזֹאת הַתּוֹרָה אֲשֶׁר שָׂם מֹשֶׁה לִפְנֵי בְּנֵי יִשְׂרָאֵל:

שְׁמַע יִשְׂרָאֵל יְהֹוָה אֱלֹהֵינוּ יְהֹוָה אֶחָד:

גַּדְּלוּ לַיְיָ אִתִּי. וּנְרוֹמְמָה שְׁמוֹ יַחְדָּו:

לְךָ יְיָ הַגְּדֻלָּה וְהַגְּבוּרָה. וְהַתִּפְאֶרֶת וְהַנֵּצַח וְהַהוֹד. כִּי כֹל בַּשָּׁמַיִם וּבָאָרֶץ. לְךָ יְיָ הַמַּמְלָכָה. וְהַמִּתְנַשֵּׂא לְכֹל לְרֹאשׁ:

ברכת התורה.

בָּרוּךְ אַתָּה יְיָ אֱלֹהֵינוּ מֶלֶךְ הָעוֹלָם. אֲשֶׁר בָּחַר בָּנוּ מִכָּל־הָעַמִּים וְנָתַן לָנוּ אֶת־תּוֹרָתוֹ. בָּרוּךְ אַתָּה יְיָ נוֹתֵן הַתּוֹרָה:

Reading from the Pentateuch.

(After the Reading of the Law.)

Praise be to thee, O Eternal, our God, Ruler of the universe, who hast given us a law of truth and implanted eternal life within us. Praise be to thee, O God, giver of the Law. Amen.

CHOIR:

God's law is perfect, inspiring the soul; God's testimony is true, making wise the simple; God's commandments are clear, cheering the heart; God's teachings are pure, giving light to the eye.

Reading from the Prophets.

(HERE MAY BE INTRODUCED ANY PRAYER FOR SPECIAL OCCASIONS.)

(Placing back the Law into the Ark.)

MINISTER:

Praise ye the Name of the Lord, for his Name alone is exalted !

CHOIR: *Hodo al eretz v'shomoyim.*

His glory is above heaven and earth. He will exalt the honor of his people, the children of Israel, his faithful worshippers. Hallelujah !

(Minister before the Ark.)

Return, O Lord, to the many thousands of Israel, thou and the ark of thy strength. A good instruction I have given you, forsake ye not my law. It is a tree of life to those who lay hold of it, and its supporters are happy. Its ways are ways of pleasantness and all its paths are peace.

CHOIR: *Hashivénu Adonoy.*

Hymn.

SERMON.

תפלת שחרית לראש השנה

אחר הקריאה.

בָּרוּךְ אַתָּה יְיָ אֱלֹהֵינוּ מֶלֶךְ הָעוֹלָם. אֲשֶׁר נָתַן לָנוּ תּוֹרַת אֱמֶת וְחַיֵּי עוֹלָם נָטַע בְּתוֹכֵנוּ. בָּרוּךְ אַתָּה יְיָ נוֹתֵן הַתּוֹרָה:

בהכנסת התורה.

יְהַלְלוּ אֶת־שֵׁם יְיָ. כִּי נִשְׂגָּב שְׁמוֹ לְבַדּוֹ:

הוֹדוֹ עַל־אֶרֶץ וְשָׁמָיִם: וַיָּרֶם קֶרֶן לְעַמּוֹ תְּהִלָּה לְכָל־חֲסִידָיו לִבְנֵי יִשְׂרָאֵל עַם קְרֹבוֹ הַלְלוּיָהּ:

וּבְנֻחֹה יֹאמַר. שׁוּבָה יְיָ רִבְבוֹת אַלְפֵי יִשְׂרָאֵל: קוּמָה יְיָ לִמְנוּחָתֶךָ אַתָּה וַאֲרוֹן עֻזֶּךָ: כֹּהֲנֶיךָ יִלְבְּשׁוּ־צֶדֶק וַחֲסִידֶיךָ יְרַנֵּנוּ: כִּי לֶקַח טוֹב נָתַתִּי לָכֶם תּוֹרָתִי אַל תַּעֲזֹבוּ: עֵץ־חַיִּים הִיא לַמַּחֲזִיקִים בָּהּ וְתֹמְכֶיהָ מְאֻשָּׁר: דְּרָכֶיהָ דַרְכֵי־נֹעַם וְכָל־נְתִיבוֹתֶיהָ שָׁלוֹם: הֲשִׁיבֵנוּ יְיָ אֵלֶיךָ וְנָשׁוּבָה חַדֵּשׁ יָמֵינוּ כְּקֶדֶם:

ORDER OF SOUNDING THE SHOFAR.

CHOIR:

Sing joyfully to the Lord, our strength! rejoice unto the God of Jacob! Raise a song, and strike the timbrel, the sweet-sounding harp, and the psaltery! Blow the trumpet at the new moon, at the full moon, also, on our festal day! For this is a statute for Israel, a law of the God of Jacob.

MINISTER:

O Lord and Father, thou hast revealed thyself unto thy people, thy glory shone forth unto our ancestors, bringing to them the light of thy truth and love. From Sinai's height thou didst cause Israel to hear the heavenly voice of thy majesty. The earth trembled, the universe stood in awe, and all creatures were hushed into silence when thou descendest to teach thy children the eternal laws of truth, freedom and morality.

Reveal thyself also unto us, O Heavenly Father. May the Shofar's solemn sounds remind us that thou alone art the Creator and Sustainer of the universe, our King, Lawgiver, and Judge; that to thee alone is due worship, honor, and adoration. Cause, O Lord, our God, the bugle-blast of freedom to be heard over all the earth; may all who still sigh under the burden of oppression hear the trumpet-sound of deliverance; and may the banner of Israel, thy people, be exalted whereever thou hast sent us to proclaim and to sanctify thy name. Praise be to thee, O Eternal, who acceptest in mercy the adoration of thy people Israel.

CHOIR:

Bachatzôtzerôs vekôl Shôfor horiu lifné hamélech Adonoy!
With clarions and the sound of trumpets sing praises unto the Lord, the King.

(THE SHOFAR IS SOUNDED.)

MINISTER, THEN CHOIR:

Happy the people that know the trumpet's sound!
They walk, O Lord, in the light of thy countenance.

CHOIR: AMEN, HALLELUJAH. Or: Ps. 150.

סדר תקיעת שופר

הַרְנִינוּ לֵאלֹהִים עוּזֵנוּ הָרִיעוּ לֵאלֹהֵי יַעֲקֹב: שְׂאוּ זִמְרָה וּתְנוּ תֹף כִּנּוֹר נָעִים עִם נָבֶל: תִּקְעוּ בַחֹדֶשׁ שׁוֹפָר בַּכֶּסֶה לְיוֹם חַגֵּנוּ: כִּי חֹק לְיִשְׂרָאֵל הוּא מִשְׁפָּט לֵאלֹהֵי יַעֲקֹב:

אֱלֹהֵינוּ וֵאלֹהֵי אֲבוֹתֵינוּ. אַתָּה נִגְלֵיתָ בַּעֲנַן כְּבוֹדֶךָ עַל עַם קָדְשֶׁךָ. בְּקוֹלוֹת וּבְרָקִים עֲלֵיהֶם נִגְלֵיתָ. וּבְקוֹל שׁוֹפָר עֲלֵיהֶם הוֹפָעְתָּ. כַּכָּתוּב בְּתוֹרָתֶךָ. וַיְהִי קוֹל הַשּׁוֹפָר הוֹלֵךְ וְחָזֵק מְאֹד מֹשֶׁה יְדַבֵּר וְהָאֱלֹהִים יַעֲנֶנּוּ בְקוֹל: אָנָּא יְיָ זָכְרֵנוּ בְּזִכָּרוֹן טוֹב לְפָנֶיךָ. תְּקַע בְּשׁוֹפָר גָּדוֹל לְחֵרוּת עוֹלָם. וְיִשְׂמְחוּ בִישׁוּעָתֶךָ כָּל יוֹשְׁבֵי תֵבֵל וְשׁוֹכְנֵי אָרֶץ. לִקְרֹא כֻלָּם בְּשֵׁם יְיָ לְעָבְדוֹ שְׁכֶם אֶחָד. כִּי אַתָּה שׁוֹמֵעַ תְּפִלָּה וּמַאֲזִין תְּרוּעָה. וְאֵין דּוֹמֶה לָּךְ. בָּרוּךְ אַתָּה יְיָ שׁוֹמֵעַ קוֹל תְּרוּעַת עַמּוֹ יִשְׂרָאֵל בְּרַחֲמִים:

הווק״ין.

תְּקִיעָה. שְׁבָרִים. תְּרוּעָה. תְּקִיעָה:

אַשְׁרֵי הָעָם יֹדְעֵי תְרוּעָה. יְיָ בְּאוֹר פָּנֶיךָ יְהַלֵּכוּן:

הַלְלוּיָהּ. הַלְלוּ אֵל בְּקָדְשׁוֹ. הַלְלוּהוּ בִּרְקִיעַ עֻזּוֹ: הַלְלוּהוּ בִגְבוּרֹתָיו. הַלְלוּהוּ כְּרֹב גֻּדְלוֹ: הַלְלוּהוּ בְּתֵקַע שׁוֹפָר. הַלְלוּהוּ בְּנֵבֶל וְכִנּוֹר: הַלְלוּהוּ בְּתֹף וּמָחוֹל. הַלְלוּהוּ בְּמִנִּים וְעֻגָב: הַלְלוּהוּ בְצִלְצְלֵי שָׁמַע. הַלְלוּהוּ בְּצִלְצְלֵי תְרוּעָה: כֹּל הַנְּשָׁמָה תְּהַלֵּל יָהּ. הַלְלוּיָהּ:

ADORATION.

Almighty God! Creator of heaven and earth! It behooves us to render praise and thanksgiving unto thee, who hast delivered us from the darkness of false belief and sent to us the light of thy truth. Thou art our God, there is no other.

We, therefore, bow the head and bend the knee before thee, Creator and Ruler of the world, and bless thy holy name!

MINISTER, THEN CHOIR AND CONGREGATION:

Vaanachnu, kôr'im, umishtáchavim, vmódim, lifné Mélech mal'ché hammelóchim, Hakkódosh boruch hu.

Thou art, in truth, our Father, our God, our Saviour, and there is none besides thee, as is written in thy law: Thou shalt know this day and reflect in thy heart that the Lord is God in heaven above as on earth below; and there is none else.

We fervently pray, O Lord our God, that we may speedily behold the glory of thy mighty power, banishing all impurities from the earth, de-troying idolatry and wickedness, and establishing thy truth among mankind; that all the inhabitants of the earth may invoke thy name, acknowledge thy unity, and understand that to thee alone every knee must bend and every tongue swear fealty.

May all thy children, O God, soon be united in a common bond of brotherhood, may the time be hastened when no religious differences will separate them, but when they will all adore thee as the universal father, worship thee in the spirit of true religion, and unite in proclaiming the unity of thy holy name.

Thus, O God, do thou reign over them for ever and ever, for the kingdom is thine, and unto thee appertain power, glory and majesty from everlasting to everlasting. As it is written: The Lord will reign for ever and ever; the Lord will be king over all the earth; on that day shall God be acknowledged One and his name One.

MINISTER, THEN CHOIR AND CONGREGATION:

Veho-yoh Adonoy lemélech al kol hoórets, bayóm hahu yih'yéh Adonoy echod, u-shemo echod.

תפלה שחרית לראש השנה

עָלֵינוּ לְשַׁבֵּחַ לַאֲדוֹן הַכֹּל. לָתֵת גְּדֻלָּה לְיוֹצֵר בְּרֵאשִׁית. שֶׁהוּא נוֹטֶה שָׁמַיִם וְיוֹסֵד אָרֶץ. וּמוֹשַׁב יְקָרוֹ בַּשָּׁמַיִם מִמַּעַל. וּשְׁכִינַת עֻזּוֹ בְּגָבְהֵי מְרוֹמִים. הוּא אֱלֹהֵינוּ אֵין עוֹד.

וַאֲנַחְנוּ כּוֹרְעִים וּמִשְׁתַּחֲוִים וּמוֹדִים לִפְנֵי מֶלֶךְ מַלְכֵי הַמְּלָכִים. הַקָּדוֹשׁ בָּרוּךְ הוּא:

אֱמֶת מַלְכֵּנוּ אֶפֶס זוּלָתוֹ. כַּכָּתוּב בְּתוֹרָתוֹ. וְיָדַעְתָּ הַיּוֹם וַהֲשֵׁבֹתָ אֶל־לְבָבֶךָ. כִּי יְיָ הוּא הָאֱלֹהִים בַּשָּׁמַיִם מִמַּעַל וְעַל־הָאָרֶץ מִתָּחַת. אֵין עוֹד:

עַל כֵּן נְקַוֶּה לְּךָ יְיָ אֱלֹהֵינוּ. לִרְאוֹת מְהֵרָה בְּתִפְאֶרֶת עֻזֶּךָ. לְהַעֲבִיר גִּלּוּלִים מִן הָאָרֶץ. וְהָאֱלִילִים כָּרוֹת יִכָּרֵתוּן. לְתַקֵּן עוֹלָם בְּמַלְכוּת שַׁדַּי. וְכָל־בְּנֵי בָשָׂר יִקְרְאוּ בִשְׁמֶךָ. לְהַפְנוֹת אֵלֶיךָ כָּל־רִשְׁעֵי אָרֶץ. יַכִּירוּ וְיֵדְעוּ כָּל־יוֹשְׁבֵי תֵבֵל. כִּי לְךָ תִּכְרַע כָּל־בֶּרֶךְ. תִּשָּׁבַע כָּל־לָשׁוֹן. לְפָנֶיךָ יְיָ אֱלֹהֵינוּ יִכְרְעוּ וְיִפֹּלוּ. וְלִכְבוֹד שִׁמְךָ יְקָר יִתֵּנוּ. וִיקַבְּלוּ כֻלָּם אֶת־עֹל מַלְכוּתֶךָ. וְתִמְלֹךְ עֲלֵיהֶם מְהֵרָה לְעוֹלָם וָעֶד. כִּי הַמַּלְכוּת שֶׁלְּךָ הִיא. וּלְעוֹלְמֵי עַד תִּמְלוֹךְ בְּכָבוֹד. כַּכָּתוּב בְּתוֹרָתֶךָ. יְיָ יִמְלֹךְ לְעֹלָם וָעֶד: וְנֶאֱמַר וְהָיָה יְיָ לְמֶלֶךְ עַל־כָּל־הָאָרֶץ. בַּיּוֹם הַהוּא יִהְיֶה יְיָ אֶחָד וּשְׁמוֹ אֶחָד:

ADDRESS TO THE MOURNERS.

Brothers and sisters, who are mourning for dear lives departed, remember your beloved ones and honor their names in the midst of the congregation of Israel. May the memory of the righteous inspire you to noble deeds and works in their honor. Rise, and praise with me the name of the most High, according to the anscient custom of our fathers.

MOURNERS' KADDISH.

May thy great and ineffable name, O Lord of life and death, be exalted and sanctified throughout the world, which thou hast created according to thy will. May thy kingdom be established in our midst, in our lifetime and in our days, and in the days of the whole house of Israel. Amen.

THE CONGREGATION:

May his great and ineffable name be blessed and glorified for ever and ever.

Praised and hallowed be thy name who hast created man in thy image and planted within him eternal life. In thy hand is the soul of every living being and the spirit of all flesh. Blessed art thou, whose hymns, praises and benedictions are repeated throughout the world. Amen.

THE CONGREGATION:

Praised be he and his glorious name.

Unto Israel, unto all the righteous and unto all who departed this life according to the will of God, may there be granted abundance of peace, and a blissful portion in the life to come, grace and mercy by the Lord of heaven and earth.

May the fullness of peace from heaven, with life and health be granted unto us and unto all Israel. Amen.

May he who establisheth peace in his heavenly spheres grant happiness and peace unto us, unto all Israel and to all mankind. Amen.

CLOSING SONG.
BENEDICTION.

קדיש דאבלים.

יִתְגַּדַּל וְיִתְקַדַּשׁ שְׁמֵהּ רַבָּא. בְּעָלְמָא דִי־בְרָא כִרְעוּתֵהּ. וְיַמְלִיךְ מַלְכוּתֵהּ. בְּחַיֵּיכוֹן וּבְיוֹמֵיכוֹן וּבְחַיֵּי דְכָל בֵּית יִשְׂרָאֵל. בַּעֲגָלָא וּבִזְמַן קָרִיב. וְאִמְרוּ אָמֵן.

יְהֵא שְׁמֵהּ רַבָּא מְבָרַךְ. לְעָלַם וּלְעָלְמֵי עָלְמַיָּא.

יִתְבָּרַךְ וְיִשְׁתַּבַּח וְיִתְפָּאַר וְיִתְרוֹמַם. וְיִתְנַשֵּׂא וְיִתְהַדָּר וְיִתְעַלֶּה וְיִתְהַלָּל שְׁמֵהּ דְּקוּדְשָׁא. בְּרִיךְ הוּא. לְעֵלָּא מִן כָּל בִּרְכָתָא וְשִׁירָתָא. תֻּשְׁבְּחָתָא וְנֶחֱמָתָא. דַּאֲמִירָן בְּעָלְמָא. וְאִמְרוּ אָמֵן:

עַל יִשְׂרָאֵל וְעַל צַדִּיקַיָּא. וְעַל־כָּל־מַן דְּאִתְפְּטַר מִן עָלְמָא הָדֵין בִּרְעוּתֵהּ דֶאֱלָהָא. יְהֵא לְהוֹן שְׁלָמָא רַבָּא וְחוּלָקָא־טָבָא לְחַיֵּי עָלְמָא דְּאָתֵי. וְחִסְדָּא וְרַחֲמֵי מִן־קֳדָם מָרֵא שְׁמַיָּא וְאַרְעָא. וְאִמְרוּ אָמֵן:

תִּתְקַבַּל צְלוֹתְהוֹן וּבָעוּתְהוֹן דְּכָל־יִשְׂרָאֵל. קֳדָם אֲבוּהוֹן דִּי בִשְׁמַיָּא. וְאִמְרוּ אָמֵן:

יְהֵא שְׁלָמָא רַבָּא מִן־שְׁמַיָּא וְחַיִּים. עָלֵינוּ וְעַל־כָּל־יִשְׂרָאֵל. וְאִמְרוּ אָמֵן:

עֹשֶׂה שָׁלוֹם בִּמְרוֹמָיו. הוּא יַעֲשֶׂה שָׁלוֹם עָלֵינוּ וְעַל כָּל יִשְׂרָאֵל. וְאִמְרוּ אָמֵן:

אֲדוֹן עוֹלָם אֲשֶׁר מָלַךְ. בְּטֶרֶם כָּל־יְצִיר נִבְרָא:
לְעֵת נַעֲשָׂה בְחֶפְצוֹ כֹּל. אֲזַי מֶלֶךְ שְׁמוֹ נִקְרָא:
וְאַחֲרֵי כִּכְלוֹת הַכֹּל. לְבַדּוֹ יִמְלוֹךְ נוֹרָא:
וְהוּא הָיָה וְהוּא הֹוֶה. וְהוּא יִהְיֶה בְּתִפְאָרָה:
וְהוּא אֶחָד וְאֵין שֵׁנִי. לְהַמְשִׁיל לוֹ לְהַחְבִּירָה:
בְּלִי רֵאשִׁית בְּלִי תַכְלִית. וְלוֹ הָעֹז וְהַמִּשְׂרָה:
וְהוּא אֵלִי וְחַי גּוֹאֲלִי. וְצוּר חֶבְלִי בְּעֵת צָרָה:
וְהוּא נִסִּי וּמָנוֹס לִי. מְנָת כּוֹסִי בְּיוֹם אֶקְרָא:
בְּיָדוֹ אַפְקִיד רוּחִי. בְּעֵת אִישָׁן וְאָעִירָה:
וְעִם רוּחִי גְּוִיָּתִי. יְיָ לִי וְלֹא אִירָא:

יִגְדַּל אֱלֹהִים חַי וְיִשְׁתַּבַּח. נִמְצָא וְאֵין עֵת אֶל מְצִיאוּתוֹ:
אֶחָד וְאֵין יָחִיד כְּיִחוּדוֹ. נֶעְלָם וְגַם אֵין סוֹף לְאַחְדּוּתוֹ:
אֵין לוֹ דְמוּת הַגּוּף וְאֵינוֹ גוּף. לֹא נַעֲרוֹךְ אֵלָיו קְדֻשָּׁתוֹ:
קַדְמוֹן לְכָל דָּבָר אֲשֶׁר נִבְרָא. רִאשׁוֹן וְאֵין רֵאשִׁית לְרֵאשִׁיתוֹ:
הִנּוֹ אֲדוֹן עוֹלָם לְכָל נוֹצָר. יוֹרֶה גְדֻלָּתוֹ וּמַלְכוּתוֹ:
שֶׁפַע נְבוּאָתוֹ נְתָנוֹ. אֶל אַנְשֵׁי סְגֻלָּתוֹ וְתִפְאַרְתּוֹ:
לֹא קָם בְּיִשְׂרָאֵל כְּמֹשֶׁה עוֹד. נָבִיא וּמַבִּיט אֶת תְּמוּנָתוֹ:
תּוֹרַת אֱמֶת נָתַן לְעַמּוֹ אֵל. עַל יַד נְבִיאוֹ נֶאֱמַן בֵּיתוֹ:
לֹא יַחֲלִיף הָאֵל וְלֹא יָמִיר דָּתוֹ. לְעוֹלָמִים לְזוּלָתוֹ:
צוֹפֶה וְיוֹדֵעַ סְתָרֵינוּ. מַבִּיט לְסוֹף דָּבָר בְּקַדְמָתוֹ:
גּוֹמֵל לְאִישׁ חֶסֶד כְּמִפְעָלוֹ. נוֹתֵן לְרָשָׁע רָע כְּרִשְׁעָתוֹ:
יִשְׁלַח לְקֵץ יָמִין פְּדוּת עוֹלָם. כָּל חַי וְיֵשׁ יַכִּיר יְשׁוּעָתוֹ:
הַכֹּל יִחְיֶה אֵל בְּרֹב חַסְדוֹ. בָּרוּךְ עֲדֵי עַד שֵׁם תְּהִלָּתוֹ:

ORDER OF PRAYERS

IN THE

HOUSE OF MOURNING.

(On the evening after the funeral it is customary to hold service in the house of mourning. The minister, or officiating reader, will select appropriate pieces from the following pages, or from the Collection of Psalms, then begin Borechu on page 117. If divine service is to be held in the morning, read Borechu on page 29 and 31; then continue from page 121, adding the Kedusha (Sanctification).

INTRODUCTORY SENTENCES.

In whatever place I will cause my name to be mentioned I will come to thee and bless thee.

The Lord is nigh to all that call upon him, that call upon him in truth.

Offer unto God the sacrifices of righteousness; call upon him in the day of trouble, and he will deliver thee.

The sacrifices of God are a broken spirit, a broken and contrite heart, O God, thou wilt not despise.

Thus saith the Lord, the High and Holy One: I dwell in the high and holy place, yet with him also that is of a contrite and humble spirit; to revive the spirit of the humble and to quicken the heart of the contrite.

Who shall ascend the hill of the Lord, who shall stand in his holy place? He that has clean hands, and a pure heart; who hath not lifted up his soul unto vanity, nor sworn deceitfully. He shall receive the blessing of the Lord, and righteousness from the God of his salvation.

RESPONSIVE READING.

Psalm 103.

Bless the Lord, O my soul! and all that is within me, bless his holy name!

Bless the Lord, O my soul! and forget not all his benefits!

Who forgiveth all thine iniquities; who healeth all thy diseases;

Who redeemeth thy life from the grave; who crowneth thee with loving kindness and tender mercies;

Who satisfieth thy old age with good, so that thy youth is renewed like the eagle's.

The Lord executeth justice and equity for all the oppressed.

He made known his ways to Moses, his doings to the children of Israel.

The Lord is merciful and kind, slow to anger and rich in mercy.

He doth not always chide, nor doth he keep his anger for ever.

He hath not dealt with us according to our sins, nor requited us according to our iniquities.

As high as are the heavens above the earth, so great is his mercy to them that fear him.

As far as the East is from the West, so far hath he removed our transgressions from us.

Even as a father pitieth his children, so the Lord pitieth them that fear him.

For he knoweth our frame, he remembereth that we are dust.

As for man, his days are as grass; as a flower of the field, so he flourisheth.

The wind passeth over it, and it is gone; and its place shall know it no more.

But the mercy of the Lord is from everlasting to everlasting to them that fear him, and his righteousness to children's children,

To such as keep his covenant, and remember his commandments to do them.

The Lord hath established his throne in the heavens, and his kingdom ruleth over all.

Bless the Lord, ye his angels, ye mighty ones who do his commands, hearkening to the voice of his word!

Bless the Lord, all ye his hosts; ye, his ministers, who do his pleasure!

Bless the Lord, all his works, in all places of his dominion! Bless the Lord, O my soul!

Psalm 23.

The Lord is my shepherd: I shall not want.

He maketh me lie down in green pastures; he leadeth me beside the still waters.

He reviveth my soul; he leadeth me in paths of safety, for his name's sake.

When I walk through the valley of the shadow of death I fear no evil, for thou art with me; thy stay and thy staff, they comfort me.

Thou preparest a table before me in the presence of my enemies. Thou anointest my head with oil; my cup runneth over.

Surely goodness and mercy shall follow me all the days of my life, and I shall dwell in the house of the Lord for ever.

MINISTER:

Borechu es Adonoy hammevoroch.
Praise ye the Lord to whom all praise is due!

CONGREGATION:

Boruch Adonoy hammevoroch l'olom voëd.
Praised be the Lord, who is praised through all eternity.

Praise be to thee, O Lord our God, Ruler of the Universe, who by his word calls in the evening and in his wisdom opens the gates of the morning. He changes the times and the seasons by his understanding, and by his will he sets the stars in their heavenly watches. He alternates the light and the darkness; he leads out the day and brings in the night, the Lord of hosts is his name. May he rule over us forevermore. Praise be to thee, O God, who bringest in the evening.

With unchanging love thou hast guided thy people Israel; thou hast revealed to us thy law which will become a blessing to all mankind. Therefore we will ever think of thy word and rejoice in thy truth. It is our light and our life; we will cling to it day and night, and will proclaim thy name and thy unity before all the nations of the earth. Do thou, O God, never withold from us thy love and thy protection. Praise be to thee, O God, our Guardian and Keeper.

CONGREGATION: Amen.

MINISTER AND CONGREGATION:

Sh'ma Yisroël, Adonoy Elohénu, Adonoy Echod.
HEAR, O ISRAEL, THE LORD OUR GOD, THE LORD IS ONE.

Boruch Shem kevod mal'chuso l'olom voëd.
Praised be the name of his glorious kingdom for evermore.

Thou shalt love the Eternal thy God with all thy heart, with all thy soul, and with all thy might. And these words, which I command thee to-day, shall be in thy heart. Thou shalt teach them diligently to thy children, and shalt talk of them when thou sittest in thy house, and when thou walkest by the way, and when thou liest down, and when thou risest up.

תפלת ערבית לחול

בָּרְכוּ אֶת יְיָ הַמְבֹרָךְ:
בָּרוּךְ יְיָ הַמְבֹרָךְ לְעוֹלָם וָעֶד:

בָּרוּךְ אַתָּה יְיָ אֱלֹהֵינוּ מֶלֶךְ הָעוֹלָם. אֲשֶׁר בִּדְבָרוֹ מַעֲרִיב עֲרָבִים. בְּחָכְמָה פּוֹתֵחַ שְׁעָרִים. וּבִתְבוּנָה מְשַׁנֶּה עִתִּים וּמַחֲלִיף אֶת הַזְּמַנִּים. וּמְסַדֵּר אֶת הַכּוֹכָבִים בְּמִשְׁמְרוֹתֵיהֶם בָּרָקִיעַ כִּרְצוֹנוֹ. בּוֹרֵא יוֹם וָלָיְלָה. גּוֹלֵל אוֹר מִפְּנֵי חֹשֶׁךְ וְחֹשֶׁךְ מִפְּנֵי אוֹר. וּמַעֲבִיר יוֹם וּמֵבִיא לָיְלָה. יְיָ צְבָאוֹת שְׁמוֹ. אֵל חַי וְקַיָּם תָּמִיד יִמְלוֹךְ עָלֵינוּ לְעוֹלָם וָעֶד. בָּרוּךְ אַתָּה יְיָ הַמַּעֲרִיב עֲרָבִים:

אַהֲבַת עוֹלָם בֵּית יִשְׂרָאֵל עַמְּךָ אָהָבְתָּ. תּוֹרָה וּמִצְוֹת חֻקִּים וּמִשְׁפָּטִים אוֹתָנוּ לִמַּדְתָּ. עַל כֵּן יְיָ אֱלֹהֵינוּ בְּשָׁכְבֵנוּ וּבְקוּמֵנוּ נָשִׂיחַ בְּחֻקֶּיךָ. וְנִשְׂמַח בְּדִבְרֵי תוֹרָתֶךָ וּבְמִצְוֹתֶיךָ לְעוֹלָם וָעֶד. כִּי הֵם חַיֵּינוּ וְאֹרֶךְ יָמֵינוּ. וּבָהֶם נֶהְגֶּה יוֹמָם וָלָיְלָה. וְאַהֲבָתְךָ אַל תָּסִיר מִמֶּנּוּ לְעוֹלָמִים. בָּרוּךְ אַתָּה יְיָ אוֹהֵב עַמּוֹ יִשְׂרָאֵל:

שְׁמַע יִשְׂרָאֵל יְהֹוָה אֱלֹהֵינוּ יְהֹוָה אֶחָד:
בָּרוּךְ שֵׁם כְּבוֹד מַלְכוּתוֹ לְעוֹלָם וָעֶד:

וְאָהַבְתָּ אֵת יְיָ אֱלֹהֶיךָ בְּכָל לְבָבְךָ וּבְכָל נַפְשְׁךָ וּבְכָל מְאֹדֶךָ: וְהָיוּ הַדְּבָרִים הָאֵלֶּה אֲשֶׁר אָנֹכִי מְצַוְּךָ הַיּוֹם עַל לְבָבֶךָ: וְשִׁנַּנְתָּם לְבָנֶיךָ וְדִבַּרְתָּ בָּם. בְּשִׁבְתְּךָ בְּבֵיתֶךָ וּבְלֶכְתְּךָ בַדֶּרֶךְ וּבְשָׁכְבְּךָ וּבְקוּמֶךָ: וּקְשַׁרְתָּם לְאוֹת עַל יָדֶךָ. וְהָיוּ לְטֹטָפֹת בֵּין עֵינֶיךָ: וּכְתַבְתָּם עַל מְזֻזוֹת בֵּיתֶךָ וּבִשְׁעָרֶיךָ:

And they shall be as a sign on thy hand and as an ornament on thy brow. And thou shalt write them upon the doorposts of thy house and on thy gates. DEUTER, CHAPT. 6. V. 4—9.)

Unchangeable and immutable is this word with us: God is everlasting; his word is true unto all generations; his commandments stand for ever. He alone is our God and none besides him.

Truly thou art our God, and we are thy people, whom thou hast delivered from the hand of mighty oppressors. Wonders without number thou hast wrought for us, and hast miraculously protected us during these many centuries. As thy arm saved us from the yoke of Egyptian slavery, so thou wast with us in all times of need and danger, when hatred and fanaticism threatened to destroy the remnant of Israel. Therefore we render thanks to thee, and praise thy name with the ancient song of our fathers:

Who is like thee among the mighty, O God, who is like thee glorified in Holiness, awe-inspiring, wonder-working!

MINISTER AND CONGREGATION:

Mi chomócho boëlim Adonoy; mi komócho, neddor bakkódesh, nóro sehillos, osé féleh.

MINISTER:

As thou hast revealed thy kingdom to our fathers, so manifest thy glorious help unto us, their children, who worship thee as their God and King, proclaiming:

The Lord will reign for ever and ever!

Adonoy yimlóch l'olom roëd.

Continue to be with us, O God, and guard us from evil. Let our lying down and our rising up be in peace. O guide us with thy good counsel; protect us from grief and need, from sorrow and anxiety, from sickness and danger; for in thee, O God, we put our trust, our gracious and merciful father. Let our going out and coming in be in peace, henceforth and forevermore. Blessed art thou, O God, Redeemer and Keeper of Israel.

CONGREGATION: **Amen.**

תפלת ערבית לחול

אֱמֶת וֶאֱמוּנָה כָּל זֹאת וְקַיָּם עָלֵינוּ. כִּי הוּא יְיָ אֱלֹהֵינוּ וְאֵין זוּלָתוֹ. וַאֲנַחְנוּ יִשְׂרָאֵל עַמּוֹ. הַפּוֹדֵנוּ מִיַּד מְלָכִים. מַלְכֵּנוּ הַגּוֹאֲלֵנוּ מִכַּף כָּל־הֶעָרִיצִים. הָעוֹשֶׂה גְדֹלוֹת עַד אֵין חֵקֶר. וְנִפְלָאוֹת עַד אֵין מִסְפָּר. הַשָּׂם נַפְשֵׁנוּ בַּחַיִּים. וְלֹא נָתַן לַמּוֹט רַגְלֵנוּ. הָעוֹשֶׂה לָּנוּ נִסִּים בְּמִצְרַיִם. אוֹתֹת וּמוֹפְתִים בְּאַדְמַת בְּנֵי חָם. וְרָאוּ בָנָיו גְּבוּרָתוֹ. שִׁבְּחוּ וְהוֹדוּ לִשְׁמוֹ. וּמַלְכוּתוֹ בְּרָצוֹן קִבְּלוּ עֲלֵיהֶם. מֹשֶׁה וּבְנֵי יִשְׂרָאֵל לְךָ עָנוּ שִׁירָה בְּשִׂמְחָה רַבָּה וְאָמְרוּ כֻלָּם:

מִי־כָמֹכָה בָּאֵלִים יְיָ מִי כָּמֹכָה נֶאְדָּר בַּקֹּדֶשׁ. נוֹרָא תְהִלֹּת עֹשֵׂה־פֶלֶא:

מַלְכוּתְךָ רָאוּ בָנֶיךָ. בּוֹקֵעַ יָם לִפְנֵי מֹשֶׁה. זֶה אֵלִי עָנוּ וְאָמְרוּ:

יְיָ יִמְלֹךְ לְעֹלָם וָעֶד:

וְנֶאֱמַר כִּי־פָדָה יְיָ אֶת־יַעֲקֹב וּגְאָלוֹ מִיַּד חָזָק מִמֶּנּוּ. בָּרוּךְ אַתָּה יְיָ גָּאַל יִשְׂרָאֵל:

הַשְׁכִּיבֵנוּ יְיָ אֱלֹהֵינוּ לְשָׁלוֹם. וְהַעֲמִידֵנוּ מַלְכֵּנוּ לְחַיִּים. וּפְרֹשׂ עָלֵינוּ סֻכַּת שְׁלוֹמֶךָ. וְתַקְּנֵנוּ בְּעֵצָה טוֹבָה מִלְּפָנֶיךָ. וְהוֹשִׁיעֵנוּ לְמַעַן שְׁמֶךָ. וְהָגֵן בַּעֲדֵנוּ וְהָסֵר מֵעָלֵינוּ אוֹיֵב דֶּבֶר וְחֶרֶב וְרָעָב וְיָגוֹן. וּבְצֵל כְּנָפֶיךָ תַּסְתִּירֵנוּ. כִּי אֵל שׁוֹמְרֵנוּ וּמַצִּילֵנוּ אָתָּה. כִּי אֵל מֶלֶךְ חַנּוּן וְרַחוּם אָתָּה. וּשְׁמוֹר צֵאתֵנוּ וּבוֹאֵנוּ לְחַיִּים וּלְשָׁלוֹם מֵעַתָּה וְעַד עוֹלָם. בָּרוּךְ אַתָּה יְיָ שׁוֹמֵר עַמּוֹ יִשְׂרָאֵל לָעַד:

DOMESTIC SERVICE.

Praise be to thee, O Eternal our God, God of our fathers, God of Abraham, Isaac, and Jacob, Almighty and Supreme Ruler of the world, who renderest just reward unto all. Thou rememberest the pious deeds of the fathers, and bringest redemption and love to their descendants; thou art our Father, our Protector, and Helper. Praise be to thee, O God, Shield of Abraham.

Thou art mighty, O Lord, thy help is ever near. Thou sustainest in kindness the living; thou upholdest the falling, healest the sick, loosest the bonds of captives, and keepest thy faith to those who sleep in the dust. Who is like unto thee, Almighty! Author of life and death, who givest salvation, and rememberest thy creatures unto life eternal! Praise be to thee, O God, who hast planted within us eternal life.

Thou art holy, and thy name is holy, and thy worshippers daily praise thy holiness. (Praise be to thee, Almighty and Holy God.)

SANCTIFICATION.
(The Congregation will rise.)

Let us sanctify the Name of the Holy One of Israel, as it is sanctified throughout the universe, and in the solemn words of our prophets we exclaim: Holy, holy, holy is the Lord of hosts, the whole earth is full of his glory.

MINISTER AND CONGREGATION:
Kodósh, Kodósh, Kodósh Adonoy Tsevoós, meló chol hoóretz k'vodo.

All creation sounds his praise continually, saying: Praised be the glory of God which fills the universe!

MINISTER AND CONGREGATION:
Boruch k'vód Adonoy mimmekomo.

The Lord shall reign for evermore, even thy God, O Zion, from generation to generation. Hallelujah!

MINISTER AND CONGREGATION:
Yimlóch Adonoy l'olom, Elohayich Zion l'dór, vodór Hallelujah.

For ever will we declare thy greatness and proclaim thy holiness, neither shall thy praise ever depart from our lips. Praise be to thee, Almighty and Holy God. Amen.

(The Congregation will be seated.)

בָּרוּךְ אַתָּה יְיָ אֱלֹהֵינוּ וֵאלֹהֵי אֲבוֹתֵינוּ. אֱלֹהֵי אַבְרָהָם אֱלֹהֵי יִצְחָק וֵאלֹהֵי יַעֲקֹב. הָאֵל הַגָּדֹל הַגִּבּוֹר וְהַנּוֹרָא. אֵל עֶלְיוֹן. גּוֹמֵל חֲסָדִים טוֹבִים. וְקֹנֵה הַכֹּל וְזוֹכֵר חַסְדֵי אָבוֹת. וּמֵבִיא גְאֻלָּה לִבְנֵי בְנֵיהֶם. לְמַעַן שְׁמוֹ בְּאַהֲבָה:

מֶלֶךְ עוֹזֵר וּמוֹשִׁיעַ וּמָגֵן. בָּרוּךְ אַתָּה יְיָ מָגֵן אַבְרָהָם:

אַתָּה גִבּוֹר לְעוֹלָם אֲדֹנָי. רַב לְהוֹשִׁיעַ: מְכַלְכֵּל חַיִּים בְּחֶסֶד. מְחַיֶּה הַכֹּל בְּרַחֲמִים רַבִּים. סוֹמֵךְ נוֹפְלִים וְרוֹפֵא חוֹלִים וּמַתִּיר אֲסוּרִים. וּמְקַיֵּם אֱמוּנָתוֹ לִישֵׁנֵי עָפָר. מִי כָמוֹךָ בַּעַל גְּבוּרוֹת. וּמִי דוֹמֶה לָּךְ. מֶלֶךְ מֵמִית וּמְחַיֶּה. וּמַצְמִיחַ יְשׁוּעָה. בָּרוּךְ אַתָּה יְיָ מְחַיֶּה הַכֹּל:

אַתָּה קָדוֹשׁ וְשִׁמְךָ קָדוֹשׁ. וּקְדוֹשִׁים בְּכָל יוֹם יְהַלְלוּךָ סֶּלָה. (בָּרוּךְ אַתָּה יְיָ הָאֵל הַקָּדוֹשׁ):

קְדוּשָׁה.

ח׳ כַּכָּתוּב עַל יַד נְבִיאֶךָ. וְקָרָא זֶה אֶל זֶה וְאָמַר:
ק׳ קָדוֹשׁ. קָדוֹשׁ. קָדוֹשׁ יְיָ צְבָאוֹת. מְלֹא כָל הָאָרֶץ כְּבוֹדוֹ:
ח׳ לְעֻמָּתָם בָּרוּךְ יֹאמֵרוּ: ק׳ בָּרוּךְ כְּבוֹד יְיָ מִמְּקוֹמוֹ:
ח׳ וּבְדִבְרֵי קָדְשְׁךָ כָּתוּב לֵאמֹר: ק׳ יִמְלֹךְ יְיָ לְעוֹלָם אֱלֹהַיִךְ צִיּוֹן לְדֹר וָדֹר. הַלְלוּיָהּ:

ח׳ לְדוֹר וָדוֹר נַגִּיד גָּדְלֶךָ. וּלְנֵצַח נְצָחִים קְדֻשָּׁתְךָ נַקְדִּישׁ. וְשִׁבְחֲךָ אֱלֹהֵינוּ מִפִּינוּ לֹא יָמוּשׁ לְעוֹלָם וָעֶד. כִּי אֵל מֶלֶךְ גָּדוֹל וְקָדוֹשׁ אָתָּה. בָּרוּךְ אַתָּה יְיָ הָאֵל הַקָּדוֹשׁ:

In thy endless mercy, O Lord, thou hast crowned the son of earth with honor and glory, and distinguished him from all other beings by an intelligent, immortal spirit. May this light within us never be dimmed through folly and sin, but shine in clear and radiant luster, a pure reflexion of its divine origin. Praise be to thee, O God, who hast graciously given us the light of reason.

Forgive us, O Father, our failings; pardon, O Lord, our transgressions; thou desirest not the destruction of the sinner; but that he shall return from his way and live; for thou art a gracious and merciful God. Praise be to thee, O God; thine is mercy and forgiveness.

Have compassion, O Lord, on all those who suffer; defend the cause of the guiltless; send healing and comfort to the sick and the sorrow-striken, for thou alone art our God and Helper; thou alone dispensest life and health. Praise be to thee, O God, who art the Redeemer of the distressed.

Bless this year with abundance; shower rain and dew upon the soil and satiate all living beings with thy goodness. Praise be to thee, O God, who blessest the years, and by whose goodness we live.

Grant, O God, that the trumpet sounds of freedom be heard throughout all the countries of the earth, and all thy children enjoy the blessings of true liberty. Remove all prejudice and injustice from thy people Israel, that his mourning may cease everywhere; let the reign of wickedness vanish like smoke and all nations of the earth recognize thee alone as their King. Praise be to thee, O Ruler of the universe who lovest right and justice.

Remember, O God, in love the just and virtuous of all nations; let all who sincerely trust in thy name rejoice in thy goodness; and may we all enjoy the happiness of thy blessing, that we may never need the gift of man, and never have to blush. Praise be to thee, O God, Shield of the righteous.

תפלה לחול

אַתָּה חוֹנֵן לְאָדָם דַּעַת. וּמְלַמֵּד לֶאֱנוֹשׁ בִּינָה. חָנֵּנוּ מֵאִתְּךָ דֵּעָה בִּינָה וְהַשְׂכֵּל. בָּרוּךְ אַתָּה יְיָ חוֹנֵן הַדָּעַת:

הֲשִׁיבֵנוּ אָבִינוּ לְתוֹרָתֶךָ. וְקָרְבֵנוּ מַלְכֵּנוּ לַעֲבוֹדָתֶךָ. וְהַחֲזִירֵנוּ בִּתְשׁוּבָה שְׁלֵמָה לְפָנֶיךָ. בָּרוּךְ אַתָּה יְיָ הָרוֹצֶה בִּתְשׁוּבָה:

סְלַח לָנוּ אָבִינוּ כִּי חָטָאנוּ. מְחַל לָנוּ מַלְכֵּנוּ כִּי פָשָׁעְנוּ. כִּי מוֹחֵל וְסוֹלֵחַ אָתָּה. בָּרוּךְ אַתָּה יְיָ חַנּוּן הַמַּרְבֶּה לִסְלוֹחַ:

רְאֵה בְעָנְיֵנוּ וְחַלְצֵנוּ. וְהָסֵר מִמֶּנּוּ יָגוֹן וַאֲנָחָה. וּכְכָל רָע גְּאָלֵנוּ לְמַעַן שְׁמֶךָ. כִּי גּוֹאֵל חָזָק אָתָּה. בָּרוּךְ אַתָּה יְיָ גּוֹאֵל יִשְׂרָאֵל:

רְפָאֵנוּ יְיָ וְנֵרָפֵא. הוֹשִׁיעֵנוּ וְנִוָּשֵׁעָה. כִּי תְהִלָּתֵנוּ אָתָּה. וְהַעֲלֵה רְפוּאָה שְׁלֵמָה לְכָל תַּחֲלוּאֵינוּ וּלְכָל מַכְאוֹבֵינוּ. כִּי אֵל רוֹפֵא נֶאֱמָן וְרַחֲמָן אָתָּה. בָּרוּךְ אַתָּה יְיָ רוֹפֵא חוֹלִים:

בָּרֵךְ עָלֵינוּ יְיָ אֱלֹהֵינוּ אֶת הַשָּׁנָה הַזֹּאת. וְאֶת כָּל מִינֵי תְבוּאָתָהּ לְטוֹבָה. וְתֵן טַל וּמָטָר לִבְרָכָה עַל פְּנֵי הָאֲדָמָה וְשַׂבְּעֵנוּ מִטּוּבֶךָ. וּבָרֵךְ שְׁנָתֵנוּ כַּשָּׁנִים הַטּוֹבוֹת. בָּרוּךְ אַתָּה יְיָ מְבָרֵךְ הַשָּׁנִים:

תְּקַע בְּשׁוֹפָר גָּדוֹל לְחֵרוּתֵנוּ עַמִּים. וְשָׂא נֵס לְקַבֵּץ גָּלֻיּוֹתֵינוּ. וּבָרֵךְ לְאֻמִּים יַחַד בִּבְרִית שָׁלוֹם וְשַׁלְוָה. אַהֲבָה וְאַחֲוָה: בָּרוּךְ אַתָּה יְיָ מְקַבֵּץ נִדָּחִים:

הוֹשִׁיבָה שׁוֹפְטֵינוּ בְּצֶדֶק. וְיוֹעֲצֵינוּ בֶּאֱמוּנָה. וְהָאֵר עֵינֵיהֶם בְּאוֹר פָּנֶיךָ. וְתֵן יִרְאָתְךָ בְּלִבָּבָם. וּמְלוֹךְ עָלֵינוּ אַתָּה יְיָ לְבַדְּךָ בְּחֶסֶד וּבְרַחֲמִים. בָּרוּךְ אַתָּה יְיָ הַמֶּלֶךְ הַמִּשְׁפָּט:

MINISTER AND MOURNERS:

We know, that we are but pilgrims upon this earth, that thou hast appointed us to walk in thy ways, to do good and work salvation here below, and at thy summons, to return unto thee into the invisible realm of the spiritual life, where thou hast treasured up salvation and eternal beautitude for those, who live in accordance with thy will. From thee we derive comfort and strength, when thou plungest our hearts into deep mourning and sorrow by severing a dearly beloved link from our closely knitted family-chain. And though we walk in the valley of the shadow of death, we fear no evil, for thou remainest the staff and stay of our immortal soul unto all eternity.

THE CONGREGATION:

Blessed art thou, O Lord, our God, in all thy dispensations; honor and glory to thy holy name, for ever and ever. Amen.

MINISTER AND MOURNERS:

O sublime Judge over life and death, thy inscrutable will has called from hence the soul of ...... At thy command it has abandoned this place, leaving behind it many mourning hearts whose love is stronger than death. May it be thy will, O Lord of all spirits, to grant the soul of our departed ...... blissful peace in thy sanctuary; may it be overshadowed by the tree of eternal life and satiated with thy goodness which thou keepest in store for the pious. Mayest thou send help to those whom thou hast striken; show thy mercy to the mourning survivors, O God, who healest the wounded and takest care of the abandoned. Grant them salvation, comfort and aid, soothe their pain with the balm of thy word, and announce peace to those who are nigh and those who are departed.

CONGREGATION:
Amen.

תפלה לחול

עַל הַצַּדִּיקִים וְעַל הַחֲסִידִים כֻּלָּם. וְעַל זִקְנֵי עַמְּךָ בֵּית יִשְׂרָאֵל. וְעַל סוֹפְרֵיהֶם וְתַלְמִידֵיהֶם. וְעַל כָּל עוֹשֵׂי הַצֶּדֶק וְאוֹהֲבֵי הַחֶסֶד. יֶהֱמוּ רַחֲמֶיךָ יְיָ אֱלֹהֵינוּ. וְתֵן שָׂכָר טוֹב לְכָל הַבּוֹטְחִים בְּשִׁמְךָ בֶּאֱמֶת. וְשִׂים חֶלְקֵנוּ עִמָּהֶם לְעוֹלָם. וְלֹא נֵבוֹשׁ כִּי בְךָ בָּטָחְנוּ. בָּרוּךְ אַתָּה יְיָ מִשְׁעָן וּמִבְטָח לַצַּדִּיקִים:

אֶת צֶמַח יְשׁוּעָתְךָ מְהֵרָה תַצְמִיחַ. וְקַרְנוֹ עַמְּךָ תָּרוּם בִּישׁוּעָתֶךָ. כִּי לִישׁוּעָתְךָ קִוִּינוּ כָּל הַיּוֹם. בָּרוּךְ אַתָּה יְיָ מַצְמִיחַ קֶרֶן יְשׁוּעָה:

שְׁמַע קוֹלֵנוּ יְיָ אֱלֹהֵינוּ. חוּס וְרַחֵם עָלֵינוּ. וְקַבֵּל בְּרַחֲמִים וּבְרָצוֹן אֶת תְּפִלָּתֵנוּ. כִּי אֵל שׁוֹמֵעַ תְּפִלּוֹת וְתַחֲנוּנִים אָתָּה. וּמִלְּפָנֶיךָ מַלְכֵּנוּ רֵיקָם אַל תְּשִׁיבֵנוּ. בָּרוּךְ אַתָּה יְיָ שׁוֹמֵעַ תְּפִלָּה:

לראש חדש וחוה״מ

אֱלֹהֵינוּ וֵאלֹהֵי אֲבוֹתֵינוּ יַעֲלֶה וְיָבֹא זִכְרוֹנֵנוּ וְזִכְרוֹן אֲבוֹתֵינוּ. וְזִכְרוֹן כָּל עַמְּךָ בֵּית יִשְׂרָאֵל לְפָנֶיךָ. לְחֵן וּלְחֶסֶד וּלְרַחֲמִים לְחַיִּים וּלְשָׁלוֹם בְּיוֹם

לר״ח רֹאשׁ הַחֹדֶשׁ | לפסח חַג הַמַּצּוֹת | לסכות חַג הַסֻּכּוֹת

הַזֶּה. זָכְרֵנוּ יְיָ אֱלֹהֵינוּ בּוֹ לְטוֹבָה. וּפָקְדֵנוּ בוֹ לִבְרָכָה. וְהוֹשִׁיעֵנוּ בוֹ לְחַיִּים. וּבִדְבַר יְשׁוּעָה וְרַחֲמִים חוּס וְחָנֵּנוּ. וְרַחֵם עָלֵינוּ וְהוֹשִׁיעֵנוּ. כִּי אֵלֶיךָ עֵינֵינוּ. כִּי אֵל מֶלֶךְ חַנּוּן וְרַחוּם אָתָּה:

Look with kindness, O God, upon Israel, thy people: may their fervent prayers, and their worship, be always acceptable to thee. Praise be to thee, O God, whom alone we adore and worship.

From age to age we render thanks unto thee and recount thy praise, for our lives committed into thy hand, for our souls entrusted to thy care, for thy marvelous works, thy wonders which are manifested every day, and for thy boundless goodness in which thou enfoldest us at all times, evening, morning and noon. We bless thee, All-Good, whose mercies never cease, whose grace is infinite; our hopes are in thee forever.

Our God, God of our fathers! Bless us with the ancient priestly benediction:

Yevorechecho Adonoy v'yishmerecho.

May the Lord bless thee and guard thee.

Yoër Adonoy ponov elecho vichunecko.

May the Lord let his countenance shine upon thee and be gracious unto thee.

Yisso Adonoy ponov elecho v'yosaim locho sholóm.

May the Lord lift up his countenance upon thee and give thee peace.

Grant peace, happiness and blessing, grace and mercy to us, and to Israel thy people, and to all thy children. Bless us all, O our Father, with the light of thy countenance; as in the light of thy countenance thou hast given us the law of life, the love of virtue and justice, mercy and peace, so may it please thee to bless us with thy peace at all times and in all seasons. Praise be to thee, O Giver of peace.

(The Congregation in silent devotion.)

O God, keep my tongue from evil, and my lips from uttering deceit, and grant that I may be meek and kind to those who bear ill-will against me. Implant humility in my heart and strengthen me with faith. Be my support when grief oppresses me and my comfort in affliction. Let thy truth illumine my path and guide me; for thou art my God and my aid; in thee I trust every day. Amen.

תפלה לחול

רְצֵה יְיָ אֱלֹהֵינוּ בְּעַמְּךָ יִשְׂרָאֵל. וְתִפִלָּתָם בְּאַהֲבָה תְקַבֵּל. וּתְהִי לְרָצוֹן תָּמִיד עֲבוֹדַת יִשְׂרָאֵל עַמֶּךָ. בָּרוּךְ אַתָּה יְיָ שֶׁאוֹתְךָ לְבַדְּךָ בְּיִרְאָה נַעֲבוֹד:

מוֹדִים אֲנַחְנוּ לָךְ. שָׁאַתָּה הוּא יְיָ אֱלֹהֵינוּ וֵאלֹהֵי אֲבוֹתֵינוּ לְעוֹלָם וָעֶד. צוּר חַיֵּינוּ מָגֵן יִשְׁעֵנוּ אַתָּה הוּא לְדוֹר וָדוֹר. נוֹדֶה לְךָ וּנְסַפֵּר תְּהִלָּתֶךָ. עַל חַיֵּינוּ הַמְּסוּרִים בְּיָדֶךָ. וְעַל נִשְׁמוֹתֵינוּ הַפְּקוּדוֹת לָךְ. וְעַל נִסֶּיךָ שֶׁבְּכָל יוֹם עִמָּנוּ. וְעַל נִפְלְאוֹתֶיךָ וְטוֹבוֹתֶיךָ שֶׁבְּכָל עֵת. עֶרֶב וָבֹקֶר וְצָהֳרָיִם. הַטּוֹב כִּי לֹא כָלוּ רַחֲמֶיךָ. וְהַמְרַחֵם כִּי לֹא תַמּוּ חֲסָדֶיךָ. מֵעוֹלָם קִוִּינוּ לָךְ:

וְעַל כֻּלָּם יִתְבָּרַךְ וְיִתְרוֹמַם שִׁמְךָ מַלְכֵּנוּ. תָּמִיד לְעוֹלָם וָעֶד. וְכֹל הַחַיִּים יוֹדוּךָ סֶּלָה וִיהַלְלוּ אֶת שִׁמְךָ בֶּאֱמֶת. הָאֵל יְשׁוּעָתֵנוּ וְעֶזְרָתֵנוּ סֶלָה. בָּרוּךְ אַתָּה יְיָ הַטּוֹב שִׁמְךָ וּלְךָ נָאֶה לְהוֹדוֹת:

אֱלֹהֵינוּ וֵאלֹהֵי אֲבוֹתֵינוּ. בָּרְכֵנוּ בַּבְּרָכָה הַמְשֻׁלֶּשֶׁת בַּתּוֹרָה. הָאֲמוּרָה מִפִּי אַהֲרֹן וּבָנָיו כֹּהֲנֵי עַם קְדוֹשֶׁךָ. כָּאָמוּר: יְבָרֶכְךָ יְיָ וְיִשְׁמְרֶךָ: יָאֵר יְיָ פָּנָיו אֵלֶיךָ וִיחֻנֶּךָּ: יִשָּׂא יְיָ פָּנָיו אֵלֶיךָ וְיָשֵׂם לְךָ שָׁלוֹם:

שִׂים שָׁלוֹם טוֹבָה וּבְרָכָה. חֵן וָחֶסֶד וְרַחֲמִים. עָלֵינוּ וְעַל כָּל יִשְׂרָאֵל עַמֶּךָ. בָּרְכֵנוּ אָבִינוּ כֻּלָּנוּ כְּאֶחָד בְּאוֹר פָּנֶיךָ. כִּי בְאוֹר פָּנֶיךָ נָתַתָּ לָּנוּ יְיָ אֱלֹהֵינוּ. תּוֹרַת חַיִּים וְאַהֲבַת חֶסֶד. וּצְדָקָה וּבְרָכָה. וְרַחֲמִים וְחַיִּים וְשָׁלוֹם. וְטוֹב בְּעֵינֶיךָ לְבָרֵךְ אֶת עַמְּךָ יִשְׂרָאֵל. בְּכָל עֵת וּבְכָל

ADORATION.

Almighty God! Creator of heaven and earth! It behcoves us to render praise and thanksgiving unto thee, who hast delivered us from the darkness of false belief and sent to us the light of thy truth. Thou art our God, there is no other.

We, therefore, bow the head and bend the knee before thee, Creator and Ruler of the world, and bless thy holy name!

MINISTER AND CONGREGATION:

Vaanachnu, kór'im, umishtdchavim, umódim, lifné Mélech mal'ché Limmelóchim, Hakkódosh boruch hu.

Thou art, in truth, our Father, our God, our Saviour, and there is none besides thee, as is written in thy law: Thou shalt know this day and reflect in thy heart that the Lord is God in heaven above as on earth below; and there is none else.

We fervently pray, O Lord our God, that we may speedily behold the glory of thy mighty power, banishing all impurities from the earth, destroying idolatry and wickedness, and establishing thy truth among mankind; that all the inhabitants of the earth may invoke thy name, acknowledge thy unity, and understand that to thee alone every knee must bend and every tongue swear fealty.

May all thy children, O God, soon be united in a common bond of brotherhood, may the time be hastened when no religious differences will separate them, but when they will all adore thee as the universal father, worship thee in the spirit of true religion, and unite in proclaiming the unity of thy holy name.

Thus, O God, do thou reign over them for ever and ever, for the kingdom is thine, and unto thee appertain power, glory and majesty from everlasting to everlasting. As it is written: The Lord will reign for ever and ever; the Lord will be king over all the earth; on that day shall God be acknowledged One and his name One.

MINISTER AND CONGREGATION:

Veho-yoh Adonoy lemélech al kol hoórets, bayóm hahu yih'yéh Adonoy echod, u-shemo echod.

תפלה לחול

עָלֵינוּ לְשַׁבֵּחַ לַאֲדוֹן הַכֹּל. לָתֵת גְּדֻלָּה לְיוֹצֵר בְּרֵאשִׁית. שֶׁהוּא נוֹטֶה שָׁמַיִם וְיוֹסֵד אָרֶץ. וּמוֹשַׁב יְקָרוֹ בַּשָּׁמַיִם מִמַּעַל. וּשְׁכִינַת עֻזּוֹ בְּגָבְהֵי מְרוֹמִים. הוּא אֱלֹהֵינוּ אֵין עוֹד.

וַאֲנַחְנוּ כֹּרְעִים וּמִשְׁתַּחֲוִים וּמוֹדִים

לִפְנֵי מֶלֶךְ מַלְכֵי הַמְּלָכִים. הַקָּדוֹשׁ בָּרוּךְ הוּא:

אֱמֶת מַלְכֵּנוּ אֶפֶס זוּלָתוֹ. כַּכָּתוּב בְּתוֹרָתוֹ. וְיָדַעְתָּ הַיּוֹם וַהֲשֵׁבֹתָ אֶל־לְבָבֶךָ. כִּי יְיָ הוּא הָאֱלֹהִים בַּשָּׁמַיִם מִמַּעַל וְעַל־הָאָרֶץ מִתָּחַת. אֵין עוֹד:

עַל כֵּן נְקַוֶּה לְךָ יְיָ אֱלֹהֵינוּ. לִרְאוֹת מְהֵרָה בְּתִפְאֶרֶת עֻזֶּךָ. לְהַעֲבִיר גִּלּוּלִים מִן הָאָרֶץ. וְהָאֱלִילִים כָּרוֹת יִכָּרֵתוּן. לְתַקֵּן עוֹלָם בְּמַלְכוּת שַׁדַּי. וְכָל־בְּנֵי בָשָׂר יִקְרְאוּ בִשְׁמֶךָ. לְהַפְנוֹת אֵלֶיךָ כָּל־רִשְׁעֵי אָרֶץ. יַכִּירוּ וְיֵדְעוּ כָּל־יוֹשְׁבֵי תֵבֵל. כִּי לְךָ תִּכְרַע כָּל־בֶּרֶךְ. תִּשָּׁבַע כָּל־לָשׁוֹן. לְפָנֶיךָ יְיָ אֱלֹהֵינוּ יִכְרְעוּ וְיִפֹּלוּ. וְלִכְבוֹד שִׁמְךָ יְקָר יִתֵּנוּ. וִיקַבְּלוּ כֻלָּם אֶת־עֹל מַלְכוּתֶךָ. וְתִמְלוֹךְ עֲלֵיהֶם מְהֵרָה לְעוֹלָם וָעֶד. כִּי הַמַּלְכוּת שֶׁלְּךָ הִיא. וּלְעוֹלְמֵי עַד תִּמְלוֹךְ בְּכָבוֹד. כַּכָּתוּב בְּתוֹרָתֶךָ. יְיָ יִמְלֹךְ לְעֹלָם וָעֶד: וְנֶאֱמַר וְהָיָה יְיָ לְמֶלֶךְ עַל־כָּל־הָאָרֶץ: בַּיּוֹם הַהוּא יִהְיֶה יְיָ אֶחָד וּשְׁמוֹ אֶחָד:

Address to the Mourners.

Brothers and sisters, who are mourning for dear lives departed, remember your beloved ones and honor their names in the midst of the congregation of Israel. May the memory of the righteous inspire you to noble deeds and works in their honor. Rise, and praise with me the name of the most High, according to the anscient custom of our fathers.

MOURNERS' KADDISH.

May thy great and ineffable name, O Lord of life and death, be exalted and sanctified throughout the world, which thou hast created according to thy will. May thy kingdom be established in our midst, in our lifetime and in our days, and in the days of the whole house of Israel. Amen.

THE CONGREGATION:

May his great and ineffable name be blessed and glorified for ever and ever.

Praised and hallowed be thy name who hast created man in thy image and planted within him eternal life. In thy hand is the soul of every living being and the spirit of all flesh. Blessed art thou, whose hymns, praises and benedictions are repeated throughout the world. Amen.

THE CONGREGATION:

Praised be he and his glorious name.

Unto Israel, unto all the righteous and unto all who departed this life according to the will of God, may there be granted abundance of peace, and a blissful portion in the life to come, grace and mercy by the Lord of heaven and earth. Amen.

THE CONGREGATION:

May the fullness of peace from heaven, with life and health be granted unto us and unto all Israel. Amen.

May he who establisheth peace in his heavenly spheres grant happiness and peace unto us, unto all Israel and to all mankind. Amen.

קדיש דאבלים.

יִתְגַּדַּל וְיִתְקַדַּשׁ שְׁמֵהּ רַבָּא. בְּעָלְמָא דִּי־בְרָא כִרְעוּתֵהּ. וְיַמְלִיךְ מַלְכוּתֵהּ. בְּחַיֵּיכוֹן וּבְיוֹמֵיכוֹן וּבְחַיֵּי דְכָל בֵּית יִשְׂרָאֵל. בַּעֲגָלָא וּבִזְמַן קָרִיב. וְאִמְרוּ אָמֵן.

יְהֵא שְׁמֵהּ רַבָּא מְבָרַךְ. לְעָלַם וּלְעָלְמֵי עָלְמַיָּא.

יִתְבָּרַךְ וְיִשְׁתַּבַּח וְיִתְפָּאַר וְיִתְרוֹמַם. וְיִתְנַשֵּׂא וְיִתְהַדָּר וְיִתְעַלֶּה וְיִתְהַלָּל שְׁמֵהּ דְּקוּדְשָׁא. בְּרִיךְ הוּא. לְעֵלָּא מִן כָּל בִּרְכָתָא וְשִׁירָתָא. תֻּשְׁבְּחָתָא וְנֶחֱמָתָא. דַּאֲמִירָן בְּעָלְמָא. וְאִמְרוּ אָמֵן:

עַל יִשְׂרָאֵל וְעַל צַדִּיקַיָּא. וְעַל־כָּל־מַן דְּאִתְפְּטַר מִן עָלְמָא הָדֵין בִּרְעוּתֵהּ דֶּאֱלָהָא. יְהֵא לְהוֹן שְׁלָמָא רַבָּא וְחוּלָקָא־טָבָא לְחַיֵּי עָלְמָא דְּאָתֵי. וְחִסְדָּא וְרַחֲמֵי מִן־קֳדָם מָרֵא שְׁמַיָּא וְאַרְעָא. וְאִמְרוּ אָמֵן:

תִּתְקַבַּל צְלוֹתְהוֹן וּבָעוּתְהוֹן דְּכָל־יִשְׂרָאֵל. קֳדָם אֲבוּהוֹן דִּי בִשְׁמַיָּא. וְאִמְרוּ אָמֵן:

יְהֵא שְׁלָמָא רַבָּא מִן־שְׁמַיָּא וְחַיִּים. עָלֵינוּ וְעַל־כָּל־יִשְׂרָאֵל. וְאִמְרוּ אָמֵן:

עֹשֶׂה שָׁלוֹם בִּמְרוֹמָיו. הוּא יַעֲשֶׂה שָׁלוֹם עָלֵינוּ וְעַל כָּל יִשְׂרָאֵל. וְאִמְרוּ אָמֵן:

RESPONSIVE READINGS.

I.

Joy in Worship.

PSALM XCII. [Abrev.]

(Tob l'hodoth l'Adonai.)

A Psalm for the Sabbath-day.

M. It is good to give thanks to the Lord, and to sing praises to thy name, O Most High!

C. To show forth thy loving kindness in the morning, and thy faithfulness every night.

For thou, O Lord, hast made me glad by thy doings; in the works of thy hands I greatly rejoice!

How great are thy works, O Lord! how deep thy purposes!

But the unwise man knoweth not this, the thoughtless can not perceive it:

When the wicked spring up like grass, and evil-doers flourish;—to be destroyed for ever!

Thou, O Lord, art for ever exalted!

For, lo! thy enemies, O Lord! thy enemies perish, and dispersed are all who do iniquity!

The righteous shall flourish like the palm-tree; they shall grow up like the cedars of Lebanon;

Planted in the house of the Lord, they shall flourish in the courts of our God.

Even in old age they bring forth fruit; they are green, and full of sap;

To show that the Lord, my rock, is upright, and there is no unrighteousness in him.

PSALM XCIII.

M.   The Lord reigneth; he is clothed with majesty; the Lord is clothed with majesty, and girded with strength;
C.   Therefore the earth standeth firm, and cannot be moved.

Thy throne was established of old; thou art from everlasting!

The floods, O Lord! lift up their voice; the floods lift up their roaring!

Mightier than the voice of many waters, are the mighty waves of the sea;

But mightiest of all is the Lord in his lofty habitation.

Thy promises are most sure; holiness becometh thy house, O Lord! for ever!

PSALM XCV. [Abrev.]

M.   O come, let us sing to the Lord; let us raise a voice of joy to the rock of our salvation!
C.   Let us come into his presence with thanksgiving, and sing joyfully to him with psalms!

For the Lord is a great God; yea, a great King over all the world.

In his hands are the depths of the earth; his also are the heights of the mountains.

The sea is his, and he made it; the dry land also his hands have formed.

O come, let us worship and bow down, let us bow down before the Lord, our Maker!

For he is our God, and we are the people of his pasture and the flock of his hand.

O that ye would now hear his voice!

PSALM XCVI.

M.   O sing to the Lord a new song; sing to the Lord, all the earth!
C.   Sing to the Lord; praise his name, show forth his salvation from day to day!

Proclaim his glory among the nations, his wonders among all people!

For the Lord is great, and highly exalted, and beside him there is no God.
For all the gods of the nations are idols; but the Lord made the heavens.
Honor and majesty are before him; glory and beauty are in his holy abode.
Give to the Lord, ye families of the people, give to the Lord glory and praise!
Give to the Lord the glory due to his name; bring an offering, and come into his courts!
O worship the Lord in holy attire! tremble before him, all the earth!
Say among the nations, the Lord is king; the world shall stand firm; it shall not be moved; he will judge the nations in righteousness.
Let the heavens be glad, and the earth rejoice; let the sea roar, and the fullness thereof;
Let the fields be joyful, with all that is therein; let all the trees of the forest rejoice;
Before the Lord! for he cometh, he cometh to judge the earth! he will judge the world with justice, and the nations with faithfulness.

PSALM XCVII.

M. The Lord reigneth, let the earth rejoice! let the multitude of isles be glad!

C. Clouds and darkness are round about him; justice and equity are the foundation of his throne.
Before him goeth a fire, which burneth up his enemies around.
His lightnings illumine the world; the earth beholdeth and trembleth.
The mountains melt like wax at the presence of the Lord, at the presence of the Lord of the whole earth.
The heavens declare his righteousness, and all nations behold his glory.
Confounded be they who worship graven images, who glory in idols! to him, all ye mighty ones, bow down!

Zion hath heard, and is glad, and the daughters of Judah exult on account of thy judgments, O Lord!

For thou, O Lord! art most high above all the earth; thou art far exalted above all powers!

Ye that love the Lord, hate evil! he preserveth the lives of his servants, and delivereth them from the hand of the wicked.

Light is sown for the righteous, and joy for the upright in heart.

Rejoice, O ye righteous, in the Lord, and praise his holy name!

PSALM XCVIII.

M. Sing to the Lord a new song; for he hath done marvellous things;

C. His own right hand and his holy arm have gotten him the victory!

The Lord hath made known his salvation; his righteousness hath he manifested in the sight of the nations.

He hath remembered his mercy and truth toward the house of Israel, and all the ends of the earth have seen the salvation of our God.

Sing unto the Lord, all the earth! break forth into joy, and exult, and sing!

Sing to the Lord with the harp, with the harp, and the voice of song!

With clarions, and the sound of trumpets, make a joyful noise before the Lord the King!

Let the sea roar, and the fulness thereof; the world, and they that dwell therein;

Let the rivers clap their hands, and the mountains rejoice together,

Before the Lord! for he cometh to judge the earth! he will judge the world, with righteousness and the nations with equity.

PSALM XCIX.

M. The Lord reigneth, let the nations tremble! he dwelleth between the cherubim, let the earth quake!

C. Great is the Lord upon Zion; he is exalted over all the nations.

Let men praise thy great and awe-inspiring name! it is holy.

Let them declare the glory of the King who loveth justice! thou hast established equity; thou dost execute justice in Jacob!

Exalt ye the Lord, our God, and bow yourselves down at his footstool! he is holy.

Moses and Aaron, with his priests, and Samuel, who called upon his name,—they called upon the Lord, and he answered them.

He spake to them in the cloudy pillar; they kept his commandments, and the ordinances which he gave them.

Thou, O Lord, our God! didst answer them; thou wast to them a forgiving God, though thou didst punish their transgressions!

Exalt the Lord, our God, and worship at his holy mountain! for the Lord, our God, is holy.

PSALM C.

M. Raise a voice of joy unto the Lord, all ye lands!

C. Serve the Eternal with gladness; come before his presence with rejoicing!

Know ye that the Eternal is God! it is he that made us, and we are his, his people, and the flock of his pasture.

Enter into his gates with thanksgiving, and his courts with praise; be thankful to him, and bless his name!

For the Lord is good; his mercy is everlasting; and his truth endureth to all generations.

PSALM CXXII.

M. I was glad when they said to me, let us go up to the house of the Lord!

C. Our feet are standing within thy gates, O Jerusalem!

Jerusalem, the rebuilt city! the city that is joined together!

Thither the tribes go up, the tribes of the Lord, according to the law of Israel, to praise the name of the Lord.

There stand the thrones of judgment, the thrones of the house of David.

Pray for the peace of Jerusalem! may they prosper who love thee!

Peace be within thy walls, and prosperity within thy palaces!

For my brethren and companions' sake will I say, Peace be within thee!

For the sake of the house of the Lord, our God, will I seek thy good!

II.
Acceptable Worship.
PSALM XV.

M. Lord, who shall abide at thy tabernacle? who shall dwell upon thy holy hill?

C. He that walketh uprightly, and doeth righteousness, and speaketh the truth from his heart;

He that slandereth not with his tongue, that doeth no injury to his friend, and uttereth no reproach against his neighbor;

In whose eyes a vile person is contemned, but who honereth them that fear the LORD; who sweareth to his own hurt, and changeth not;

He that lendeth not his money upon usury, and taketh not a bribe against the innocent: he that doeth these things shall never be moved.

PSALM LXXXIV.

M. How lovely are thy tabernacles, O Lord of hosts!

C. My soul longeth, yea, fainteth, for the courts of the Lord; my heart and my flesh cry aloud for the living God.

Even the sparrow findeth an abode, and the swallow a nest, for their young, by thy altars, O Lord of hosts, my king and my God!

Happy they who dwell in thy house, they will continually praise thee!

Happy the man whose glory is in thee, in whose heart are thy ways!

Passing through the valley of tears, they make it a fountain; and the early rain covereth it with blessings.

They go on from strength to strength; every one of them appeareth before God in Zion.

Hear my prayer, O Lord, God of hosts! give ear, O God of Jacob!

Look down, O God! our shield, and behold the face of thy anointed!

For a day spent in thy courts is better than a thousand without:

I would rather stand on the threshold of the house of my God, than dwell in the tents of wickedness.

For the Lord God is a sun and a shield; the Lord giveth grace and glory;

No good thing doth he withhold from those who walk uprightly.

O Lord of hosts! happy the man who trusteth in thee!

PSALM XXXIII.

M. Rejoice, O ye righteous, in the Lord! for praise becometh the upright.

C. Praise the Lord with the harp; sing to him with musical instruments!

Sing to him a new song; play skilfully amid the sound of trumpets!

For the word of the Lord is right, and all his acts are faithful.

He loveth justice and equity; the earth is full of the goodness of the Lord.

By the word of the Lord were the heavens made, and all the hosts of them by the breath of his mouth.

He gathereth the waters of the sea, as a heap; he layeth up the deep in storehouses.

Let all the earth fear the Lord; let all the inhabitants of the world stand in awe of him!

For he spake, and it was done; he commanded, and it stood fast.

The Lord bringeth the devices of the nations to nothing; he frustrateth the designs of kingdoms.

The purposes of the Lord stand for ever; the designs of his heart, to all generations.

Happy the nation whose God is the Lord; the people whom he hath chosen for his inheritance.

The Lord looketh down from heaven; he beholdeth all the children of men;

From his dwelling-place he beholdeth all the inhabitants of the earth, —

He that formed the hearts of all, and observeth all their works.

A king is not saved by the number of his forces, nor a hero by the greatness of his strength.

The horse is a vain thing for safety, nor can he deliver his master by his great strength.

Behold, the eye of the Lord is upon them that fear him,— upon them that trust in his goodness;

To save them from the power of death, and keep them alive in famine.

The hope of our souls is in the Lord; he is our help and our shield.

Yea, in him doth our heart rejoice; in his holy name we have confidence.

May thy goodness be upon us, O Lord! according as we trust in thee!

III.

The Glory of God.

PSALM XXIX.

(Habu l'Adonai bene Elim.)

M. Give unto the Lord, O ye sons of the mighty! give unto the Lord glory and praise!

C. Give unto the Lord the glory due to his name; worship the Lord in holy attire!

The voice of the LORD is heard above the waters; the God of glory thundereth,—the Lord above the great waters.

The voice of the Lord is powerful; the voice of the Lord is full of majesty;

The voice of the Lord breaketh the cedars; yea, the Lord breaketh the cedars of Lebanon;

Yea, he maketh them to leap like a calf,—Lebanon and Sirion like a young buffalo.

The voice of the Lord divideth the flames of fire.

The voice of the Lord maketh the wilderness tremble; yea, the Lord maketh the wilderness of Kadesh tremble.

The voice of the Lord causes the wild deer to start, and layeth bare the forests; while, in his temple, every one declareth his glory.

The Lord dwelleth above the floods; yea, the Lord is king for ever.

The Lord will give strength to his people; the Lord will bless his people with peace.

PSALM XXIV.

M. The earth is the Lord's, and all that is therein; the world and they who inhabit it.

C. For he hath founded it upon the seas, and established it upon the floods.

Who shall ascend the hill of the Lord? and who shall stand in his holy place?

He that hath clean hands and a pure heart; who hath not inclined his soul to falsehood, nor sworn deceitfully.

He shall receive a blessing from the Lord, and favor from the God of his salvation.

This is the race of those that seek him; those that seek thy face, O God of Jacob.

Lift up your heads, O ye gates! lift yourselves up, ye everlasting doors, that the king of glory may come!

"Who is the king of glory?" The Lord, strong and mighty; the Lord, mighty in battle.

Lift up your heads, O ye gates! lift yourselves up, ye everlasting doors, that the king of glory may enter in!
"Who is this King of glory?" The Lord, God of hosts, he is the king of glory.

PSALM XIX.

M. The heavens declare the glory of God; the firmament showeth forth the work of his hands.

C. Day uttereth instruction unto day, and night showeth knowledge unto night.

They have no speech nor language, and their voice is not heard;

Yet their sound goeth forth to all the earth, and their words to the ends of the world.

In them hath he set a tabernacle for the sun, which like a bridegroom he cometh forth from his chamber, and rejoiceth, like a hero, to run his course.

He goeth forth from the extremity of heaven, and maketh his circuit to the end of it; and nothing is hid from his heat.

The law of the Lord is perfect, reviving the soul; the precepts of the Lord are sure, making wise the simple;

The statutes of the Lord are right, rejoicing the heart; the commandments of the Lord are pure, enlightening the eyes;

The fear of the Lord is clean, enduring for ever; the judgments of the Lord are true and righteous altogether.

More precious are they than gold; yea, than much fine gold; sweeter than honey and the honeycomb.

By them also is thy servant warned, and in keeping of them there is great reward.

Who knoweth his own offences? O, cleanse thou me from secret faults!

Keep back also thy servant from presumptuous sins; let them not have dominion over me!

Then shall I be upright, and free from gross transgression.

May the words of my mouth and the meditation of my heart be acceptable in thy sight, O Lord, my strength and my redeemer.

PSALM VIII.

M. O Eternal, our God! how excellent is thy name in all the earth! thou hast set thy glory above the heavens.

C. Out of the mouths of babes and sucklings hast thou founded thy might, to put thy adversaries to shame, and to silence the enemy and avenger.

When I consider thy heavens, the work of thy hands, the moon and the stars which thou hast established:

What is man, that thou art mindful of him, and the son of man that thou carest for him?

Yet thou hast made him little lower than God; thou hast crowned him with glory and honor.

Thou hast given him dominion over the works of thy hands; thou hast put all things under his feet,—

All sheep and cattle, yea, and the beasts of the forest;

The birds of the air, and the fishes of the sea, and whatever passeth through the paths of the deep.

O Eternal, our God, how excellent is thy name in all the earth!

PSALM LXXXIX.

M. I will sing of the mercies of the Lord for ever; I will make known thy faithfulness to all generations!

C. For I know that thy mercy endureth for ever; thou hast established thy truth like the heavens.

The heavens shall praise thy wonders, O Lord! and the assembly of the holy ones thy truth!

Who in the heavens can be compared to the Lord? who is like the Eternal among the mighty?

A God greatly feared in the assembly of the holy ones, and held in reverence above all who are around him?

O Lord, God of hosts! who is mighty like thee, O Lord? and thy faithfulness is round about thee.

Thou rulest the raging of the sea; when the waves thereof rise, thou stillest them!

The heavens are thine; thine also is the earth; the world and all that is therein, thou didst found them.

The North and the South were created by thee;

Thine is a mighty arm; strong is thy hand, and high thy right hand.

Justice and equity are the foundation of thy throne; mercy and truth go before thy face.

Happy the people that know the trumpet's sound! they walk, O Lord, in the light of thy countenance;

In thy name they daily rejoice, and in thy righteousness they glory!

For thou art the glory of their strength; yea, through thy favor we are exalted.

IV.

The Goodness of God.

PSALM XXXIV.

M. I will bless the Lord at all times; his praise shall continually be in my mouth.

C. In the Lord doth my soul boast; let the afflicted hear, and rejoice!

O magnify the Lord with me, and let us exalt his name together!

I sought the Lord, and he heard me, and delivered me from all my fears.

Look up to him, and ye shall have light; your faces shall never be ashamed.

This afflicted man cried, and the Lord heard, and saved him from all his troubles.

The angels of the Lord encamp around those who fear him, and deliver them.

O taste, and see how good is the Lord! happy the man who trusteth in him!

O fear the Lord, ye his servants! for to those who fear him there shall be no want.

Young lions may want, and suffer hunger; but they who fear the Lord want no good thing.

Come, ye children, hearken to me! I will teach you the
fear of the Lord.
Who is he that loveth life, and desireth many days, in
which he may see good?
Guard well thy tongue from evil, and thy lips from speaking
guile!
Depart from evil, and do good; seek peace, and pursue it!
The eyes of the Lord are upon the righteous, and his ears
are open to their cry.
But the face of the Lord is against evil-doers, to cut off
their remembrance from the earth.
The righteous cry, and the Lord heareth, and delivereth
them from all their troubles.
The Lord is near to them that are of a broken heart, and
saveth such as are of a contrite spirit.
Many are the afflictions of the righteous; but the Lord
delivereth him from them all.
He guardeth all his bones; not one of them shall be
broken.
Calamity destroyeth the wicked, and they who hate righteousness suffer for it.
The Lord redeemeth the life of his servants, and none that
put their trust in him will suffer of it.

PSALM XXXV. [Abrev.]

M. Thy goodness, O Lord! reacheth to the heavens, and thy
faithfulness to the clouds;

C. Thy righteousness is like the high mountains; thy judgments are like the great deep; thou, O Lord, preservest man and beast!
How precious is thy loving-kindness, O God! Yea, the
sons of men seek refuge under the shadow of thy
wings.
They are satisfied with the abundance of thy house, and
thou causest them to drink of the full stream of thy
pleasures.
For with thee is the fountain of life; through thy light we
see light.

O continue thy loving-kindness to them that know thee, and thy favor to the upright in heart!

PSALM CXI.

M. Praise ye the Lord! I will praise the Lord with my whole heart, in the assembly of the righteous, and in the congregation.

C. The works of the Lord are great; sought out by all who have pleasure in them.

His deeds are honorable and glorious, and his righteousness endureth for ever.

He hath established a memorial of his wonders; the Lord is gracious and full of compassion.

He giveth food to them that fear him; he is ever mindful of his covenant.

He showed his people the greatness of his works, when he gave them the inheritance of nations.

The deeds of his hands are truth and justice; all his commandments are sure;

They stand firm for ever and ever, being founded on truth and justice.

He sent redemption to his people; he established his covenant for ever; holy, and awe-inspiring is his name.

The fear of the Lord is the beginning of wisdom; a good understanding have all they who keep his commandments; his praise endureth for ever.

PSALM CVI. [Abrev.]

M. Praise ye the Lord! O give thanks to the Lord, for he is good; for his mercy endureth for ever!

C. Who can utter the mighty deeds of the Lord? who can show forth all his praise?

Happy are they who have regard to justice, who practise righteousness at all times!

Remember me, O Lord! with the favor promised to thy people; O visit me with thy salvation!

That I may see the prosperity of the nation, that I may rejoice in the joy of thy people, that I may glory with thine inheritance!

PSALM CIII.

M. Bless the Lord, O my soul! and all that is within me, bless his holy name!

C. Bless the Lord, O my soul! and forget not all his benefits!
Who forgiveth all thine iniquities; who healeth all thy diseases;
Who redeemeth thy life from the grave; who crowneth thee with loving-kindness and tender mercies;
Who satisfieth thy old age with good, so that thy youth is renewed like the eagle's.
The Lord executeth justice and equity for all the oppressed.
He made known his ways to Moses, his doings to the children of Israel.
The Lord is merciful and kind, slow to anger and rich in mercy.
He doth not always chide, nor doth he keep his anger for ever.
He hath not dealt with us according to our sins, nor requited us according to our iniquities,
As high as are the heavens above the earth, so great is his mercy to them that fear him.
As far as the East is from the West, so far hath he removed our transgressions from us.
Even as a father pitieth his children, so the Lord pitieth them that fear him.
For he knoweth our frame, he remembereth that we are dust.
As for man, his days are as grass; as a flower of the field, so he flourisheth.
The wind passeth over it, and it is gone; and its place shall know it no more.
But the mercy of the Lord is from everlasting to everlasting to them that fear him, and his righteousness to children's children,
To such as keep his covenant, and remember his commandments to do them.
The Lord hath established his throne in the heavens, and his kingdom ruleth over all.

Bless the Lord, ye his angels, ye mighty ones who do his commands, hearkening to the voice of his word!

Bless the Lord, all ye his hosts; ye, his ministers, who do his pleasure!

Bless the Lord, all his works, in all places of his dominion! Bless the Lord, O my soul!

V.

Time and Eternity.

PSALM XC.

M. Lord! thou hast been our refuge, in all generations!

C. Before the mountains were brought forth, or ever thou hadst formed the earth and the world, even from everlasting to everlasting thou art God!

But man thou turnest again to dust, and sayst, "Return, ye children of men!"

For a thousand years are, in thy sight, as yesterday when it is past, and as a watch in the night.

Thou carriest him away as with a flood; he is a dream; in the morning he springeth up like grass,

Which flourisheth and shooteth up in the morning, and in the evening is cut down, and withered.

For we are consumed by thy anger, and by thy wrath are we destroyed.

If thou settest our iniquities before thee, our secret sins in the light of thy countenance:

Then in thine anger all our days vanish away; we spend our years like a thought.

The days of our life are threescore years and ten, and by reason of strength may be fourscore years:

Yet is the pride of them weariness and sorrow; for it vanisheth swiftly, and we fly away.

Yet who attendeth to the power of thy anger? who with due reverence regardeth thy indignation?

Teach us so to number our days, that we may apply our hearts to wisdom!

Desist, O Lord! How long—? have compassion upon thy servants!

Satisfy us speedily with thy mercy, that we may rejoice and be glad all our days!

Make us glad according to the time in which thou hast afflicted us; according to the years in which we have seen adversity!

Let thy deeds be known to thy servants, and thy glory to their children!

Let the favor of the Lord our God be upon us, and establish for us the work of our hands; yea, the work of our hands, establish thou it!

PSALM XXXIX. [Abrev.]

M. Lord, make me to know my end, and the number of my days, that I may know how frail I am!

C. Behold, thou hast made my days as a hand-breadth, and my life is as nothing before thee; yea, every man in his firmest state is altogether vanity.

Surely every man walketh in a vain show; surely he disquieteth himself in vain; he heapeth up riches, and knoweth not who shall gather them.

What, then, O Lord! is my hope? my hope is in thee!

Deliver me from all my transgressions; let me not be the reproach of scoffers!

Yet I am dumb; I open not my mouth; for thou hast done it!

But remove from me thy infliction; for I am perishing by the blow of thy hand.

When thou with rebukes dost chasten man for iniquity, thou causest his glory to waste away like a moth! surely every man is vanity.

Hear my prayer, O Lord! give ear to my cry; be not silent at my tears! for I am but a stranger with thee, a sojourner, as all my fathers were.

O spare me, that I may recover strength, before I go away, and be no more!

PSALM XCI.

M. He who dwelleth under the shelter of the Most High will abide in the shadow of the Almighty.

C. I say to the Lord, thou art my refuge and my fortress; my God, in whom I trust.

Surely he will deliver thee from the snare of the fowler, and from the wasting pestilence;

He will cover thee with his pinions, and under his wings shalt thou find refuge; his faithfulness shall be thy shield and buckler.

Thou shalt not be afraid of the terror of the night, nor of the arrow that flieth by day;

Nor of the pestilence that walketh in darkness, nor of the plague that destroyeth at noonday.

A thousand may fall by thy side, and ten thousand at thy right hand; but thee it shall not touch.

Thou shalt only behold with thy eyes, and see the recompense of the wicked.

Because thou hast made the Lord thy refuge, and the Most High thy habitation,

No evil shall befall thee, nor any plague come near thy dwelling.

For he will give his angels charge over thee, to guard thee in all thy ways.

They shall bear thee up in their hands, lest thou dash thy foot against a stone.

Thou shalt tread upon the lion and the adder; the young lion and the dragon shalt thou trample under foot.

"Because he loveth me, I will deliver him; I will set him on high, because he knoweth my name.

When he calleth upon me, I will answer him; I will be with him in trouble; I will deliver him, and bring him to honor.

With long life will I satisfy him, and show him my salvation."

VI.

The Universal Presence of God.

PSALM CXXXIX. [Abrev.]

M. O Lord! thou hast searched me and known me!
C. Thou knowest my sitting-down and my rising-up; thou understandest my thoughts from afar!
Thou seest my path and my lying-down, and art acquainted with all my ways!
For before the word is upon my tongue, behold, O Lord! thou knowest it altogether!
Thou besettest me behind and before, and layest thy hand upon me!
Such knowledge is too wonderful for me; it is high, I cannot attain to it!
Whither shall I go from thy spirit, and whither shall I flee from thy presence?
If I ascend into heaven, thou art there! if I make my bed in the underworld, behold, thou art there!
If I take the wings of the morning, and dwell in the remotest parts of the sea,
Even there shall thy hand lead me, and thy right hand shall hold me!
If I say, "Surely the darkness shall cover me"; even the night shall be light about me.
Yea, the darkness hideth not from thee, but the night shineth as the day; the darkness and the light are both alike to thee!
I will praise thee; for I am fearfully and wonderfully made; marvellous are thy works, and this my soul knoweth full well!
My frame was not hidden from thee, when yet unborn, when I was curiously shaped in the depths of the earth.
Thy eyes did see my substance, while yet unformed, and in thy book was every thing written; my days were appointed before one of them existed.

How precious to me are thy thoughts, O God! how great is the sum of them!

If I should count them, they would outnumber the sand; when I awake, I am still with thee!

Search me, O God! and know my heart; try me, and know my thoughts;

And see if the way of trouble be within me, and lead me in the way everlasting!

PSALM CIV.

M. Bless the Lord, O my soul! O Lord, my God! thou art very great! thou art clothed with glory and majesty!

C. He covereth himself with light as with a garment; he spreadeth out the heavens like a curtain;

He layeth the beams of his palaces in the waters; he maketh the clouds his chariot; he rideth upon the wings of the wind.

He maketh the winds his messengers, the flaming lightnings his ministers.

He established the earth on its foundations; it shall not be moved for ever.

Thou didst cover it with the deep as with a garment; the waters stood above the mountains!

They give drink to all the beasts of the forest; in them the wild animals quench their thirst.

At thy rebuke they fled; at the voice of thy thunder they hasted away.

The mountains rose, the valleys sank, in the place which thou didst appoint for them.

Thou hast established a bound which the waters may not pass, that they may not return, and cover the earth.

He sendeth forth the springs in brooks; they run among the mountains;

About them the birds of heaven have their habitation; they sing among the branches.

He watereth the hills from his clouds; the earth is satisfied with the fruit of thy works!

He causeth grass to spring up for cattle, and herbage for the service of man, to bring forth food out of the earth,

And wine that gladdeneth the heart of man, and bread that strengtheneth man's heart.

The trees of the Lord are full of sap, the cedars of Lebanon which he hath planted;

There the birds build their nests; in the cypresses the stork hath her abode.

The high hills are a refuge for the wild goats, and the rocks for the conies.

He appointed the moon to mark seasons; the sun knoweth when to go down.

Thou makest darkness, and it is night, when all the beasts of the forest go forth.

The young lions roar for prey, and seek their food from God.

When the sun ariseth, they withdraw themselves, and lie down in their dens.

Man goeth forth, to his work, and to his labor, until the evening.

O Lord! how manifold are thy works! in wisdom hast thou made them all! the earth is full of thy riches!

Lo! this great and wide sea! in it are moving creatures without number, animals, small and great.

There go the ships; there is the leviathan, which thou hast made to play therein.

All these wait on thee, to give them their food in due season.

Thou givest it to them, they gather it; thou openest thy hand, they are satisfied with good.

Thou hidest thy face, they are confounded; thou takest away their breath, they die, and return to the dust.

Thou sendest forth thy spirit, they are created, and thou renewest the face of the earth.

The glory of the Lord shall endure for ever; the Lord rejoiceth in his works;

He looketh on the earth, and it trembleth; he toucheth the hills, and they smoke.

I will sing to the Lord as long as I live, I will sing praise to my God while I have my being.

May my meditation be acceptable to him! I will rejoice in the Lord.

May sinners cease from the earth, and the wicked be no more!

Bless the Lord, O my soul! praise ye the Lord!

VII.
Seeking God.
PSALM LXIII. [Abrev.]

M. O God, thou art my God! earnestly do I seek thee! my soul thirsteth, my flesh longeth for thee, in a dry, thirsty land, where there is no water!

C. Thus I look toward thee in thy sanctuary, to behold thy power and thy glory!

For thy loving-kindness is better than life; therefore my lips shall praise thee!

Thus will I bless thee, while I live; in thy name will I lift up my hands!

My soul shall be satisfied as with marrow and fatness, and with joyful lips my mouth shall praise thee,

When I think of thee upon my bed, and meditate on thee in the night-watches.

For thou art my help, and in the shadow of thy wings I rejoice.

My soul cleaveth to thee; thy right hand holdeth me up.

PSALM V. [Abrev.]

M. Give ear to my words, O Lord; have regard to my prayer!

C. Listen to the voice of my supplication, my King and my God! for to thee do I address my prayer.

In the morning shalt thou hear my voice, O Lord! in the morning will I address my prayer to thee, and look for help.

For thou art not a God that hath pleasure in wickedness; the unrighteous man dwelleth not with thee.

The haughty shall not stand in thy sight; thou hatest all that do iniquity.

Thou destroyest them that speak falsehood; the man of blood and deceit the Lord abhorreth.

But I, through thy great goodness, will come to thy house; in the fear of thee will I worship at thy holy temple.

Lead me, O Lord! in thy righteousness, make thy path straight before my face!

Let all, that put their trust in thee, rejoice; let them ever shout for joy, because thou defendest them; let them, that love thy name, be joyful in thee!

For thou, O Lord! dost bless the righteous; with favor dost thou encompass him, as with a shield.

PSALM XVI.

M. Preserve me, O God! for to thee do I look for help.

C. I have said to the Lord, thou art my Lord; I have no happiness beyond thee!

The holy that are in the land, and the excellent,—in them is all my delight.

They who hasten after false gods shall have multiplied sorrows; their drink-offerings of blood I will not offer, nor will I take their names upon my lips.

The Lord is my portion and my cup; thou wilt maintain my lot!

My portion hath fallen to me in pleasant places; yea, I have a goodly inheritance.

I will bless the Lord, who careth for me; yea, in the night my heart admonisheth me.

I set the Lord before me at all times; since he is at my right hand, I shall not fall.

Therefore my heart is glad, and my spirit rejoiceth; yea, my flesh dwelleth in security.

For thou wilt not give me up to the underworld; nor wilt thou suffer thy holy one to see the corruption.

Thou wilt show me the path of life; in thy presence is fulness of joy; at thy right hand are pleasures for evermore.

PSALM XXV.

M. To thee, O Lord! do I lift up my soul.

C. O my God! I trust in thee; let me not be put to shame! let not my enemies triumph over me!

Yea, none that hope in thee shall be put to shame: they shall be put to shame who wickedly forsake thee.

Cause me to know thy ways, O Lord! teach me thy paths!

Lead me in thy truth, and teach me! For thou art the God from whom cometh my help; in thee do I trust at all times!

Remember thy loving-kindness, O Lord! and thy tender mercy, which thou hast exercised of old!

Remember not the faults and transgressions of my youth: according to thy mercy remember thou me, for thy goodness' sake, O Lord!

Good and righteous is the Lord; therefore showeth he to sinners the way.

The humble he guideth in his statutes, and the contrite he teacheth his way.

All the doings of the Lord are mercy and truth, to those who keep his covenant and his precepts.

For thy name's sake, O Lord, pardon my iniquity; for it is great!

Who is the man that feareth the Lord? him doth he show the way which he should choose.

He shall himself dwell in prosperity, and his offspring shall inherit the land.

The friendship of the Lord is with them that fear him, and he will teach them his covenant.

My eyes are ever directed to the Lord, for he will pluck my feet from the net.

Look upon me, and have pity on me; for I am desolate and afflicted!

Lighten the sorrows of my heart, and deliver me from my troubles!

Look upon my affliction and distress, and forgive all my sins!

Guard thou my life, and deliver me! let me not be put to shame, for I have trusted in thee!

Let integrity and uprightness preserve me, for on thee do I rest my hope!

Redeem Israel, O God! from all his troubles!

PSALM XLIII.

M. As the hart panteth for the water-brooks, so panteth my soul for thee, O God!

C. My soul thirsteth for God, the living God: when shall I come, and appear before God?

My tears have been my food day and night, while they say to me continually, "Where is thy God?"

When I think of it, I pour out my soul in grief; how I once walked with the multitude, walked slowly with them to the house of God, amid sounds of joy and praise with the festive multitude!

Why art thou cast down, O my soul? and why art thou disquieted within me? hope thou in God; for I shall yet praise him, him, my deliverer and my God!

Deep calleth unto deep at the noise of thy waterfalls; all thy waves and billows have gone over me!

Once the Lord commanded his kindness by day, and by night his praise was with me,— thanksgiving to the God of my life.

Now I say to God, my rock, why hast thou forgotten me? why go I mourning on account of the oppression of the enemy?

Like the crushing of my bones are the reproaches of the enemy, while they say to me continually, "Where is thy God?"

Why art thou cast down, O my soul? and why art thou disquieted within me? hope thou in God; for I shall yet praise him, him, my deliverer and my God!

Judge me, O God! and defend my cause against a merciless nation! deliver me from unjust and deceitful men!

Thou art the God of my refuge: why dost thou cast me off! why go I mourning on account of the oppression of the enemy?

O send forth thy light and thy truth; let them guide me; let them lead me to thy holy mountain, and to thy dwelling-place!

Then will I go to the altar of God, to the God of my joy and exultation; yea, upon the harp will I praise thee, O Lord, my God!

Why art thou cast down, O my soul? and why art thou disquieted within me? hope thou in God; for I shall yet praise him, him, my deliverer and my God!

PSALM CI.

M. I will sing of mercy and justice; to thee, O Lord! will I sing!

C. I will have regard to the way of uprightness: when thou shalt come to me, I will walk within my house with an upright heart.

I will set no wicked thing before my eyes; I hate the work of evil-doers; it shall not cleave to me.

The perverse in heart shall be far from me; I will not know a wicked person.

Whoso slandereth his neighbor in secret, him will I remove; him that hath a haughty look and a proud heart I will not endure.

My eyes shall be upon the faithful of the land, that they may dwell with me; he that walketh in the way of uprightness shall be with me.

He who practiseth deceit shall not dwell in my house; he who telleth lies shall not remain in my sight.

PSALM CXIX. [Abrev.]

M. Teach me, O Lord, the way of thy statutes, and I shall keep it unto the end.

C. Give me understanding and I shall keep thy law, yea, I shall keep it with my whole heart.

Make me to go in the path of thy commandments, for therein is my desire.

Turn away my eyes from beholding vanity, and quicken thou me in thy way.

Thy hands have made me and fashioned me, give me understanding that I may learn thy commandments

Let thy tender mercies come unto me, that I may live, for thy law is my delight.

Order my footsteps in thy word, and let not any sin have dominion over me.

O Lord! thy word endureth forever, being established like the heavens:

Thy truth remaineth from generation to generation. Thou has laid the foundation of the earth, and it abideth.

Oh, how I love thy law, it is my meditation all the day.

How sweet are thy words unto my taste, yea, sweeter than honey unto my mouth.

Thy word is a lamp unto my feet, and a light unto my path.

The going forth of thy word giveth light, it giveth understanding to the simple.

Thy testimonies are wonderful, therefore doth my soul keep them.

Thy righteousness is an everlasting righteousness, and thy law is the truth.

Let my prayer come before thee, O Lord! give me understanding according to thy word.

My lips shall speak thy praise, when thou hast taught me thy statutes.

I have longed for thy salvation, O Lord, and in thy law is my delight.

The righteousness of thy testimonies is everlasting; Oh, grant me understanding and I shall live.

Thy testimonies are my heritage forever; quicken me, O Lord! according to thy loving kindness.

VIII.

Thanksgiving.

PSALM CV. [Abrev.]

M. O give thanks unto the Lord; call upon his name; make known his deeds among the people!

C. Sing unto him; sing psalms unto him; tell ye all of his wondrous works!

Glory ye in his holy name; let the hearts of them that seek the Lord rejoice!

Seek the Lord, and his majesty; seek his face continually!

Remember the wonders he hath wrought, his miracles and the judgments of his mouth,

Ye offspring of Abraham his servant, ye children of Jacob his chosen!

The Eternal, he is our God, his judgments are over all the earth.

He remembereth his covenant for ever, and the promise to a thousand generations;

The covenant which he made with Abraham, and the oath which he gave to Isaac;

Which he confirmed to Jacob for a decree, and to Israel for an everlasting covenant.

"To thee," said he, "will I give the land of Canaan for the lot of your inheritance."

When they were yet few in number, very few, and strangers in the land;

When they went from nation to nation, from one kingdom to another people,

He suffered no man to oppress them; yea, he rebuked kings for their sakes.

"Touch not," said he, "mine anointed, and do my prophets no harm."

PSALM LXVI. [Abrev.]

M. Shout joyfully unto God, all ye lands!

C. Sing ye the honor of his name; make his praise glorious!

Say unto God, How wonderful are thy doings! through the greatness of thy power thy enemies are suppliants to thee!

Let all the earth worship thee; let it sing praise to thee, let it sing praise to thy name!

Come, behold the works of God! how wonderful his doings among the sons of men!

He turned the sea into dry land, they went through the deep on foot; then we rejoiced in him.

By his power he ruleth forever; his eyes are fixed upon the nations; let not the rebellious exalt themselves!

O bless our God, ye nations, and make the voice of his praise to be heard!

It is he who preserveth our lives, and suffereth not our feet to stumble.

Thou hast, indeed, proved us, O God! thou hast tried us as silver is tried.

Thou broughtest us into a snare, and didst lay a heavy burden upon our backs;

Thou didst cause men to ride upon our heads, and we have gone through fire and water: but thou hast brought us to a place of abundance.

I will go into thy house with offerings; I will pay thee my vows, —

The vows which my lips uttered, which my mouth promised in my trouble.

Come and hear, all ye who fear God, and I will relate what he hath done for me!

I called upon him with my mouth, and praise is now upon my tongue.

If I had meditated wickedness in my heart, the Lord would not have heard me:

But surely God hath heard me; he hath had regard to the voice of my supplication.

Blessed be God, who did not reject my prayer, nor withhold his mercy from me!

PSALM LXV. [Abrev.]

M. To thee belongeth trust, to thee praise, O God in Zion! and to thee shall the vow be performed!

C. O thou that hearest prayer! to thee shall all flesh come and worship!

Happy is he whom thou choosest, and bringest near thee to dwell in thy courts!

May we be satisfied with the blessings of thy house, thy holy temple!

By wonderful deeds dost thou answer us in thy goodness, O God, our salvation!

Who art the confidence of all the ends of the earth, and of the most distant seas!

Thou makest fast the mountains by thy power, being girded with strength!

Thou stillest the roar of the sea, the roar of its waves, and the tumult of the nations.

They who dwell in the ends of the earth are awed by thy signs;

Thou makest the outgoings of the morning and of the evening to rejoice!

Thou visitest the earth and waterest it; thou enrichest it exceedingly; the river of God is full of water.

Thou suppliest the earth with corn, when thou hast thus prepared it.

Thou waterest its furrows, and breakest down its ridges; thou makest it soft with showers, and blessest its increase.

Thou crownest the year with thy goodness; thy footsteps drop fruitfulness;

They drop it upon the pastures of the plains, and the hills are girded with gladness.

The pastures are clothed with flocks, and the valleys are covered with corn; they shout, yea, they sing for joy.

PSALM LXXV.

M. We give thanks to thee, O God! we give thanks to thee, and near is thy name; men shall declare thy wondrous deeds!

C. "When I see my time, then will I judge with equity. The earth trembleth, and all her inhabitants; but I uphold her pillars."

I say to the proud, Behave not proudly! to the wicked, Lift not up your horn!

Lift not up your horn on high, and speak not with a stiff neck!

For promotion cometh ne'ther from the East, nor from the West, nor from the South;
But it is God that judgeth; he putteth down one, and exalteth another.
For in the hand of the Lord there is a cup; the wine is foaming and full of spices, and of it he poureth out;
Even to the dregs shall all the wicked of the earth drink it.
Therefore I will extol him for ever; I will sing praise to the God of Jacob.
"I will bring down all the power of the wicked; but the righteous shall lift up their heads."

PSALM CXXXVIII.

M. I will praise thee with my whole heart; before the mighty ones will I sing praise to thee;

C. I will worship toward thy holy temple, and praise thy name for thy goodness and thy truth; for thy promise thou hast magnified above all thy name!

In the day when I called, thou didst hear me; thou didst strengthen me, and encourage my soul.

All the kings of the earth shall praise thee, O Lord! when they hear the promises of thy mouth!

Yea, they shall sing of the ways of the Lord; for great is the glory of the Lord.

The Lord is high, yet he looketh upon the humble, and the proud doth he know from afar.

Though I walk through the midst of trouble, thou wilt revive me;

Thou wilt stretch forth thy hand against the wrath of my enemies; thou wilt save me by thy right hand!

The Lord will perform all things for me; thy goodness, O Lord! endureth for ever: forsake not the works of thy hands!

PSALM CVII. [Abrev.]

M. O give thanks to the Lord, for he is good; for his mercy endureth for ever!

C. Let the redeemed of the Lord say it, whom he hath redeemed from the hands of the enemy;

Whom he had gathered from the lands, from the East, the West, the North and the South.

They were wandering in the wilderness, in a desert, they found no way to a city to dwell in.

They were hungry and thirsty, and their souls fainted within them.

Then they cried to the Lord in their trouble, and he delivered them out of their distress.

He led them in a straight way, till they came to a city where they might dwell.

O let them praise the Lord for his goodness, for his wonderful works to the children of men!

For he satisfieth the thirsty, and the hungry he filleth with good.

They dwelt in darkness and the shadow of death, being bound in affliction and iron;

Because they disobeyed the commands of God, and contemned the will of the Most High;

Their hearts he brought down by hardship; they fell down and there was none to help.

But they cried to the Lord in their trouble, and he saved them out of their distresses;

He brought them out of darkness and the shadow of death, and brake their bands asunder.

O let them praise the Lord for his goodness, for his wonderful works to the children of men!

For he hath broken the gates of brass, and cut the bars of iron asunder.

Let them offer the sacrifices of thanksgiving, and declare his works with joy!

Whoso is wise, let him observe this, and have regard to to the loving-kindness of the Lord!

PSALM CXXXVI. [Abrev.]

M. O give thanks to the Lord! for he is kind; for his goodness endureth for ever!

C. O give thanks to the God of heaven; for his goodness endureth for ever!

O give thanks to the Lord of lords; for his goodness endureth for ever!

To him that alone doeth great wonders; for his goodness endureth for ever!

To him that made the heavens with wisdom; for his goodness endureth for ever!

To him that spread out the earth upon the waters; for his goodness endureth for ever!

To him that made the great lights; for his goodness endureth for ever!

The sun to rule the day; for his goodness endureth for ever!

The moon and stars to rule the night; for his goodness endureth for ever!

To him that smote the Egyptians; for his goodness endureth for ever!

And brought Israel from the midst of them; for his goodness endureth for ever!

With a strong hand and an outstreched arm; for his goodness endureth for ever!

To him who led his people through the wilderness, for his goodness endureth for ever!

Who remembered us in our low estate; for his goodness endureth for ever!

And redeemed us from our enemies; for his goodness endureth for ever!

Who giveth food unto all; for his goodness endureth for ever!

O give thanks to the God of heaven; for his goodness endureth for ever!

IX.
Prayer.
PSALM IV.

M. Hear me, when I call, O God of my righteousness! thou hast helped me, when I was in trouble, — have pity upon me, hear my prayer!

C. How long, O men! will ye dishonor my dignity? How long will ye love vanity, and seek disappointment?

Know ye that the Lord hath exalted one that is devoted to him; the Lord will hear, when I call upon him.

Stand in awe, and sin no more; commune with your hearts upon your beds, and desist!

Offer sacrifices of righteousness, and put your trust in the Lord!

There are many who say, who will show us any good? Lord, lift thou up the light of thy countenance upon us!

Thou puttest gladness into my heart, greater than theirs, when their corn and wine are abundant.

I will lay me down in peace, and sleep; for thou alone, O Lord! makest me dwell in safety.

PSALM XVII. [Abrev.]

M. Hear the righteous cause, O Lord! attend to my cry; give ear to my prayer from lips without deceit!

C. May my sentence come forth from thy presence; may thy eyes behold uprightness!

Provest thou my heart, visitest thou me in the night, triest thou me like gold, thou shalt find nothing!

My thoughts do not vary from my lips, as to the deeds of men, through the word of thy lips I have kept me from the paths of the destroyer.

Support my steps in thy paths, that my feet may not slip!

I call upon thee, O God! for thou wilt hear me; incline thy ear to me, and listen to my prayer!

Show forth thy loving-kindness, O thou that savest by thy right hand, those that seek refuge in thee from their adversaries!

Guard me as the apple of the eye; hide me under the shadow of thy wings.

And I through righteousness shall see thy face, I shall be satisfied with the light of thy countenance.

PSALM LXI. [Abrev.]

M. Hear my cry, O God! attend to my prayer!

C. From the extremity of the land I cry unto thee in deep sorrow of heart;

Lead me to the rock that is higher than I.

For thou art my refuge, my strong tower against the enemy.

I shall dwell in thy tabernacle for ever; I will seek refuge under the covert of thy wings.

For thou, O God! wilt hear my vows, and give me the inheritance of those who fear thy name.

PSALM LXVII.

M. O God! be merciful to us, and bless us, and cause thy face to shine upon us!

C. That thy doings may be known on earth, and thy saving power to all the nations.

Let the nations praise thee, O God! yea, let all the nations praise thee!

Let all the nations be glad, and shout for joy! for justly dost thou judge the people, and govern the nations on the earth.

Let all the nations praise thee, O God! yea, let all the nations praise thee!

For the earth has yielded her increase, and God, our Lord hath blessed us.

May God continue to bless us, and may all the ends of the earth fear him!

X.
In the Day of Trouble.
PSALM XX.

M. May the Lord hear thee in the day of trouble; may the name of the God of Jacob defend thee!

C. May he send thee help from his sanctuary, and strengthen thee out of Zion!

May he have regard to all thy offerings, and accept thy sacrifice!

May he grant thee thy heart's desire, and fulfill all thy purposes!

We will rejoice in thy protection, and in the name of our God will we set up our banners, when the Lord hath fulfilled all thy petitions.

Now I know that the Lord helpeth his anointed; that he heareth him from his holy heaven, and aideth him with the saving strength of his right hand.

Some glory in chariots, and some in horses, but we in the name of the Lord our God.

They stumble and fall, but we stand and are erect.

The Lord save us! may he hear us when we call!

PSALM VI. [Abrev.]

M. O Lord! rebuke me not in thy anger; chasten me not in thy hot displeasure!

C. Have pity upon me, O Lord! for I am weak; heal me, O Lord! for my bones tremble!

My soul, also, is sore troubled; and thou, O Lord! how long —?

Return, O Lord! and deliver me; O, save me according to thy mercy!

For in death no praise is given to thee; in the underworld who can give thee thanks?

I am weary with my groaning; all the night I make my bed to swim, and drench my couch with my tears.

My eye is wasted with grief; it hath become old because of all my enemies.

Depart from me, all ye that do iniquity; for the Lord heareth the voice of my weeping.

The Lord heareth my supplication; the Lord accepteth my prayer.

PSALM XXII. [Abrev.]

M. My God, my God! why hast thou forsaken me? Why so far from my aid, and from the words of my cry?

C. O my God! I cry during the day, but thou hearest not; in the night also, but I have no rest.

And yet thou art holy, dwelling amid the praises of Israel!

Our fathers trusted in thee; they trusted, and thou didst save them.

They called upon thee, and were delivered; they trusted in thee, and were not put to shame.

But I am a worm, and not a man; the reproach of men, and the scorn of the people.

All who see me scoff at me; they open wide their lips, they shake the head.

"He trusted in the Lord, let him help him; let him deliver him, since he delighted in him!"

Surely thou art he that didst bring me into the world; thou didst make me lie secure upon my mother's breast!

Upon thee have I cast myself from my birth; thou hast been my God from my earliest breath!

Oh, be not far from me, for trouble is near; for there is none to help!

My strength is dried up like an earthen vessel, and my tongue cleaveth to my jaws;

Thou hast brought me to the dust of death!

But be not thou far from me, O Lord! O my strength! make haste to my aid!

I will proclaim thy name to my brethren; in the midst of the congregation will I praise thee.

Praise him, ye worshippers of the Lord! extol him, all ye race of Jacob, and fear him, all ye race of Israel!

For he hath not despised nor abhorred the misery of the afflicted.

Nor hath he hid his face from him; but when he cried unto him, he heard.

My praise shall be of thee in the great congregation; I will pay my vows before them that fear him!

The afflicted shall eat, and be satisfied; they that seek the Lord shall praise him; your hearts shall be glad for ever and ever!

All the ends of the earth shall remember, and turn to the Lord; all the families of the nations shall worship before thee!

PSALM LXXXVIII.

M. O Lord, God of my salvation! to thee do I cry by day, and by night is my prayer before thee!

C. Let my supplication come before thee; incline thy ear to my cry!

For my soul is full of misery, and my life draweth near to the underworld.

I am counted with those who are going down to the pit; I am like one who hath no strength.

I am left to myself as among the dead, like the slain who lie in the grave, whom thou no more rememberest, and who are cut off from thy [protecting] hand.

Thou hast placed me in a deep pit, in a dark and deep abyss.

Thy wrath presseth hard upon me, and thou afflictest me with all thy waves!

Thou hast put my acquaintances far from me, yea, thou hast made me their abhorrence: I am shut up, and cannot go forth.

My eyes languish by reason of my affliction. I call upon thee daily, O Lord! to thee do I stretch out my hands!

Dost thou show wonders to the dead? shall the dead arise, and praise thee?

Shall thy goodness be declared in the grave, or thy faithfulness in the place of corruption?

Shall thy wonders be known in the dark, and thy justice in the land of forgetfulness?

To thee do I cry, O Lord! In the morning doth my cry come before thee.

Why, O Lord! dost thou cast me off? why hidest thou thy face from me?

I have been afflicted and languishing from my youth; I suffer thy terrors, and am distracted.

Thy fierce wrath overwhelmeth me; thy terrors utterly destroy me.

They surround me daily like water, they compass me about together.

Lover and friend hast thou put far from me; My acquaintances are withdrawn from my sight.

PSALM LXXVII.

M. I call upon God; I cry aloud for help; I call upon God, that he would hear me!

C. In the day of my trouble I seek the Lord; in the night is my hand stretched forth continually; my soul refuseth to be comforted.

I remember God, and am disquieted; I think of him, and my spirit is overwhelmed.

Thou keepest my eyelids from closing; I am distressed, so that I cannot speak!

I think of the days of old, — the years of ancient times.

I call to remembrance my songs in the night; I meditate in my heart, and my spirit inquireth:

Will the Lord be angry for ever? will he be favorable no more?

Is his mercy utterly withdrawn for ever? doth his promise fail from generation to generation?

Hath God forgotten to be gracious? Hath he in anger shut up his compassion?

Then I say, "This is my affliction, a change in the right hand of the Most High."

I remember the deeds of the Lord, I think of thy wonders of old.

I meditate on all thy works, and talk of thy doings.

Thy ways, O God! are holy! who is so great as our God?

Thou art a God who doest wonders; thou hast manifested thy power among the nations.

With thy strong arm thou didst redeem thy people,— the sons of Jacob and Joseph.

The waters saw thee, O God! the waters saw thee, and feared, and the deep trembled.

The clouds poured out water, the skies sent forth thunder, and thy arrows flew.

Thy thunder roared in the whirlwind; the lightning illumined the world; the earth trembled and shook.

Thy way was through the sea, and thy path through great waters; and thy footsteps could not be found.

Thou didst lead thy people like a flock; by the hands of Moses and Aaron.

PSALM LV. [Abrev.]

M. Give ear to my prayer, O God! hide not thyself from my supplication!

C. Attend unto me, and hear me! I wander about mourning and wailing.

My heart trembleth in my bosom, and the terrors of death have fallen upon me.

Fear and trembling have seized me, and horror hath overwhelmed me.

Then I say, O that I had wings like a dove! for then would I fly away, and be at rest.

Behold, I would wander far away, and take up my abode in a wilderness.

I would hasten away to a shelter from the rushing wind and tempest.

As for me, I will call upon God, and the Lord will save me.

At evening, at morn, and at noon I mourn and sigh, and he will hear my voice.

He will deliver me in peace from my conflict; for many have risen up against me.

God will hear me, he that hath been judge of old.

"Cast thy burden upon the Lord, and he will sustain thee; he will never suffer the righteous to fall!"

PSALM LXXXVI.

M. Incline thy ear, O Lord! and hear me, for I am poor and distressed!

C. Preserve my life, for I am devoted to thee! save, O thou my God! thy servant who trusteth in thee!

Have pity upon me, O Lord! for to thee do I cry daily!

Revive the soul of thy servant, for to thee, O Lord! do I lift up my soul!

For thou, O Lord, art good, and ready to forgive; yea, rich in mercy to all that call upon thee!

Give ear, O Lord! to my prayer, and attend to the voice of my supplication!

In the day of my trouble I call upon thee, for thou dost answer me!

Among the mighty there is none like thee, O Lord! and there are no works like thy works!

All the nations which thou hast made must come and worship before thee, O Lord! and glorify thy name!

For great art thou, and wondrous are thy works; thou alone art God!

Teach me, O Lord! thy way, that I may walk in thy truth; unite all my heart to fear thy name!

I will praise thee, O Lord, my God! with my whole heart; I will give glory to thy name for ever!

For thy kindness to me hath been great; thou hast delivered me from the depths of the underworld!

O God! the proud have risen against me; bands of cruel men seek my life, and set not thee before their eyes.

But thou, O Lord! art a God full of compassion and kindness, long-suffering, rich in mercy and truth!

Look upon me, and have compassion upon me! give thy strength to thy servant, and save the son of thy handmaid!

Show me a token for good, that my enemies may see it and be confounded; because thou, O Lord! helpest and comfortest me!

PSALM CXLII.

M. I cry unto the Lord with my voice; with my voice to the Lord do I make my supplication.

C. I pour out my complaint before him; I declare before him my distress.

When my spirit is overwhelmed within me, thou knowest my path! In the way which I walk, they have hid a snare for me.

I look on my right hand, and behold, but no man knoweth me; refuge faileth me, no one careth for me.

I cry unto thee, o Lord! I say, thou art my refuge, my portion in the land of the living.

Attend to my cry, for I am brought very low; deliver me from my persecutors, for they prevail against me!

Bring me out of prison, that I may praise thy name! the righteous shall gather around me, when thou shalt show me thy favor.

PSALM CXLIII. [Abrev.]

M. Hear my prayer, O Lord! give ear to my supplications! in thy faithfulness, and in thy righteousness, answer me!

C. Enter not into judgment with thy servant; for before thee no man living is righteous.

My spirit is overwhelmed within me; my heart within me is desolate.

I remember the days of old; I meditate on all thy works; I muse on the deeds of thy hands.

I stretch forth my hands unto thee; my soul thirsteth for thee, like a parched land.

Hear me speedily, O Lord! my spirit faileth; hide not thy face from me, lest I become like those who go down to the pit!

Cause me to see thy loving-kindness speedily; for in thee do I trust!

Make known to me the way which I should take; for to thee do I lift up my soul!

Deliver me, O Lord! from mine enemies; for in thee do I seek refuge!

Teach me to do thy will; for thou art my God! let thy good spirit lead me in a plain path!
Revive me, O Lord! for thy name's sake! in thy righteousness, bring me out of my distress!

XI.
Repentance and Forgiveness.

PSALM CXXX.

M. Out of the depths do I cry to thee, O Lord!
C. O Lord! listen to my voice, let thy ears be attentive to my supplication!
If thou, O Lord, shouldst treasure up transgressions, O Lord, who could stand?
But with thee is forgiveness, that thou mayst be feared.
I trust in the Lord; my soul doth trust, and in his promise do I confide.
My soul waiteth for the Lord more than they who watch for the morning;
Yea, more than they who watch for the morning!
O Israel! trust in the Lord! for with the Lord is mercy, and with him is plenteous redemption.
He will redeem Israel from all his iniquities.

PSALM XXXII.

M. Happy is he whose transgression is forgiven, whose sin is pardoned!
C. Happy the man to whom the Lord imputeth not iniquity, and in whose spirit there is no guile!
While I kept silence, my bones were wasted, by reason of my groaning all the day long.
For day and night thy hand was heavy upon me; my moisture dried up, as in summer's drought.
At length I acknowledged to thee my sin, and did not hide my iniquity.
I said, "I will confess my transgression to the Lord"; and thou forgavest the iniquity of my sin!

Therefore shall every pious man pray to thee, while thou mayst be found; surely the floods of great waters shall not come near him.

Thou art my hiding-place; thou preservest me from trouble; thou compassest me about with songs of deliverance.

"I will instruct thee, and show thee the way thou shouldst go; I will give thee counsel, and keep my eye upon thee.

Be ye not like the horse and the mule, which have no understanding.

Whose mouths must be pressed with the bridle and curb, because they will not come near thee!"

The wicked hath many sorrows; but he that trusteth in the Lord is encompassed with mercies.

Rejoice in the Lord, and be glad, ye righteous, shout for joy, all ye that are upright in heart!

PSALM LI. [Abrev.]

M. Be gracious unto me, O God! according to thy loving kindness; according to the greatness of thy mercy, blot out my transgressions!

C. Wash me thoroughly from my iniquity, and cleanse me from my sin!

For I acknowledge my transgressions, and my sin is ever before me.

Against thee, thee only, have I sinned, and in thy sight have I done evil;

So that thou art just in thy sentence, and righteous in thy judgment.

Behold! thou desirest truth in the heart; so teach me wisdom in my inmost soul!

Make me to hear joy and gladness, so that the bones which thou hast broken may rejoice!

Hide thy face from my sins, and blot out all my iniquities!

Create within me a clean heart, O God! renew within me a steadfast spirit!

Cast me not away from thy presence, and take not thy holy spirit from me!

Restore to me the joy of thy protection, and strenghten me with a willing spirit !

Then will I teach thy ways to transgressors, and sinners shall be converted to thee.

Deliver me from the guilt of blood, O God, the God of my salvation ! that my tongue may sing aloud of thy goodness !

O Lord ! open thou my lips, that my mouth may show forth thy praise !

For thou desirest not sacrifice, else would I give it ; thou delightest not in burnt-offerings.

The sacrifice which God loveth is a broken spirit ; a broken and contrite heart, O God ! thou wilt not despise !

XII.
Trust.
PSALM XI. [Abrev.]

M. In the Lord do I put my trust. Why say ye to me, "Flee, like a bird, to your mountain ?

C. For, lo ! the wicked bend their bow; they make ready their arrows on the string, to shoot in secret at the upright in heart.

If the pillars be broken down, what can the righteous do ?"

The Lord is in his holy palace ; the Lord's throne is in heaven ;

His eyes behold, his eyelids prove the children of men.

The Lord trieth the righteous ; but the wicked, and the lover of violence, his soul hateth.

For the Lord is righteous ; he loveth righteousness ; the upright shall see his countenance.

PSALM XXIII.

M. The Lord is my shepherd : I shall not want.

C. He maketh me lie down in green pastures; he leadeth me beside the still waters.

He reviveth my soul ; he leadeth me in paths of safety, for his name's sake.

When I walk through the valley of the shadow of death I fear no evil; for thou art with me; thy stay and thy staff, they comfort me.

Thou preparest a table before me in the presence of my enemies. Thou anointest my head with oil; my cup runneth over.

Surely goodness and mercy shall follow me all the days of my life, and I shall dwell in the house of the Lord for ever.

PSALM XXVII. [Abrev.]

M. The Lord is my light and my salvation; whom shall I fear?

C. The Lord is the shield of my life; of whom shall I be afraid?

When the wicked came upon me to devour me, even my persecutors and enemies, they stumbled and fell.

Though a host should encamp against me, my heart shall not fear; though war should rise against me, yet will I be confident.

One thing have I desired of the Lord; that do I yet seek; that I may dwell in the house of the Lord all the days of my life,

To behold the grace of the Lord, and to gaze upon his temple.

For in the day of trouble he will hide me in his pavilion; ye, in the secret place of his tabernacle will he shelter me; he will set me upon a rock.

Hear my voice, O Lord! when I cry unto thee; have pity upon me, and answer me!

When I think of thy precept, "Seek ye my face!" thy face, Lord, do I seek.

O hide not thou thy face from me; cast not thy servant away in displeasure!

Thou hast been my help, do not leave me; do not forsake me, O God, my helper!

For though my father and my mother may forsake me; but the Lord will take me up.

Teach me thy way, O Lord! and lead me in the right path!

Give us not up to the will of our adversaries! for false witnesses have risen up against us, and such as breathe out injustice.

I trust that I shall see the goodness of the Lord in the land of the living.

Hope thou in the Lord! be of good courage; let thy heart be strong; hope thou in the Lord!

PSALM XXXI. [Abrev.]

M. In thee, O Lord! do I trust; let me never be put to shame; according to thy goodness deliver me!

C. Bow down thy ear to me; help me speedely! be to me a strong rock, a high fortress, for my deliverance.

For thou art my rock and my high fortress; be also my guide, and lead me, for thy name's sake!

Draw me out of the net which they have secretly laid for me, for thou art my strength!

Into thy hand I commit my life; thou wilt deliver me, O Lord, thou God of truth!

I hate those who regard lying vanities, and put my trust in the Lord.

I will be glad and rejoice in thy mercy, that thou hast looked upon my trouble, and hast had regard to my distress;

That thou hast not given me up to the hands of my enemies, but hast set my feet in a wide place.

Have mercy upon me, O Lord! for I am in trouble! my face is consumed with grief; yea, my spirit and my body.

For my life is wasted with sorrow, and my years with sighing;

My strength faileth by reason of my affliction, and my bones are consumed on account of all my troubles.

But I trust in thee, O Eternal! I say, "Thou art my God!"

My destiny is in thy hand; deliver me from the power of my enemies and persecutors!

Let thy face shine upon thy servant, and save me through thy mercy!

Let me not be put to shame, O Lord! for I have called upon thee;

Let the wicked be put to shame; let them be silenced in the grave!

Let lying lips be put to silence, which speak proud things against the righteous, with haughtiness and contempt!

O how great is thy goodness, which thou treasurest up for them that fear thee;

Which thou showest to them that trust in thee, before the sons of men!

Thou hidest them in the secret place of thy presence from the machinations of men;

Thou shelterest them in thy pavilion from the violence of tongues.

Praised be the Lord; for he hath shown me his wonderful kindness, as in a fortified city!

I said in my distress, "I am cut off before thy eyes";

But thou didst hear the voice of my supplication, when I cried unto thee.

O love the Lord, all ye his servants; for the Lord preserveth the faithful, and requiteth the proud in full measure!

Be of good courage; let your hearts be strong, all ye who trust in the Lord!

PSALM XL. [Abrev.]

M. I trusted steadfastly in the Lord, and he listened, and heard my cry.

C. He drew me out of a horrible pit, out of the miry clay; he set my feet upon a rock, and made my steps firm.

He hath put into my mouth a new song, a song of praise to our God.

Many shall see, and fear, and put their trust in the Lord.

Happy the man who maketh the Lord his trust, and resorteth not to men of pride and falsehood!

Many, O Lord, my God! are the wonderful works which thou hast done;

Many have been thy gracious purposes towards us; none can be compared to thee!

Would I declare and rehearse them, they are more than can be numbered.

In sacrifice and oblation thou hast no pleasure; my ears thou hast opened; burnt-offering and sin-offering thou requirest not.

Therefore I said, "Lo, I come; in the scroll of the book it is prescribed to me;

O my God! to do thy will is my delight, and thy law dwelleth in my heart!"

I have proclaimed thy righteousnes in the great assembly, lo, I have not restrained my lips, O Lord! thou knowest!

I hide not thy justice in my heart; I declare thy faithfulness and thy salvation; I conceal not thy mercy and truth from the great assembly.

Withdraw not from me thy tender mercies, O Lord! may thy loving-kindness and thy truth continually preserve me!

Let all who seek thee be glad and rejoice in thee! let those who love thy protection ever say, "Great is the Eternal!"

I am poor and afflicted, yet the Lord thinketh of me; thou art my help and my deliverer; my God! make no delay!

PSALM XLVI.

M. God is our refuge and strength; an ever present help in trouble.

C. Therefore will we not fear, though the earth be changed; though the mountains tremble in the heart of the sea;

Though its waters roar and be troubled, and the mountains shake with the swelling thereof.

A river with its streams shall make glad the city of God, the holy dwelling-place of the Most High.

God is in the midst of her; she shall not be moved; God will help her, and that full early.

The nations raged; kingdoms were moved; he uttered his voice, the earth melted.

The Lord of hosts is with us; the God of Jacob is our refuge.

Come, behold the doings of the Lord; what desolations he hath made in the earth!

He causeth wars to cease to the end of the earth; he hath broken the bow, and snapped the spear asunder, and burned the chariots in fire.

"Desist, and know that I am God; I will be exalted among the nations, I will be exalted throughout the earth!"

The Lord of hosts is with us; the God of Jacob is our refuge.

PSALM LXII. [Abrev.]

M. Truly my soul resteth on God alone; from him cometh my deliverance!

C. He alone is my rock and my salvation; he is my safeguard, I shall not fall!

From God cometh my help and my glory: my strong rock, my refuge, is God.

Trust in him at all times, ye people! pour out your hearts before him! God is our refuge!

Truly men of low degree are vanity, and men of high degree are a lie;

Placed in the balance, they are all lighter than naught.

Trust not in extortion; place no vain hopes in greed; if riches increase, set not your heart upon them!

Once hath God promised, twice have I heard it, that power belongeth unto God.

To thee also, O Lord! belongeth mercy; for thou dost render to every man according to his work!

PSALM LXXI. [Abrev.]

M. In thee, O Lord! do I put my trust! let me never be put to shame!

C. In thy goodness deliver and rescue me; incline thy ear to me, and save me!

Be thou the rock of my abode, where I may continually resort!

Thou hast granted me deliverance; for thou art my rock and my fortress!

Save me, O my God! from the hand of the wicked,—from the hand of the unjust and the cruel!

For thou art my hope, O Eternal our God! thou hast been my trust from my youth!

Upon thee have I leaned from my birth; from my earliest breath thou hast been my support; my song hath been continually of thee!

I am a wonder to many, but thou art my strong refuge.

Let my mouth be filled with thy praise; yea, all the day long, with thy glory.

Cast me not off in my old age; forsake me not, when my strength faileth!

O God! be not far from me! come speedily to my aid, O my God!

But I will hope continually; I shall yet praise thee more and more.

My mouth shall speak of thy goodness,—of thy sure protection all the day long; for thy mercies are more than I can number.

I will celebrate thy mighty deeds, O Lord! I will make mention of thy goodness, of thine only!

O God! thou hast taught me from my youth, and thus far have I declared thy wondrous deeds;

And now, when I am old and gray-headed, O God, forsake me not,

Until I make known thy arm to the next generation,— thy mighty power to all that are to come!

For thy goodness, O God! reacheth to the heavens; wonderful things doest thou! O God! who is like unto thee?

Thou hast suffered us to see great and grievous troubles; thou wilt again give us life, and wilt bring us back from the depths of the earth!

Thou wilt increase my greatness; thou wilt again comfort me!

Then will I praise thee with psaltery; even thy faithfulness, O my God!

To thee will I sing with the harp, O Holy One of Israel!

My lips shall rejoice, when I sing to thee, and my soul, which thou hast redeemed from death;

My tongue also shall continually speak of thy righteousness:

For all who seek my hurt are brought to shame and confounded.

PSALM CXXI.

M. I lift up my eyes to the hills: whence cometh my help?

C. My help cometh from the Lord, who made heaven and earth.

He will not suffer thy foot to stumble; thy guardian doth not slumber.

Behold, the guardian of Israel doth neither slumber nor sleep.

The Lord is thy guardian; the Lord is thy shade at thy right hand.

The sun shall not smite thee by day, nor the moon by night.

The Lord will preserve thee from all evil; he will preserve thy life.

The Lord will preserve thy going out and thy coming in, from this time forth for ever.

PSALM CXXV.

M. They who trust in the Lord shall be as Mount Zion, which cannot be moved, which standeth for ever.

C. As the mountains are round about Jerusalem, so the Lord is round about his people, henceforth even for ever!

For the sceptre of the wicked shall not remain upon the portion of the righteous, lest the righteous put forth their hands to iniquity.

Do good, O Lord! to the good, to them that are upright in heart!

But such as turn aside to their crooked ways, — may the Lord destroy them with the evil-doers!

Peace be to Israel!

XIII.

Consolation.

PSALM XXX.

M. I will extol thee, O Lord! for thou hast lifted me up, and hast not suffered my enemies to rejoice over me.

C. O Lord, my God! I called upon thee, and thou hast healed me!

O Lord! thou hast raised me up from destruction; thou hast kept me alive, that I should not go down to the grave!

Sing unto the Lord, O ye his servants! and praise his holy name!

For his anger endureth but a moment, but his favor through life;

Though in the evening sorrow be a guest, yet joy cometh in the morning.

I said in my prosperity, "I shall never be moved!"

Thou, O Lord! by thy favor, hast made my mountain strong; thou didst hide thy face, and I was troubled!

I cried unto thee, O Lord! to the Lord I made supplication:

What will my death profit thee, that I should go down to the grave?

Can dust praise thee? can it declare thy faithfulness?

Hear, O Lord! and have pity upon me! be thou, O Lord, my helper!"

Thou didst turn my mourning into joy; thou didst loose my sackcloth, and gird me with gladness.

Therefore I will sing praise to thee, and not be silent; O Lord my God! I will give thanks to thee for ever!

PSALM LVII.

M. Have pity upon me, O God! have pity upon me, for in thee doth my soul seek refuge!

C. Yea, in the shadow of thy wings do I take shelter, until these calamities be overpast!

I call upon God the Most High, upon God, who performeth all things for me;

He will send from heaven, and save me; he will put to
 shame him that panteth for my life;
God will send forth his mercy and his truth.
My life was in the midst of lions; I dwelt among them that
 breathe out fire;
Among men whose teeth are spears and arrows, and whose
 tongue is a sharp sword.
Exalt thyself, O God! above the heavens, and thy glory
 above all the earth!
They have prepared a net for my steps; my soul is bowed
 down;
They have digged a pit before me, but into it they have
 themselves fallen.
My heart is strengthened, O God! my heart is strength-
 ened! I will sing and give thanks.
Awake, my soul! awake, psaltery and harp! I will wake
 with the early dawn.
I will praise thee, O Lord! among the nations; I will
 sing to thee among the kingdoms!
For thy mercy reacheth to the heavens, and thy truth to
 the clouds!
Exalt thyself, O God! above the heavens, and thy glory
 above all the earth!

PSALM CXXVI. [Abrev.]

M. When the Lord brought back the captivity of Zion, we
 were like them that dream.
C. Then was our mouth filled with laughter, and our tongue
 with singing.
Then said they among the nations, "The Lord hath done
 great things for them!"
Yea, the Lord hath done great things for us, for which we
 are glad.
They who sow in tears shall reap in joy.
Yea, he goeth forth weeping, bearing his seed; he shall
 surely come back rejoicing, bringing in his harvest.

XIV.
The Justice of God.
PSALM LXXXII.

M. God standeth in his assembly, he judgeth in the midst of the mighty ones.

C. "How long will ye judge unjustly, and favor the cause of the wicked?

Defend the poor and the fatherless; do justice to the wretched and the needy!

Deliver the poor and the destitute; save them from the hand of the wicked!

They are without knowledge and without understanding; they walk in darkness;

Therefore all the foundations of the land are shaken.

I have said, Ye are sons of God, and all of you children of the Most High;

But ye shall die like men, and fall like the rest of the princes."

Arise, O God! judge the earth! for all the nations are thy possession.

PSALM XXXVII. [Abrev.]

M. Be not thou angry on account of the wicked, nor be envious of those who do iniquity.

C. For soon shall they be cut down like grass, and wither like a green herb.

Trust in the Lord, and do good; abide in the land, and delight in faithfulness.

Place thy delight in the Lord, and he will give thee thy heart's desires.

Commit thy way to the Lord; trust in him, and he will give thee success!

He will cause thy justice to shine forth like the light, and thy righteousness like the noonday's brightness.

Hope thou patiently on the Lord, and in him place thy trust!

Be not angry on account of the prosperous, — on account of him that deviseth deceit!

Cease from anger; give not way to wrath; be not provoked, so as to do evil!

For evil-doers shall be rooted out; but they who trust in the Lord, they shall inherit the land.

Yet a little while, and the wicked shall be no more; thou mayst look for his place, and he will not be found.

But the meek shall inherit the land, and delight in the fulness of prosperity.

Better is the little of the righteous man than the great abundance of the wicked;

The Lord careth for the life of the upright, and their inheritance shall endure for ever.

They shall not be ashamed in the evil time, and in the days of famine they shall have enough.

The wicked borroweth, and repayeth not; but the righteous is merciful and bountiful.

The steps of a good man are directed by the Lord; who delighteth himself in his way.

Though he fall, he shall not be utterly cast down, for the Lord holdeth him by the hand.

I have been young, and now am old; yet have I not seen the righteous forsaken, nor his offspring begging bread.

He is ever merciful and lendeth, and his offspring shall be blessed.

Depart from evil, and do good; so thou shalt dwell in the land for ever.

The mouth of the righteous uttereth wisdom, and his tongue speaketh what is right.

The law of his God is in his heart; his footsteps shall not slip.

Trust in the Lord, and keep his way, and he will exalt thee to the possession of the land

I have seen a wicked man in great power, and spreading himself like a green cedar;

But he passed away, and, lo! he was no more; yea, I sought him, but he was not found.

Mark the righteous man, and behold the upright, that posterity is to the man of peace!

But transgressors will all be destroyed; the posterity of the wicked shall be rooted out.

The salvation of the just is from the Lord, he is their strength in the time of trouble.

The Lord will help and deliver them; he will deliver them from their enemies, and save them, because they trust in him.

PSALM XII.

M. Help, O Lord; for the goodly man ceaseth; the faithful are failing among men.

C. They speak falsehood one to another; with flattering lips, with a double heart do they speak.

May the Lord punish all the flattering lips, and the tongue which speaketh proud things!

Who say, "With our tongues will we prevail; our lips are our reliance; who is lord over us?"

The wicked walk on every side, when the vilest of men are exalted.

For the oppression of the poor and the sighing of the wretched,

Now will I stand up, saith the Lord; I will set in safety him whom they puff at.

The words of the Lord are pure; like silver purified in a furnace on the earth, seven times refined.

Thou, O Lord! wilt watch over them; thou wilt preserve them from this generation for ever.

PSALM LXXIII.

M. Truly, God is good to Israel, — to those who are pure in heart.

C. Yet my feet almost gave way; my steps had well nigh slipped:

For I was envious of the proud, when I saw the prosperity of the wicked.

For they have no pains even to their death; their bodies are in full health.

They have not the woes of other men, neither are they smitten like other men.

Therefore pride encircleth their neck as a collar; violence covereth them as a garment.

From their bosom issueth their iniquity; the designs of their hearts burst forth.

They mock, and speak of malicious oppression; their words are haughty:

They stretch forth their mouth to the heavens, and their tongue goeth through the earth;

Therefore his people walk in their ways, and they drink from full fountains.

And then say, "How doth God know? how can there be knowledge with the Most High?"

Behold these are the ungodly! yet they are ever prosperous; they heap up riches.

Verily I have cleansed my heart in vain; in vain have I washed my hands in innocence.

For every day have I been smitten; every morn have I been chastened.

If I should resolve to speak like them, surely I should be treacherous to the family of thy children.

So, when I studied to know this, it was painful to my eyes;

Until I went into the sanctuary of God, and considered what was their end.

Behold! thou hast set them on slippery places; thou castest them down into unseen pits.

How are they brought to desolation in a moment, and utterly consumed with sudden destruction!

As a dream when one awaketh, thou, O Lord! when thou risest, wilt make their vain show a derision.

When my heart was vexed and I was pierced in my reins:

Then was I stupid and without understanding; I was like one of the brutes before thee.

Yet I am ever under thy care; by my right hand thou dost hold me up.

Thou wilt guide me with thy counsel, and at last receive me in glory.

Whom have I in heaven but thee, and whom on earth do
 I love in comparison with thee?
Though my flesh and my heart fail, God is the strength of
 my soul, and my portion for ever.
For, lo! they who are far from thee perish; thou destroyest all who estrange themselves from thee.
But it is good for me to draw near to God; I put my trust
 in the Lord, my God, that I may declare all thy
 works.

XV.

Beatitudes.

PSALM I.

M. Happy the man who walketh not in the counsel of the
 unrighteous,
C. Nor standeth in the way of sinners, nor sitteth in the seat
 of scoffers;
But whose delight is in the law of the Lord, and who
 meditateth on his precepts day and night.
He is like a tree planted by streams of water, that bringeth
 forth its fruit in its season,
Whose leaves also do not wither: all that he doeth shall
 prosper.
Not so the unrighteous; they are like chaff, which the
 wind driveth away.
Therefore the wicked shall not stand in judgment, nor
 sinners in the assembly of the just.
For the Lord knoweth the way of the righteous, but the
 way of the wicked leadeth to ruin.

PSALM XLI. [Abrev.]

M. Happy is he who hath regard to the poor! the Lord will
 deliver him in time of trouble.
C. The Lord will preserve him, and keep him alive; he shall
 be happy on the earth;
Thou wilt not give him up to the will of his enemies!

The Lord will strengthen him upon the bed of disease;
all his bed thou wilt change in his sickness.

I said, O Lord! be merciful to me! heal me, for I have sinned against thee!

PSALM CXII. [Abrev.]

M. Praise ye the Lord! happy the man who feareth the Lord, who taketh delight in his commandments!

C. His posterity shall be mighty on the earth; the race of the righteous shall be blessed.

Wealth and riches shall be in his house; his righteousness shall endure for ever.

To the righteous shall arise light out of darkness; he is gracious and full of compassion and righteousness.

Happy the man who hath pity and lendeth! he shall sustain his cause in judgement;

Yea, he shall never be moved: the righteous shall be in everlasting remembrance.

He is not afraid of evil tidings; his heart is firm, trusting in the Lord.

His heart is firm; he hath no fear, till he see his wishes fulfilled.

He hath scattered blessings; he hath given to the poor; his righteousness shall endure for ever;

His horn shall be exalted with honor.

PSALM CXXXI.

M. O Lord! my heart is not haughty, nor my eyes lofty; I employ not myself on great things, or things too wonderful for me!

C. Yea, I have stilled and quieted my soul as a weaned child upon his mother; my soul within me is like a weaned child.

O Israel! trust in the Lord, henceforth even for ever!

PSALM CXXXIII.

M. Behold, how good and pleasant it is for brethren to dwell together in unity!

C. It is like precious perfume upon the head, which ran down upon the beard of Aaron;

Which went down to the very border of his garments;
Like the dew of Hermon, like that which descendeth upon the mountains of Zion.
For there the Lord commandeth a blessing, even life for evermore.

PSALM CXXVII.

M. Except the Lord build the house, the builders labor in vain;
C. Except the Lord guard the city, the watchman waketh in vain;
In vain ye rise up early, and go to rest late, and eat the bread of care!
The same giveth he to his beloved one in sleep.
Behold! sons are an inheritance from the Lord, and children are his blessing.
As arrows in the hand of the warrior, so are the sons of valiant men:
Happy the man that hath his quiver full of them! they shall not be put to shame, when they speak with adversaries in the gate.

PSALM CXXVIII.

M. Happy is he who feareth the Lord, who walketh in his ways;
C. Thou shalt eat the labor of thy hands; happy shalt thou be, and it shall be well with thee!
Thy wife shall be like a beautiful vine within thy house! thy children like olive-branches round about thy table.
Behold! thus happy is the man who feareth the Lord!
The Lord shall bless thee out of Zion, and thou shalt see the prosperity of Jerusalem all the days of thy life;
Yea, thou shalt see thy children's children; peace be to Israel!

XVI.
National.

PSALM XLIV. [Abrev.]

M. O God! we have heard with our ears, our fathers have told us, what deeds thou didst in their days, in the days of old.
C. With thy own hand didst thou drive out the nations, and plant our fathers;

Thou didst subdue the nations, and cause our fathers to flourish.

For not by their own swords did they gain possession of the land.

Nor did their own arms give them victory; but thy right hand, and thy arm, and the light of thy countenance; for thou didst favor them!

Thou art my king, O God! O send deliverance to Jacob!

Through thee we may triumph over our enemies; through thy name we may conquer our adversaries!

I trust not in my bow, nor can my sword save me.

But it is thou only who savest us from our enemies, and puttest to shame those who hate us!

In God will we glory continually; yea, we will praise thy name forever!

PSALM XLVII.
(For the Choir.)

M. O clap your hands, all ye nations! Shout unto God with the voice of triumph!

C. For wonderful is the Lord, the Most High, the great King over all the earth.

He hath subdued nations under us, and kingdoms under our feet;

He hath chosen for us an inheritance, the glory of Jacob, whom he loved.

Go up unto God with a shout; unto the Lord with the sound of the trumpet.

Sing praises to God, sing praises! sing praises to our King, sing praises!

For God is King of all the earth; sing to him hymns of praise!

God reigneth over the nations; God sitteth upon his holy throne.

The princes of the nations gather themselves together to the people of the God of Abraham;

For the mighty ones of the earth belong to God; he is supremely exalted.

PSALM LX. [Abrev.]

M. O God! thou hast forsaken us; thou hast broken us into pieces; thou hast been angry! O revive us again!

C. Thou hast made the land tremble; thou hast rent it; O heal its breaches, for it tottereth!

Thou hast caused thy people to see hard things; thou hast made us drink the wine of reeling.

Lift up a banner for them that fear thee, for the sake of thy faithfulness, that they may escape!

That thy beloved may be delivered, save with thy right hand, and answer me!

God promiseth in his holiness; I will rejoice.

PSALM LXVIII. [Abrev.]

M. Let God arise, and his enemies are scattered, and they who hate him flee before him!

C. As smoke is dispersed, so thou dispersest them; as wax melteth before the fire, so perish the wicked before the face of God.

But the righteous are glad and rejoice in his presence, yea, they exult exceedingly.

Sing unto God; sing praises to his name! prepare a way for him who rideth through the desert!

The Eternal is his name; be joyful in his presence!

The father of the fatherless, and the protector of the widow, is God in his holy habitation.

God causeth the forsaken to dwell in houses; he leadeth forth to prosperity them that are bound;

But the rebellious shall dwell in a barren land.

O God! when thou didst go before thy people, when thou didst march through the wilderness,

The earth quaked, and the heavens dropped at the presence of God;

This Sinai trembled at the presence of God, the God of Israel.

Thou, O God! didst send a plentiful rain; thou didst strengthen thy wearied inheritance.

Thy people established themselves in the land; thou, O God! in thy goodness, didst prepare it for the needy!

The Lord gave the song of victory of the maidens publishing glad tidings to the mighty host.

"The kings, with their armies have fled, — have fled! and the matron at home divideth the spoil.

Truly ye may repose yourselves in the stalls, like the wings of a dove covered with silver, and her feathers with shining gold."

Praised be the Lord daily! when we are heavy-laden, the Mighty One is our help.

Our God is a God of salvation; from the Lord, our God, cometh deliverance of death.

Rebuke the wild beast of the reeds, scatter thou the nations that delight in war!

Ye kingdoms of the earth, sing unto God; sing praise to the Lord;

To him who rideth upon the ancient heaven of heavens; behold, he uttereth his voice, his mighty voice!

Give glory to God, whose majesty is in Israel, and whose might is above the clouds!

Powerful art thou, O God! from thy sanctuary! the God of Israel giveth strength and power to his people.

Praised be God!

PSALM LXXX.

M. Give ear, O Shepherd of Israel! thou who leadest Joseph like a flock, thou who dwellest above the cherubims, shine forth!

C. Before Ephraim and Benjamin and Manasseh, stir up thy strength, and come and save us!

Bring us back to thee, O God! and cause thy face to shine upon us, that we may be saved!

O Lord, God of hosts! how long wilt thou be angry against the prayer of thy people?

For thou causest them to eat the bread of tears, and givest them tears to drink, in full measure.

Thou hast made us the object of strife to our neighbors, and our enemies hold us in derision.

Bring us back to thee, O God of hosts! and cause thy face to shine upon us that we may be saved!

Thou didst bring a vine out of Egypt; thou didst expel the nations, and plant it.

Thou didst prepare a place for it; it spread its roots, and filled the land.

The mountains were covered with its shade, and its branches were like the cedars of God.

It sent out its boughs to the sea, and its branches to the river.

Why hast thou now broken down its hedges, so that all who pass by do pluck from it?

The boar from the wood doth waste it, and the wild beast from the forest doth devour it.

O God of hosts! return, we beseech thee, look down from heaven, and behold, and have regard to this vine!

Protect what thy right hand planted; the branch which thou madest strong for thyself!

It is burnt with fire; it is cut down; under thy rebuke they perish.

May thy hand be over the man of thy right hand, the man whom thou madest strong for thyself!

So will we no more turn back from thee: revive us, and upon thy name alone will we call!

Bring us back unto thee, O Lord, God of hosts! and cause thy face to shine upon us, that we may be saved!

PSALM LXXXI. [Abrev.]

M. Sing joyfully to God, our strength! shout with gladness to the God of Jacob!

C. Raise a song, and strike the timbrel, the sweet-sounding harp, and the psaltery!

Blow the trumpet at the new moon, at the full moon, also, on our festal day!

For this is a statute for Israel, a law of the God of Jacob;

He appointed it as a memorial in Joseph, when he went out of the land of Egypt, where he heard a language he knew not.

"I relieved thy shoulders from their burden; thy hands were removed from the hod.

Thou didst call in trouble, and I delivered thee; in the secret place of thunder I answered thee; I proved thee at the waters of Meribah.

Hear, O my people! and I will admonish thee! O Israel! that thou wouldst hearken to me!

Let there be no strange god within thee, nor worship thou any foreign god!

I, the Eternal, am thy God, who brought thee out of the land of Egypt: open wide thy mouth, and I will satiate thee!"

PSALM LXXXV. [Abrev.]

M. O Lord! thou hast been favorable to thy land; thou hast brought back the captives of Jacob;

C. Thou didst forgive the iniquity of thy people, and cover all their sins!

Thou didst take away all thy displeasure, and abate the fierceness of thy wrath.

Show us thy compassion, O Lord! and grant us thy salvation!

I will hear what God the Lord will speak, truly he will speak peace to his people, and to his servants; only let them not turn again to folly!

Yea, his salvation is near to those who fear him, that glory may dwell in our land.

Mercy and truth shall meet together, righteousness and peace shall kiss each other;

Truth shall spring out of the earth; righteousness shall look down from heaven.

Yea, the Lord will give prosperity, and our land shall yield her increase.

Righteousness shall go before him, and set us in the way of his steps.

PSALM CXXIX. [Abrev.]

M. Much have they afflicted me from my youth, may Israel now say:

C. Much have they afflicted me from my youth, yet have they not prevailed against me.

The ploughers ploughed up my back; they made long their furrows;

But the Lord was righteous; he cut asunder the cords of the wicked.

PSALM CXXIV.

M. Had not the Lord been on our side, now may Israel say,

C. Had not the Lord been on our side, when men rose up against us,

Then had they swallowed us up alive, when their wrath burned against us;

Then the waters had overwhelmed us, the stream had gone over our soul;

The proud waters had gone over our soul.

Blessed be the Lord, who hath not given us a prey to their teeth!

We have escaped like a bird from the snare of the fowler; the snare is broken, and we have escaped.

Our help is in the name of the Lord, who made heaven and earth.

XVII.

Praise.

PSALM CXLV.

M. I will extol thee, my God, the King! I will praise thy name for ever and ever!

C. Every day will I bless thee, and praise thy name for ever and ever!

Great is the Lord, and greatly to be praised; yea, his greatness is unsearchable.

One generation shall praise thy works to another, and shall declare thy mighty deeds.

I will speak of the glorious honor of thy majesty, and of thy wonderful works.

Men shall speak of the might of thy wonderful deeds, and I will declare thy greatness;

They shall pour forth the praise of thy great goodness, and sing of thy righteousness.

The Lord is gracious, and full of compassion, slow to anger, and rich in mercy.

The Lord is good to all, and his tender mercies are over all his works.

All thy works praise thee, O Lord! and thy holy ones bless thee!

They speak of the glory of thy kingdom, and talk of thy power;

To make known to the sons of men his mighty deeds, and the glorious majesty of his kingdom.

Thy kingdom is an everlasting kingdom, and thy dominion endureth throughout all generations.

The Lord upholdeth all that fall, and raiseth up all that are bowed down.

The eyes of all wait upon thee, and thou givest them their food in due season;

Thou openest thy hand, and satisfiest the desire of every living thing.

The Lord is righteous in all his ways, and merciful in all his works.

The Lord is nigh to all that call upon him, to all that call upon him in truth.

He fulfilleth the desire of them that fear him; he heareth their cry, and saveth them.

The Lord preserveth all that love hm; but all the wicked he will destroy.

My mouth shall speak the praise of the Lord; and let all flesh bless his holy name for ever and ever!

PSALM CXLVI.

HALLELUJAH.

M. Praise ye the Lord! praise the Lord, my soul!

C. I will praise the Lord, as long as I live; I will sing praises to my God, while I have my being.

Put not your trust in princes, in the son of man, in whom is no help!

His breath goeth forth; he returneth to the dust; in that very day his plans perish.

Happy is he that hath the God of Jacob for his help; whose hope is in the Lord, his God;

Who made heaven and earth, the sea, and all that is therein; who keepeth truth forever;

Who executeth judgment for the oppressed; who giveth food to the hungry.

The Lord setteth free the prisoners; the Lord openeth the eyes of the blind;

The Lord raiseth up them that are bowed down; the Lord loveth the righteous.

The Lord preserveth the strangers; he relieveth the fatherless and the widow; but the way of the wicked he perverteth.

The Lord shall reign forever; thy God, O Zion! to all generations! praise ye the Lord!

PSALM CXLVII.

M. Praise ye the Lord! for it is good to sing praise to our God; for it is pleasant, and praise is becoming.

C. The Lord buildeth up Jerusalem; he gathereth together the dispersed of Israel.

He healeth the broken in heart, and bindeth up their wounds.

He counteth the number of the stars; he calleth them all by their names.

Great is our Lord, and mighty in power; his wisdom is infinite.

The Lord lifteth up the lowly; he casteth the wicked down to the ground.

Sing to the Lord with thanksgiving; sing praises upon the harp to our God!

Who covereth the heavens with clouds, who prepareth rain for the earth, who causeth grass to grow upon the mountains.

He giveth to the cattle their food, and to the young ravens, when they cry.

He delighteth not in the strength of the horse, he taketh not pleasure in the legs of a man.

The Lord taketh pleasure in those who fear him, in those who trust in his mercy.

Praise the Lord, O Jerusalem! praise thy God, O Zion!

For he hath strengthened the bars of thy gates; he hath blessed thy children within thee.

He maketh peace in thy borders, and satisfieth thee with the finest of the wheat.

He sendeth forth his command to the earth; his word runneth swiftly.

He giveth snow like wool, and scattereth the hoarfrost like ashes.

He casteth forth his ice like morsels; who can stand before his cold?

He sendeth forth his word, and melteth them; he causeth his wind to blow, and the waters flow.

He publisheth his word to Jacob, his statutes and laws to Israel.

He hath dealt in this manner with no other nation; and, as for his ordinances, they have not known them.

Praise ye the Lord!

PSALM CXLVIII.
[For the Choir.]

M. Praise ye the Lord! praise the Lord from the heavens! praise him in the heights!

C. Praise him, all ye his angels! praise him, all ye his hosts!

Praise ye him, sun and moon! praise him, all ye stars of light!

Praise him, ye heavens of heavens! ye waters, that are above the heavens!

Let them praise the name of the Lord; for he commanded, and they were created.

He hath also established them forever; he hath given them a law, and they transgress it not.

Praise the Lord from the earth, ye sea-monsters, and all deeps!

Fire and hail, snow and vapor; thou tempest, that fulfillest his word!

Ye mountains, and all hills! fruit-trees, and all cedars!

Ye wild beasts, and all cattle! ye creeping things, and winged birds!

Ye kings, and all peoples, princes, and all judges of the earth!

Young men and maidens, old men and children!

Let them praise the name of the Lord! for his name alone is exalted; his glory is above the earth and the heavens.

He exalteth the horn of his people, the glory of all his godly ones, of the children of Israel, a people near him.

Praise ye the Lord!

PSALM CL.
[For the Choir.]

M. Praise ye the Lord! praise God in his sanctuary! praise him in his glorious firmament!

C. Praise him for his mighty deeds! praise him according to his excellent greatness!

Praise him with the sound of trumpets! praise him with the psaltery and harp!

Praise him with the timbrel and dance! praise him with stringed instruments and flutes!

Praise him with the clear-sounding cymbals! praise him with the high-sounding cymbals!

Let every thing that hath breath praise the Lord!

Praise ye the Lord!

CHILDREN'S PRAYER.

MORNING PRAYER.

שְׁמַע יִשְׂרָאֵל יְיָ אֱלֹהֵינוּ יְיָ אֶחָד

Hear, O Israel, God our Lord, God is One.

Moses commanded us a law, the inheritance of the congregation of Jacob.

I give thanks to thee, O God, for thy loving kindness toward me. Thou hast watched over my life while I was asleep, and thou hast awakened me to life and usefulness. Be with me this day and ever more, that I may become righteous and good, and deserve the love of my dear parents, and find favor in the sight of God and men. Amen.

NIGHT PRAYER.

To thee, O God, I commit my spirit and my body before I lie down to rest. Let me slumber gently through the night and restore me to life and light. Bless my dear parents...... and all my teachers. Amen.

Hear, O Israel, God our Lord, God is One!

GRACE BEFORE MEALS.

Be praised, O God, Ruler of the universe, who causest the earth to bring forth nourishment for man, and in thy paternal love satisfiest us with thy goodness. Amen.

GRACE AFTER MEALS.

Be praised, O Lord, for thy boundless kindness, which sustains everything and supplies us with food and drink. Thou openest thy hand and satisfiest every living being. Thy great mercy has never suffered us to want nourishment, and henceforth too, mayest thou give us the sustenance of life. Be praised, O God, dispenser of all good gifts. Amen.

www.ingramcontent.com/pod-product-compliance
Lightning Source LLC
Chambersburg PA
CBHW020909230426
43666CB00008B/1380